I0823062

Pope Leo XIV

The Election of a Pope in Pictures

EWTN Publishing, Inc.
Irondale, Alabama

Cover design: Emma Helstrom

Front cover image: Rear View of Pope Leo XIV from Balcony (0080511052025 Vatican Media)

Back cover images: Images used in the back-cover collage are listed
in the image credits on pages 108-110, and marked with an asterisk.

EWTN Publishing, Inc.
5817 Old Leeds Road, Irondale, AL 35210

Distributed by Sophia Institute Press, Box 5284, Manchester, NH 03108.

Hardcover ISBN: 978-1-68278-449-5

Ebook ISBN: 978-1-68278-450-1

Library of Congress Control Number: 2025945448

First printing

Table of Contents

1. The Death of Pope Francis 7

The Passing of a Pope 7

The Camerlengo's Duties 7

Novemdiales: Mourning and Prayer in the Heart of the Church 11

The Funeral Mass and Burial of Pope Francis 11

2. *Sede Vacante*: The Vacant See 17

The Unoccupied Throne of Peter 17

Vatican City Under Stewardship 17

Gathering the College: General Congregations 20

Sacred Traditions of a Vacant See 23

3. The Sacred Conclave 29

In the Sistine Chapel: *Missa pro Eligendo Pontifice* and "*Extra Omnes!*" 29

The Balloting Rituals: Scrutineers, Smoke Signals, and the Watchful World 30

The Election of Pope Leo XIV 33

The Room of Tears 35

Habemus Papam! 36

The First Papal Blessing: *Urbi et Orbi* 39

4. The First Days of Pope Leo XIV 45

Mass and Meeting with the College of Cardinals 45

Pope Leo XIV's First Public *Regina Caeli* and Messages 45

Engaging the World: First Acts and Outreach 51
Continuity and New Beginnings. 52

5. Installation of the New Pope 67
The Inauguration Mass: A New Pontificate Begins 67
The Chair of Peter and the City of Rome 76

Conclusion: A Church That Endures. 91

Appendix I: Pope Leo XIV's Coat of Arms. 97

Appendix II: Indulgenced Prayer for the Supreme Pontiff, by Pope Leo XIII 99

Appendix III: Papal Election Timeline 103

Image Credits. 108

Pope Leo XIV

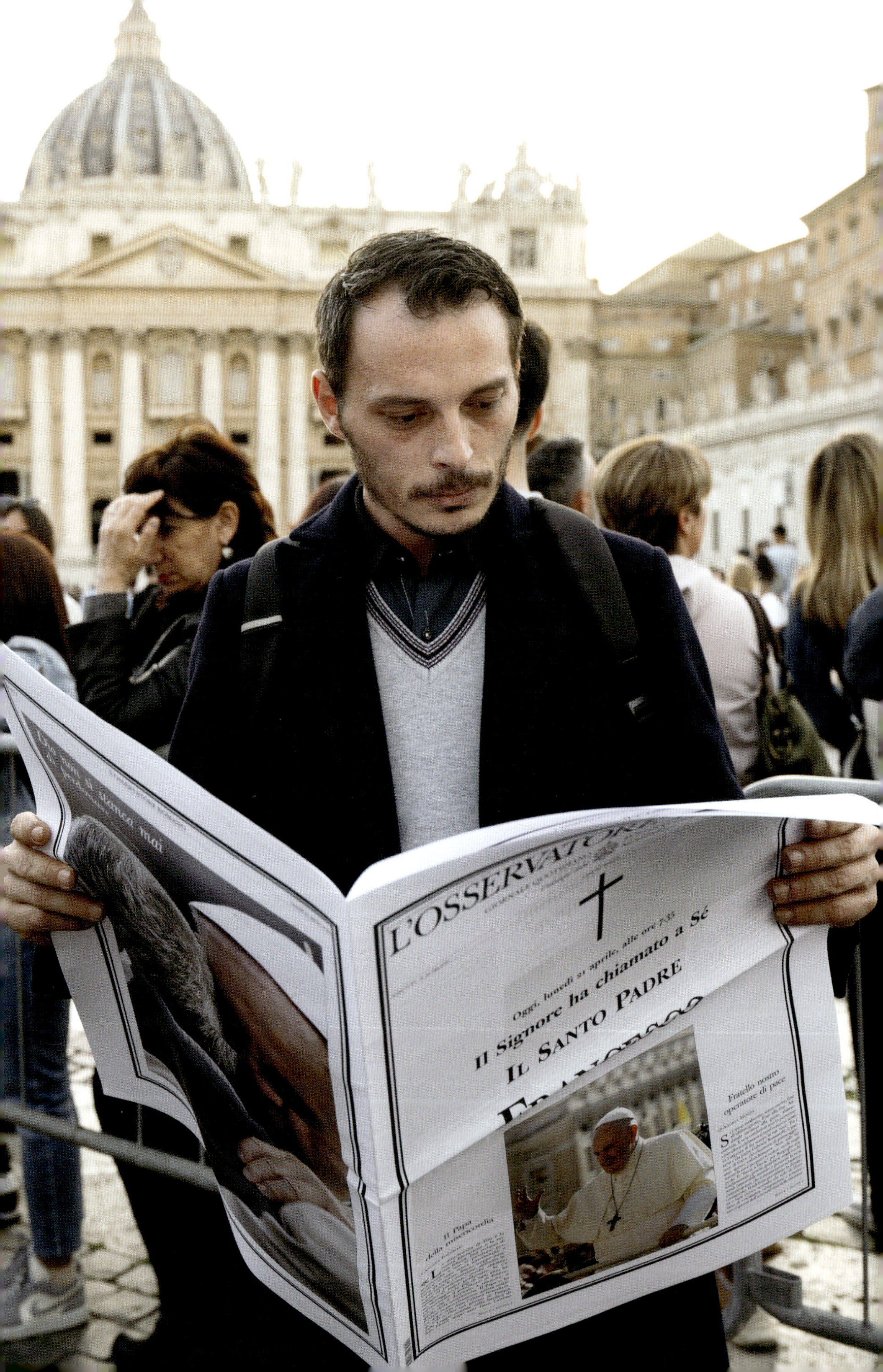
Dio non si stanca mai
L'OSSERVATORE
Oggi, lunedì 21 aprile, alle ore 7.35
Il Signore ha chiamato a Sé
Il Santo Padre
Fratello nostro
operatore di pace
Il Papa
della misericordia

CHAPTER ONE

The Death of Pope Francis

The Passing of a Pope

On the somber morning of April 21, 2025, news spread that Pope Francis had passed away, marking the end of a pontificate and the beginning of a sacred interregnum.

According to ancient protocol refined over centuries, the Cardinal Camerlengo—in this case the Irish-born American Cardinal Kevin Farrell—officially confirmed the Pope's death after calling him three times by his baptismal name. According to the centuries-old tradition, when the Camerlengo received no response, he announced, "*Vere, Franciscus mortus est*—Truly, Francis is dead." He then formally announced, "The Bishop of Rome, Francis, [has] returned to the house of the Father." As news of the pronouncement spread, church bells began to toll in mourning across Rome and the world, and the faithful began to gather in prayer, both for the soul of the deceased Pontiff and for the future of the Church. And in St. Peter's Square, more than anywhere else, thousands of pilgrims knelt to pray the Rosary and sing hymns, united in grief and hope.

The Camerlengo's Duties

With the Pope's passing, all eyes turned to the Camerlengo, the official entrusted with managing the interregnum. In a time-honored sequence, Cardinal Farrell assumed this role and solemn duty. His duties included ensuring that a death certificate was drawn up, among other ancient tasks that symbolically end a pontificate. In the presence of papal household officials, he removed and later destroyed the Ring of the Fisherman, the Pope's signet ring used to seal documents (to prevent its misuse). He also ordered the papal seal destroyed.

Next, following tradition, he sealed the papal apartments by draping red ribbons across the doors and affixing them with wax seals. No one could enter the private study or bedroom of the Holy Father until a new Pope decided otherwise, protecting the sanctity of the late Pope's personal quarters. (Because Pope Francis primarily resided in the Domus Sanctae Marthae guesthouse rather than the Apostolic

LEFT *In front of St. Peter's Basilica, a man reading a newspaper announcing the death of Pope Francis.*

Palace, where Popes have traditionally lived, the Camerlengo sealed both locations.) By sealing the apartments and securing the papal residences at the Vatican, the Lateran, and at Castel Gandolfo, the Camerlengo overtly demonstrated that the See of Peter was now vacant.

Concurrently, letters were dispatched and phone calls made: the Dean of the College of Cardinals was informed and in turn notified cardinals worldwide—as well as ambassadors and Heads of State—that Pope Francis had died. These actions, though administrative, were carried out with deference and deep reverence. Each ritual—the breaking of the ring, the sealing of doors, the manner of notification—spoke to the Catholic sense of continuity, preservation of the ancient, and respect for the Papal Office. Collectively, and through these gestures, the Church bid farewell to Pope Francis—even as She prepared to safeguard his legacy and move forward.

Notably, no one assumes the powers of the Pope in this moment. There is no such thing as a "vice Pope." The Camerlengo's role is one of stewardship, not rule: he maintains the essential functions of Vatican administration with a small team, but he cannot introduce new policies or teachings.

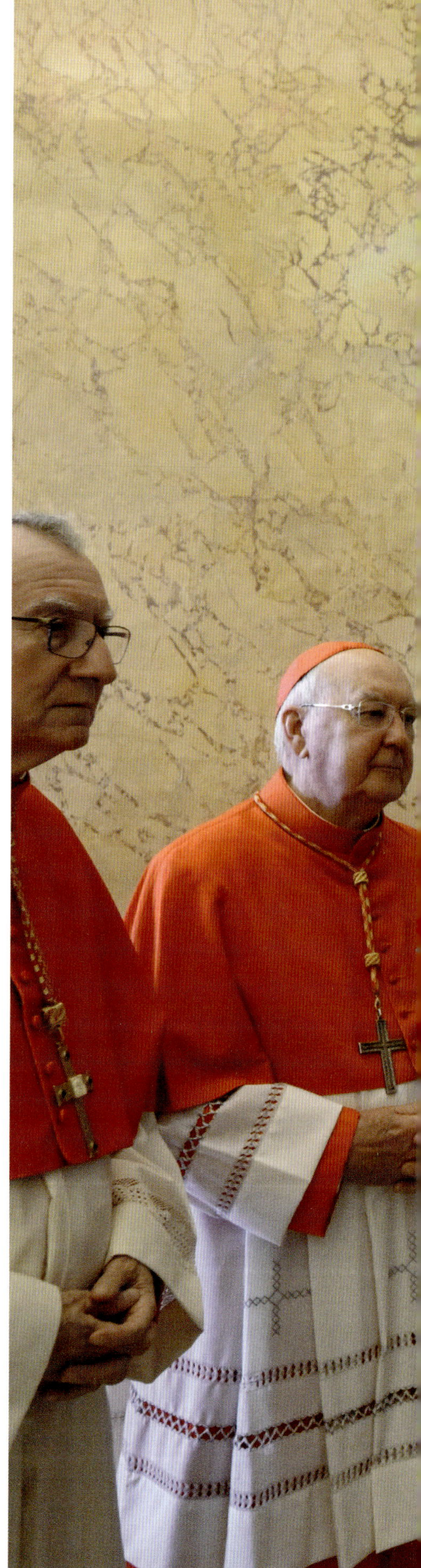

***RIGHT** The doors of the papal apartments being ceremoniously sealed following Pope Francis' death.*

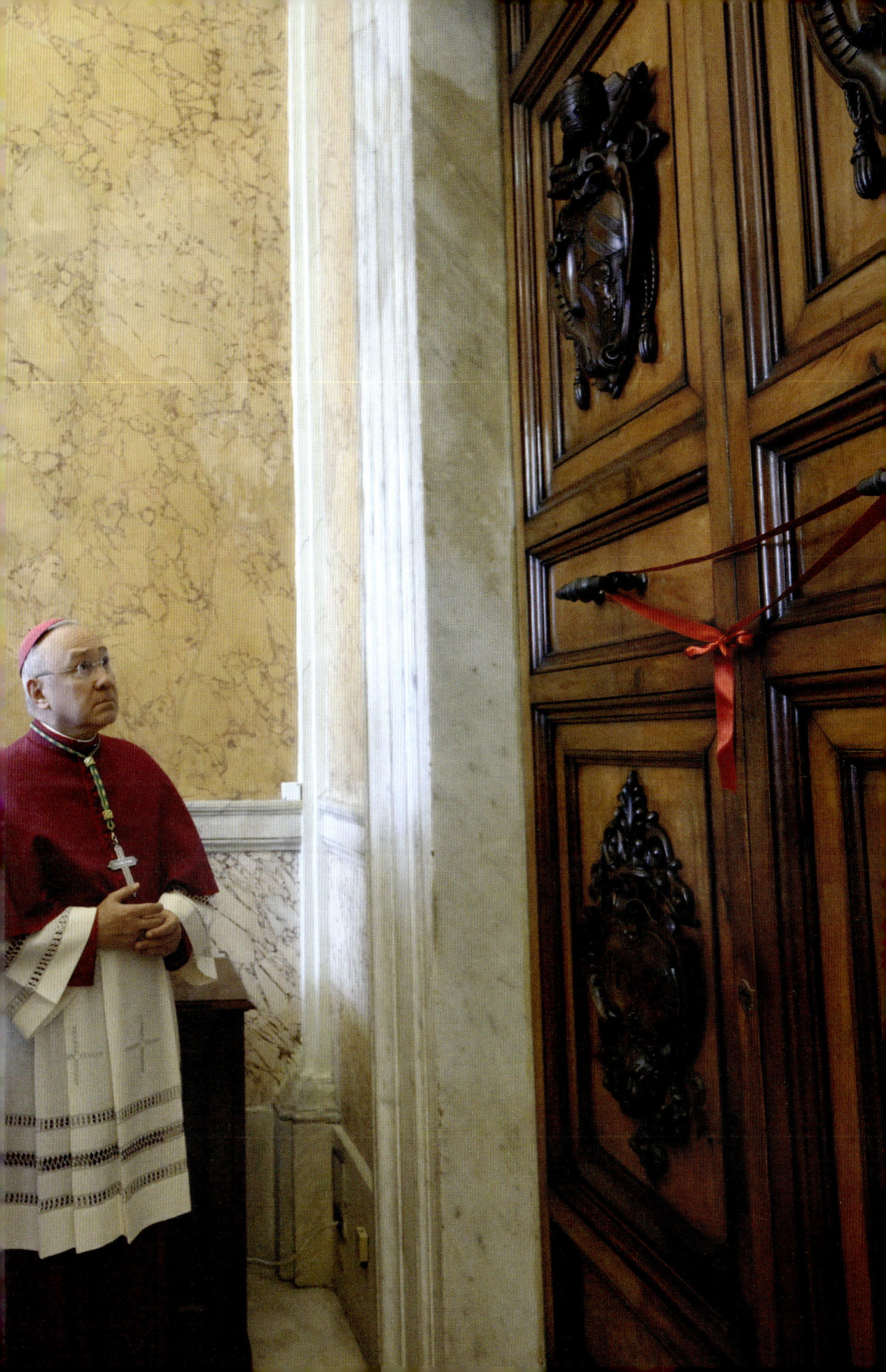

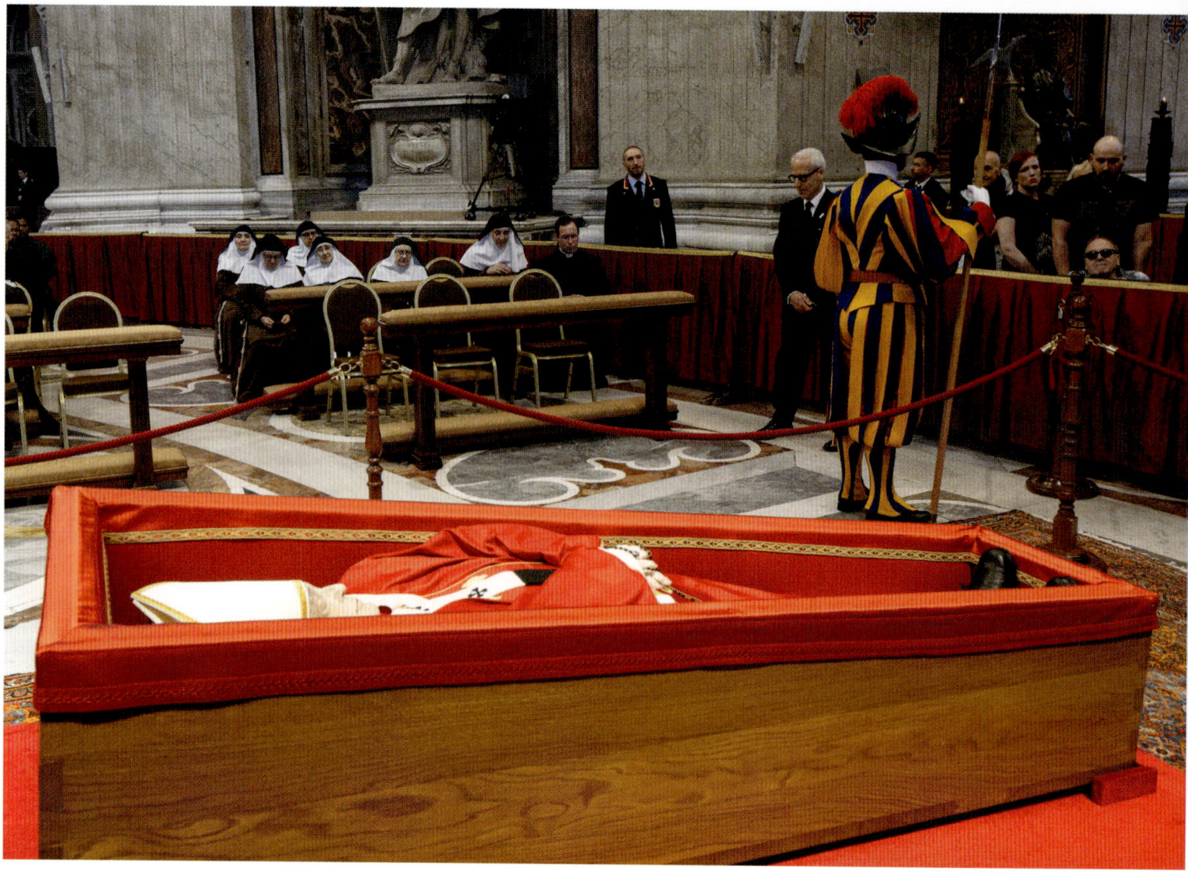

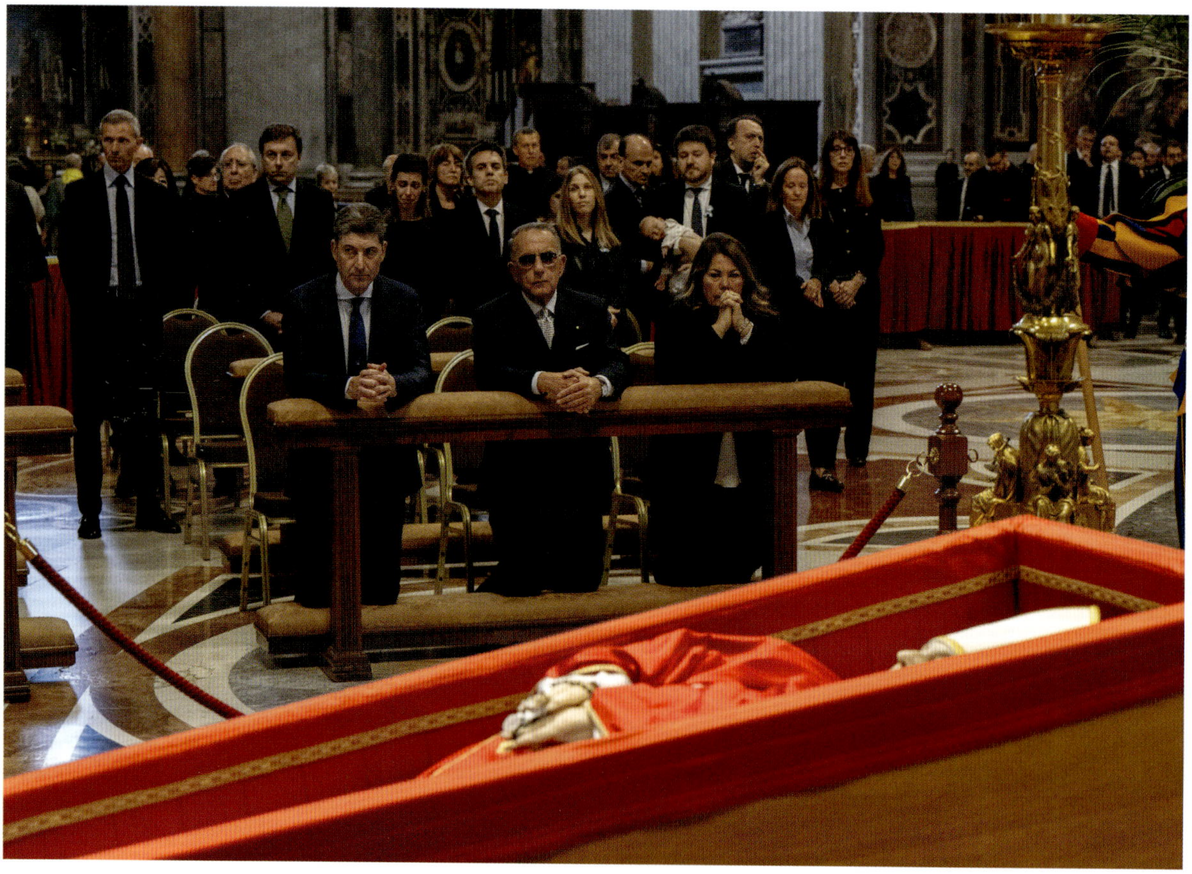

Novemdiales: Mourning and Prayer in the Heart of the Church

As the faithful around the world mourned Pope Francis' death, they watched as the Camerlengo's duties signified the official period of *Sede Vacante*: the Seat of St. Peter was vacant. But this did not mean that the prayer life of the Church was suspended. Rather, it intensified.

The late Pope's body was gently prepared for his funeral, washed and vested in papal liturgical garments. Before being moved to St. Peter's Basilica, it was laid in a simple open casket in the chapel of Domus Sanctae Marthae for private viewing and prayer by Vatican officials and members of the Pontifical Household. His remains were then moved to St. Peter's Basilica to lie in state. In accordance with Pope Francis' request, and in a departure from the way Popes have been buried in the past, his body was not placed on a elevated catafalque; instead, it rested in a plain open coffin, slightly propped up for viewing. Swiss Guards, in their distinctive uniforms, took up their watch at the head of the casket, honoring and guarding the fallen Pontiff.

During the three days in which Pope Francis' body lay in state, more than 250,000 pilgrims streamed into St. Peter's Basilica to pay their last respects, waiting in line for hours in the Roman spring air for the chance to kneel briefly and offer a prayer. Dignitaries and Heads of State from around the world also came to Rome, joining ordinary Catholics in a remarkable outpouring of love and respect. Each evening, the atmosphere in the Basilica was prayerful and hushed; soft Latin chants and hymns from around the world echoed as mourners shuffled forward. Vatican officials ensured that every detail—down to the placement of candles and the guarding of the body—reflected centuries-old protocol and the profound esteem due to the Successor of Peter.

During the *Novemdiales*—the nine-day period of mourning that began on April 26 with the Pope's funeral—a different cardinal presided over a Requiem Mass for the repose of the late Pope's soul each day. Churches around the globe likewise offered memorial Masses, uniting the Church Universal in mourning and prayers. The city of Rome itself observed an official period of mourning; flags flew at half-mast, and the illumination of monuments was subdued, underscoring that the Bishop of Rome had departed.

The Funeral Mass and Burial of Pope Francis

On the evening of April 25, the actions preceding the burial ritual took place. In a striking moment, attendants draped a white silk veil over Pope Francis' face, signifying his

TOP LEFT *Pope Francis' body lying in state at St. Peter's Basilica.* ***BOTTOM LEFT*** *Mourners praying for the repose of the soul of Pope Francis as his body lies in state.*

farewell to this life. A small parchment document, called a *Rogito*, written in Latin and summarizing his life and pontificate, was read aloud, then rolled and sealed in a metal tube to be buried with him. Following tradition, a red leather pouch containing commemorative medals and coins minted during Francis' papacy was placed beside him in the coffin. Though in earlier times deceased Popes were interred in three nested coffins (cypress, lead, and oak), Pope Francis had requested that his body be laid in a single cypress coffin, lined only with zinc. During the Mass, the coffin was borne by some of the *Gentiluomo di Sua Santità*—Papal Gentlemen (a group of about 150 men who closely attended the needs of Pope Francis during his pontificate).

On the fifth day after the Pope's death, the official Funeral Mass—known as the *Missa exequialis*—was celebrated in St. Peter's Square (following Pope Francis' wish for an open-air Liturgy). Under a mild sky and before a crowd of hundreds of thousands, Cardinal Giovanni Battista Re, the Dean of the College of Cardinals, served as the principal celebrant, leading the assembled Cardinals and Patriarchs in offering the Church's final farewell. The sight was both somber and majestic: a plain, cypress coffin lay before the altar, bearing the late Pope's coat of arms, as choirs intoned the ancient Gregorian chant, "*Requiem aeternam dona eis, Domine*—Eternal rest grant unto him, O Lord." During the Mass, incense swirled and rose toward the sky, symbolizing prayers for Pope Francis' soul: "Let my prayer be counted as incense before thee,and the lifting up of my hands as an evening sacrifice!" (Ps. 141:2). Passages from Scripture recounted Christ's promise of Resurrection, as well as St. Peter's pastoral charge. After Holy Communion, a poignant silence fell; and then the Litany of the Saints was sung and the coffin was aspersed with holy water and incensed one final time—a commendation that entrusted the Pope's soul to God.

According to his personal wishes, Pope Francis was laid to rest not in St. Peter's Basilica, but in the Basilica of St. Mary Major, a church he loved dearly for its devotion to the Blessed Mother. Though Popes have been buried outside of St. Peter's, he was the first one since Leo XIII (who died in 1903) to make that choice. He is the eighth Pope buried at St. Mary Major.

The *Novemdiales* of mourning began with the funeral and continued for eight more days with additional Masses for the repose of the soul of Pope Francis. And at the end of the ninth day, the period of official mourning concluded. The Church, though still grieving, turned Her gaze to the next step: the preparation for a conclave to elect Pope Francis' successor.

TOP LEFT *A candlelight vigil for the recovery of Pope Francis after he was hospitalized on February 14, 2025.* ***TOP RIGHT*** *Mourners pray the Rosary in St. Peter's Square.* ***BOTTOM*** *Cardinal Giovanni Battista Re blessing the coffin of Pope Francis during the funeral Mass.*

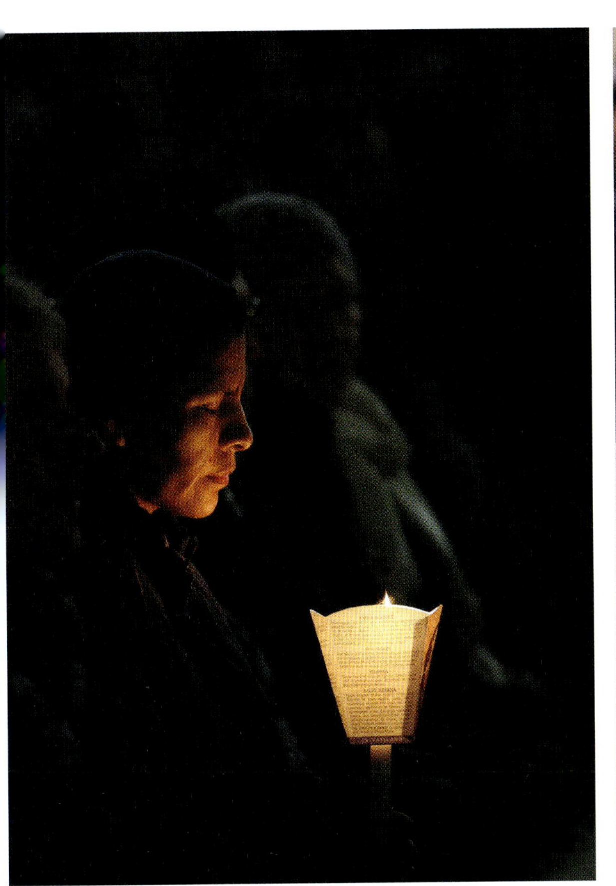

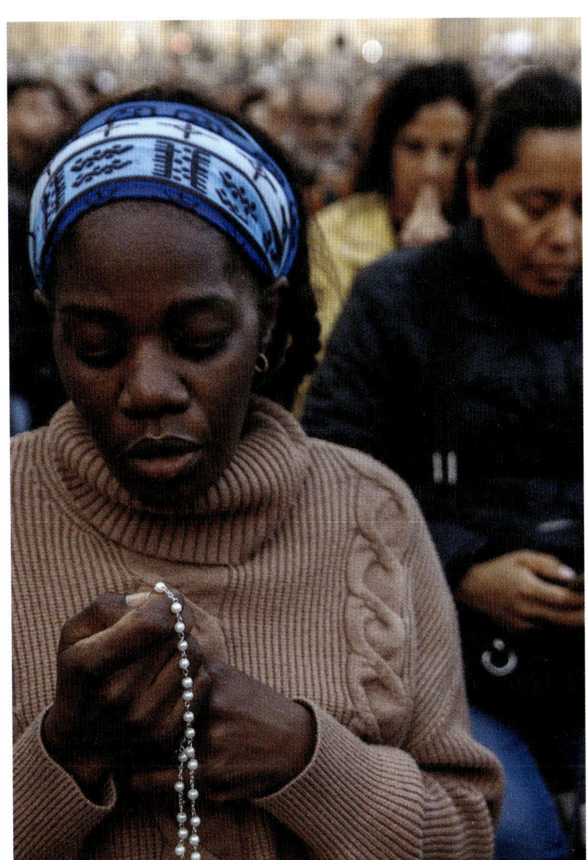

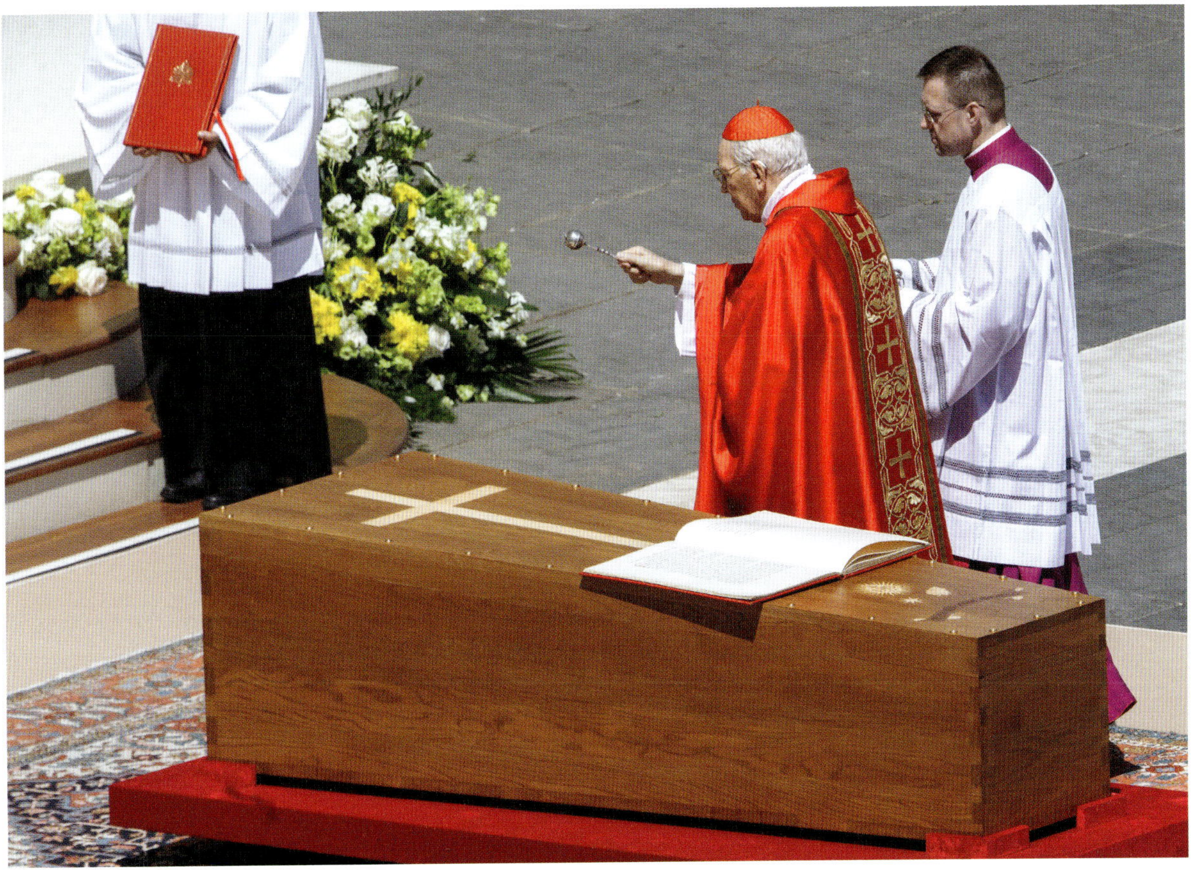

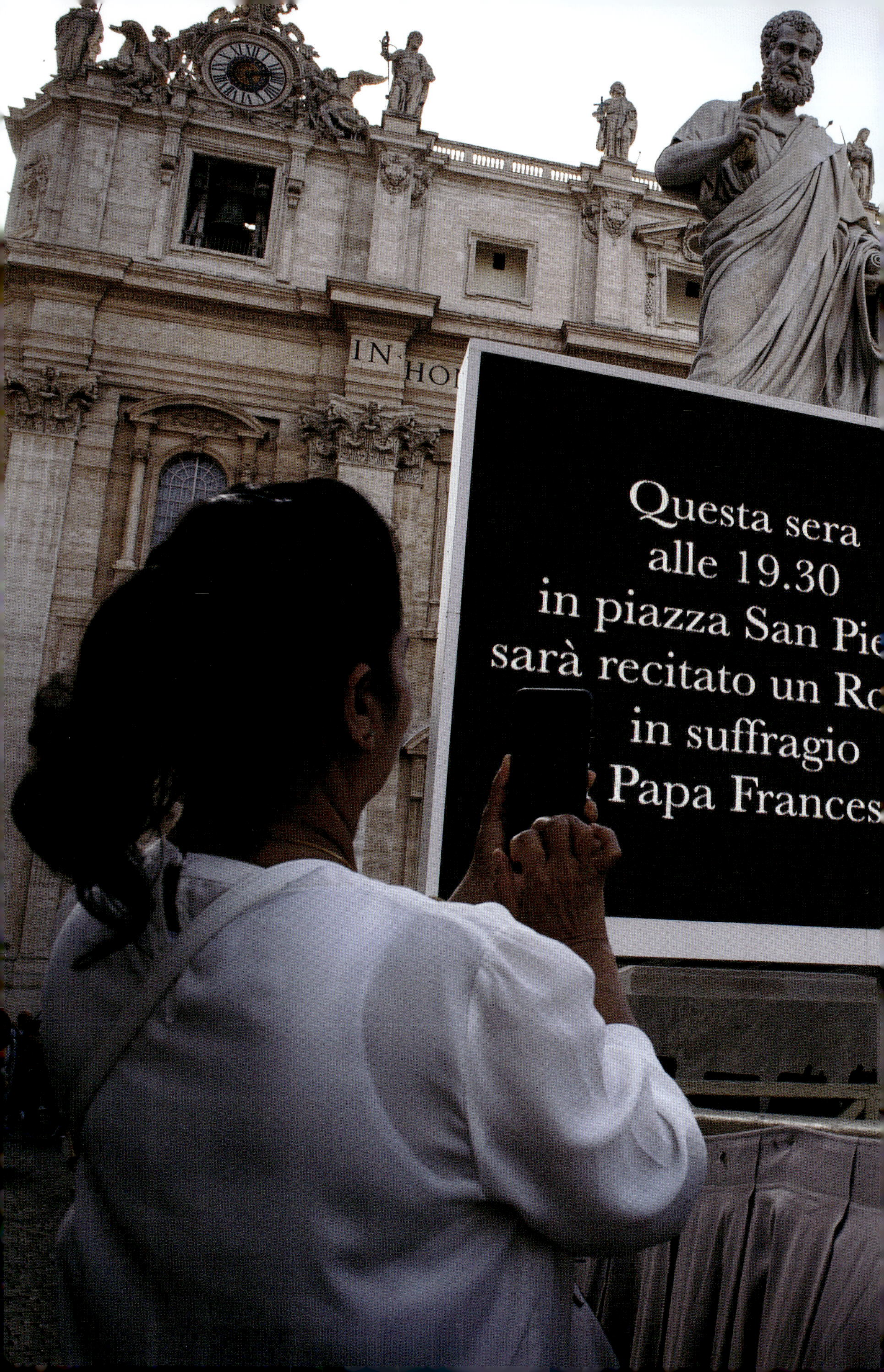
IN·HO
Questa sera
alle 19.30
in piazza San Pie
sarà recitato un Ro
in suffragio
Papa Frances

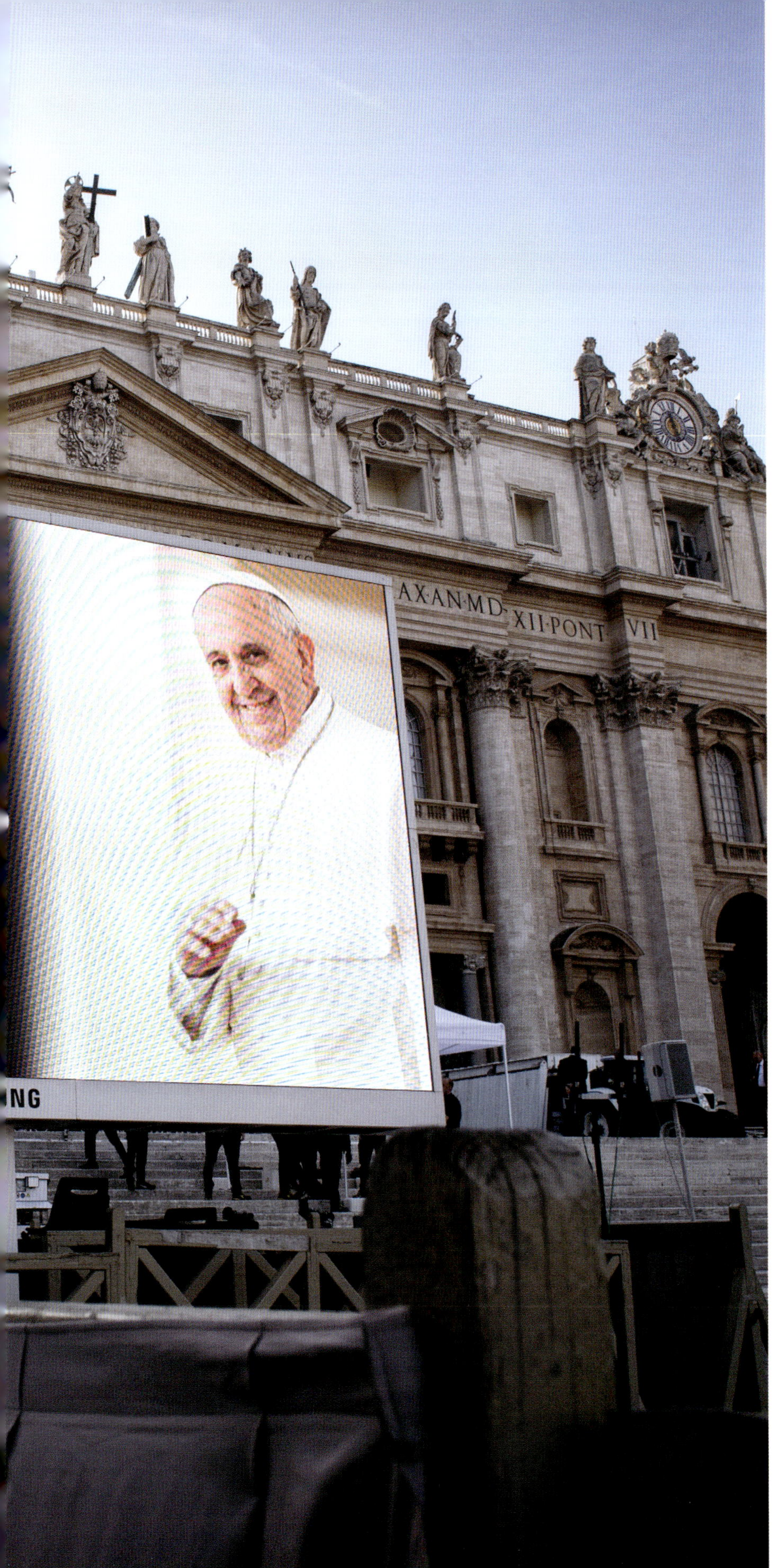

LEFT *A billboard informing the faithful of a Rosary to be prayed for the repose of the soul of Pope Francis, April 21, 2025.*

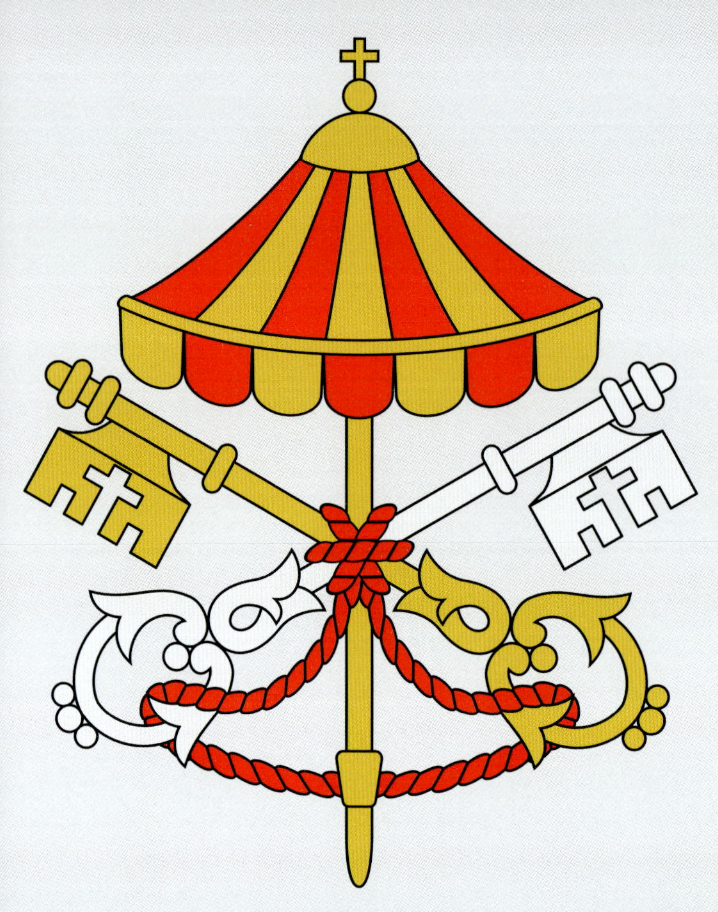

The coat of arms for the *Sede Vacante*. To signify the absence of a Pope, the papal tiara is removed and replaced with the *umbraculum*.

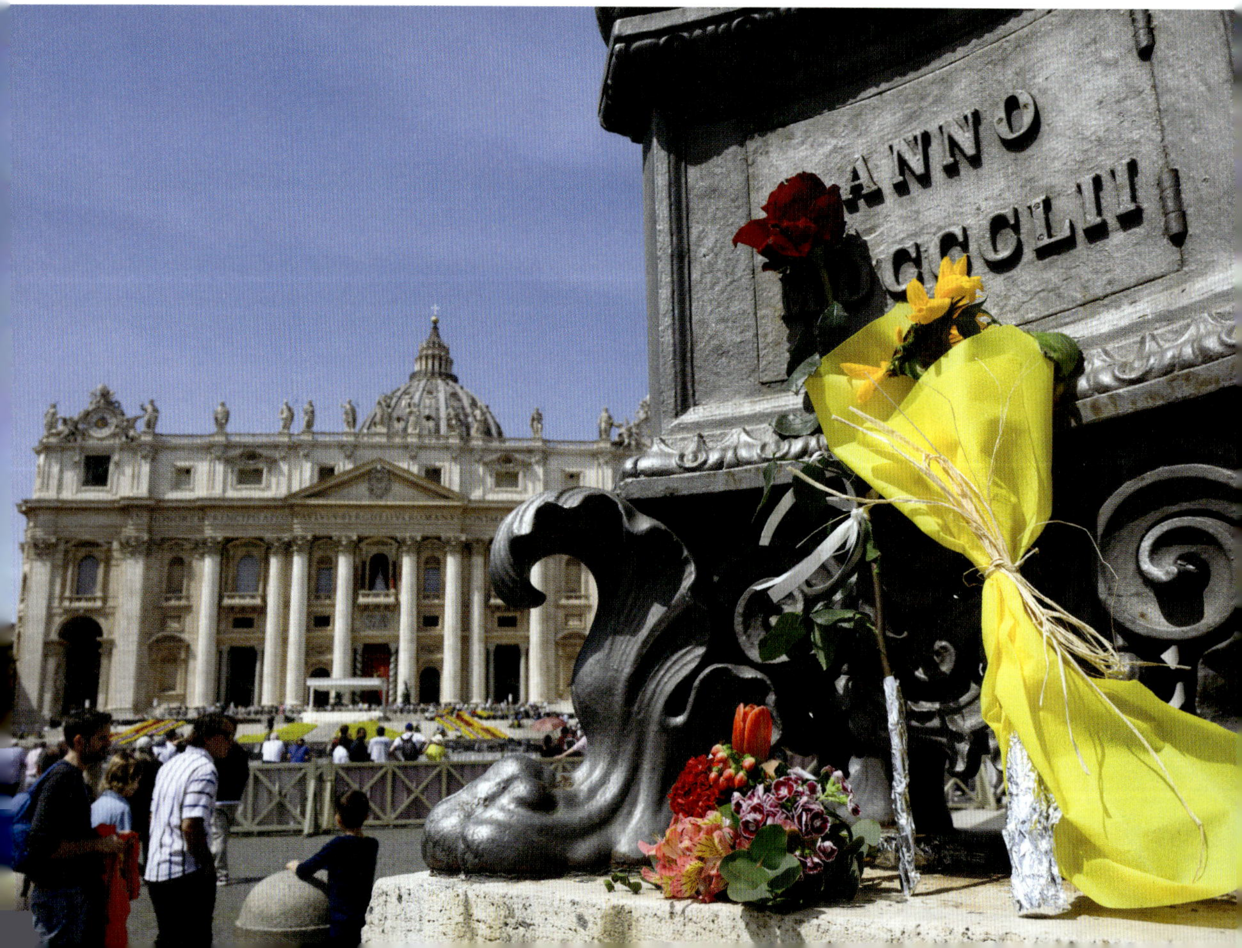

CHAPTER TWO

Sede Vacante: The Vacant See

The Unoccupied Throne of Peter

During this time, the traditional papal coat of arms is altered: the tiara (papal crown) is replaced by the *umbraculum* (a gold-and-red-striped canopy or umbrella), accompanied by the crossed Keys of St. Peter. This symbol, seen on Vatican documents and websites during the vacancy, signifies the temporary status of the governance of the Church. It is a visual reminder to the faithful that the See of Rome—the Chair of the Pope—is empty, awaiting its next occupant. The Apostolic Palace was silent, and the famous window from which each Pope gives his weekly Angelus address was shuttered. And the Swiss Guards, whose primary duty is the Pope's personal protection, ceremonially stood down from their usual posts at the papal apartment (though they continued to guard the entrances of Vatican City and to honor the late Pope's remains).

This period of *Sede Vacante*—rich in pageantry and precision—has been described as a "tightly choreographed series of events, refined over the centuries." It balances grief with hope, as the Church both mourns the past and prepares for the future.

Importantly, no major decisions or appointments can be made during *Sede Vacante*. The governance of the Church is in a "caretaker mode," handling only routine matters. Papal authority in teaching and governance is suspended until the new Pope is elected, as the Church waits in prayerful expectation. Nevertheless, pilgrims still visit, Masses are still offered, and the world's attention begins to focus on the upcoming conclave. This remarkable situation—the Church without a living Pope—is solemn, but not chaotic; it is guided by detailed rules set forth in Church law. Each step in the interregnum is meant to ensure continuity and prepare for a smooth transfer of the Keys of Peter to the next Pontiff.

Vatican City Under Stewardship

During *Sede Vacante*, day-to-day administration of the Vatican and the Church's essential functions falls to certain key figures and bodies, all operating under clear guidelines and limits. The College of Cardinals as a whole carries a great responsibility in this

LEFT *Flowers in honor of Pope Francis in St. Peter's Square.*

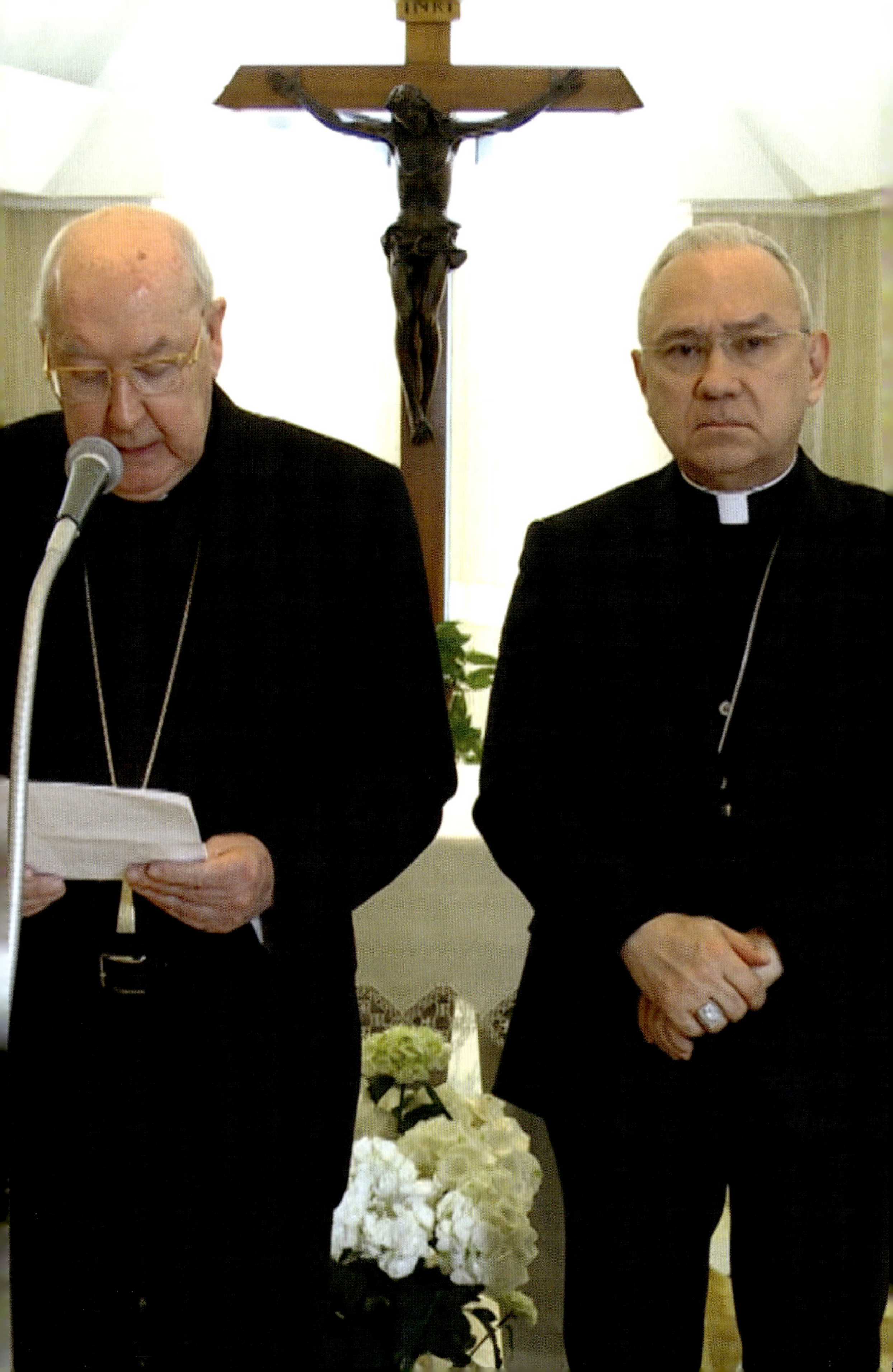

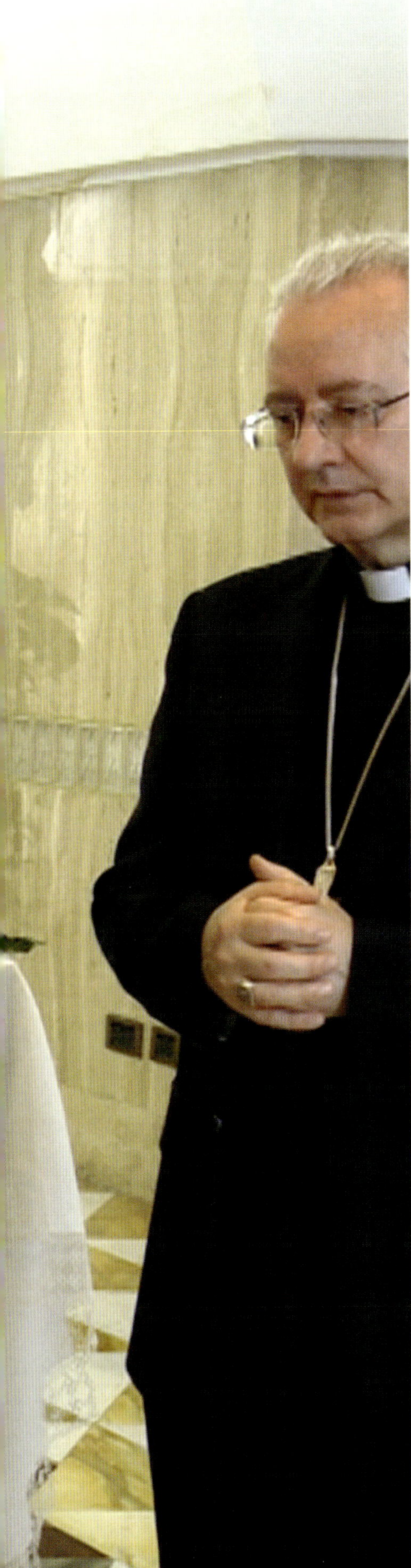

period, but they must act in unison, and with restraint.

As is the custom, the Cardinal Camerlengo (Cardinal Farrell) remained the central steward, responsible for the Vatican's temporal goods and for an orderly progression of events leading to the upcoming election. He was assisted by three cardinals, chosen by drawing lots, in accordance with the dictates of Church law. These three cardinals were changed every several days. Together with the Cardinal Camerlengo, these rotating individuals ensured that the "lights stayed on" (literally and figuratively)—that the Vatican City State and Roman Curia continued basic operations, but without making any long-term decisions. They oversaw everything from the continued celebration of liturgies to the security of the Apostolic Palace. In these roles, Cardinal Farrell and his assistants acted as calm administrators, not as new leaders; their charge was to govern only in urgent matters, until a new Pope took the helm.

All heads of Vatican departments (dicasteries) automatically lost their authority when the Pope died. This is by design (and for the particular reason of preventing any single person from wielding undue power in the Pope's absence), underlining that the Supreme Pontiff alone unifies all authority. There were a few exceptions: the Major Penitentiary (in charge of certain internal matters of conscience), the Vicar General

LEFT *Cardinal Kevin Farrell, the Cardinal Camerlengo, announces the death of Pope Francis, April 21, 2025.*

for Rome, the Vicar for Vatican City, and the Papal Almoner (who oversees daily charity to the poor) all continued their pastoral or charitable work without interruption. They ensured that spiritual care and charity in Rome carried on. Additionally, the Master of Papal Liturgical Celebrations temporarily coordinated the funeral rites and the liturgies during the vacancy. These remaining officials acted in accord with the College of Cardinals.

During the *Sede Vacante*, the Cardinals avoided any actions intended to fill a "power vacuum"; rather, the Church functioned like a ship under interim officers, steady on course until the new captain would arrive.

Gathering the College: General Congregations

Within days of Pope Francis' death, Vatican City saw the arrival of Cardinals from around the globe to participate in the impending conclave (at the time of the conclave, there were 252 cardinals worldwide, but only those under the age of 80 were permitted to take part in the conclave). Before they entered the Sistine Chapel to vote, these Princes of the Church engaged in a series of meetings known as the General Congregations of Cardinals. Beginning on the day after the Pope's death and continuing for two weeks, these twelve Congregations were closed-door sessions in which Cardinals collectively reflected on the Church's needs and prepared for the election. Within the Vatican, Cardinals in simple black cassocks and red *zucchetti* (skullcaps) came together in the mornings and afternoons. They opened and closed each session with prayer, invoking the Holy Spirit's guidance. The mood in these gatherings was fraternal and solemn, yet hopeful.

During the General Congregations, Cardinals discussed a wide range of topics facing the Church. According to reports, they spoke about external challenges—ongoing wars and worldwide conflicts, the plight of migrants and refugees, the persecution of Christians in certain regions—as well as internal issues within the Church. They revisited Pope Francis' projects, such as the continued implementation of synodality, and they assessed pressing administrative concerns, such as Vatican finances and the clergy abuse reforms. While explicit campaigning or politicking is forbidden in these meetings (the Cardinals may not form voting blocs or make promises), they are typically free to exchange views frankly. Many Cardinals stepped to the microphone to share reflections on the kind of Pope the Church needed at this juncture: a

TOP LEFT *Cardinal Pietro Parolin signing the* Rogito *before it is placed in the papal coffin.* ***TOP RIGHT*** *Cardinal Kevin Joseph Farrell.* ***BOTTOM LEFT*** *Cardinals walking together leading up to the General Congregations.* ***BOTTOM RIGHT*** *Cardinals gathering for the General Congregations leading up to the conclave.*

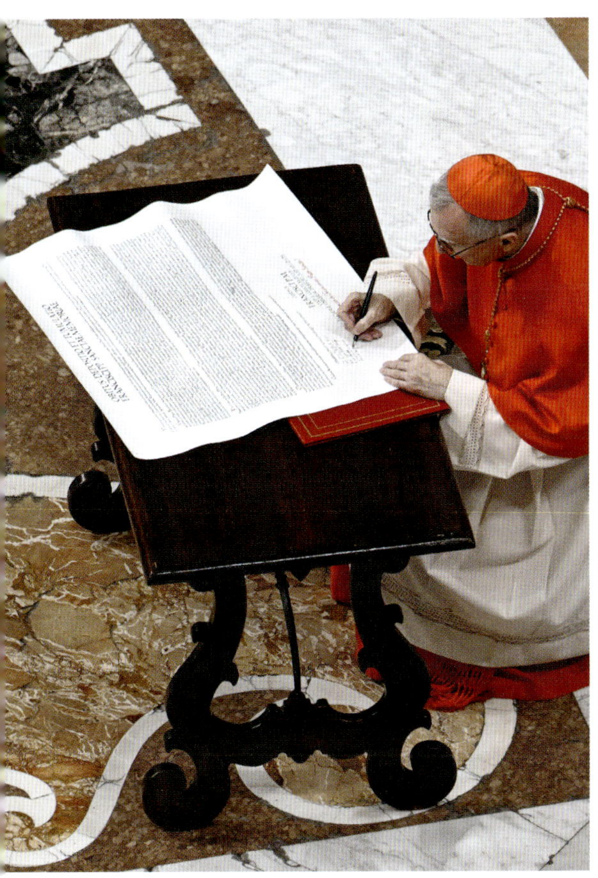

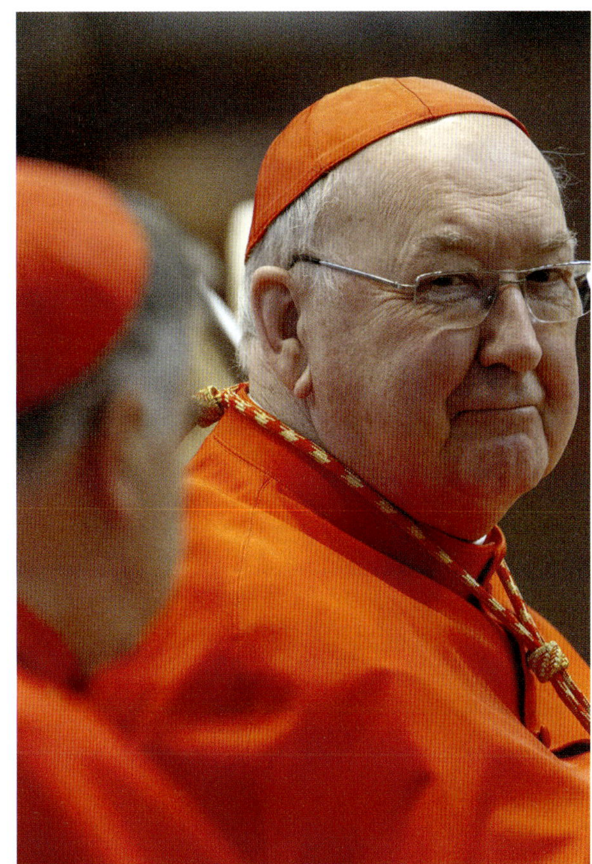

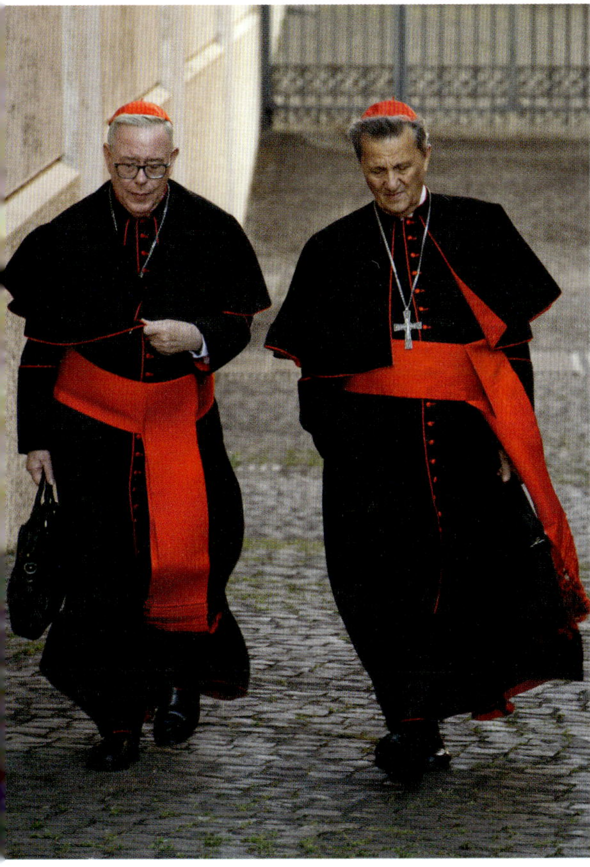

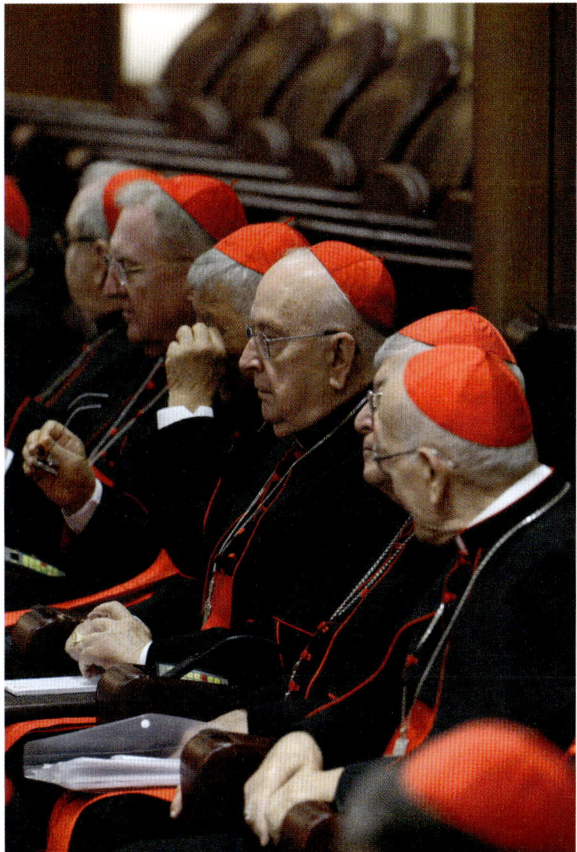

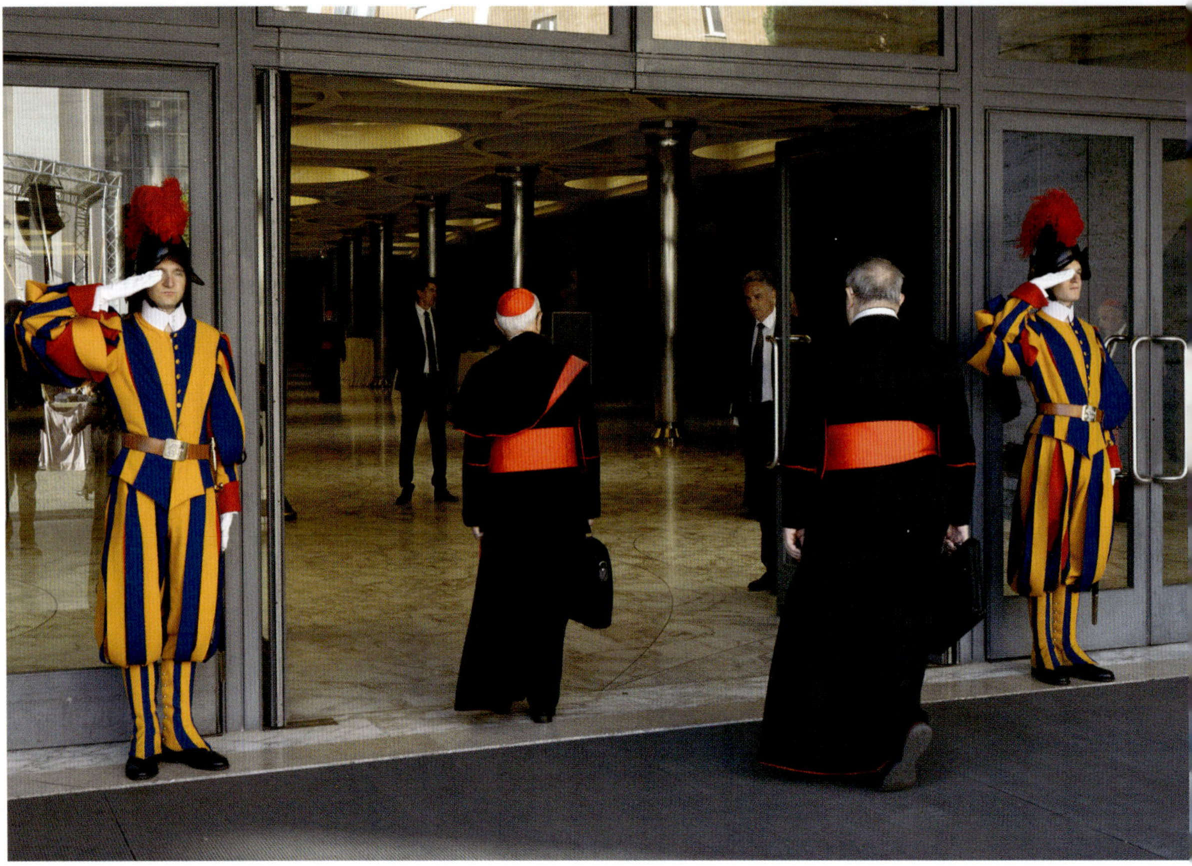

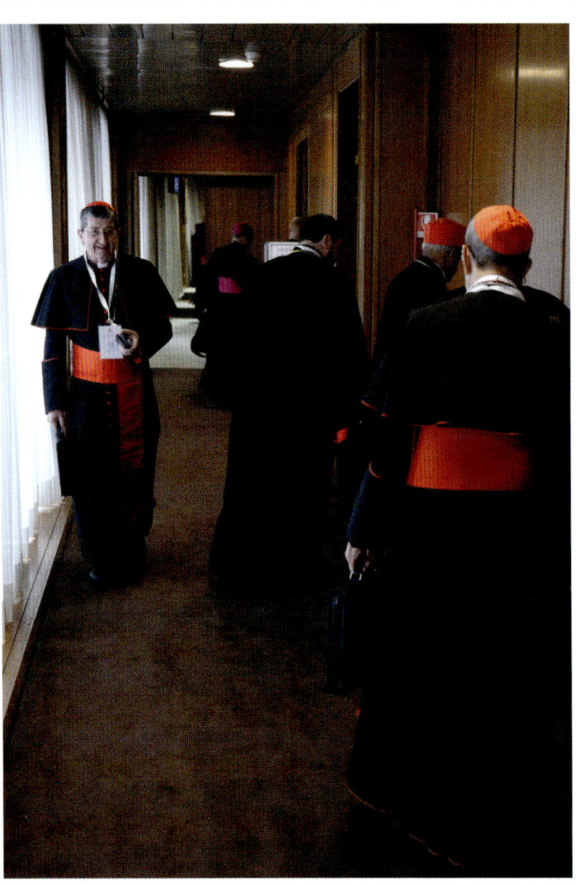

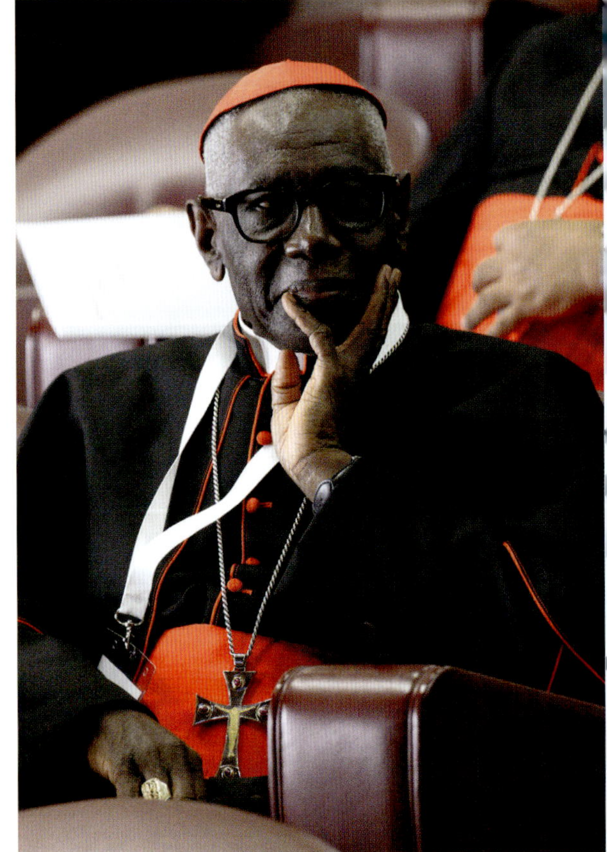

shepherd who is capable of bridging divides, a humble servant, a vigorous evangelist, perhaps even someone from a region of the world that has never produced a Pope. As Pope St. John Paul II noted in *Universi Dominici Gregis*, Cardinals are permitted "to exchange views concerning the election" during this period—indeed it is expected they will do so prayerfully—but all formal "lobbying" or pacts are strictly prohibited.

Each evening after the meetings, Cardinals offered Mass in Rome's churches and visited Pope Francis' tomb at St. Mary Major to pray. The faithful of Rome, for their part, lit candles at parish altars and kept vigils for the Cardinal-electors, trusting that God's Hand was guiding the imminent choice of a new Pope.

By the end of the General Congregations, the Cardinals had set a date for the start of the conclave. In accordance with Church law, the conclave begins between fifteen and twenty days after a Pope's death; this window of time allows for the mourning and burial of the Pope and for the arrival of Cardinals from all the corners of the world. In this case, the Cardinals chose to begin the conclave on May 7, 2025.

Sacred Traditions of a Vacant See

Even as these meetings were taking place, the Vatican observed several unique traditions that occur only during *Sede Vacante*, underscoring both the continuity and the sense of expectation in this period.

One such tradition is the installation of the Sistine Chapel chimney. In the days before the conclave, technicians climbed to the roof of the Sistine Chapel to fit a small metal stovepipe atop it—the very chimney through which the famous smoke signals of the conclave would rise. The sight of this chimney going up caused a stir among pilgrims: it made the coming election feel imminent and real. Photographers captured images of workers testing the two stoves inside the chapel (one stove for burning ballots, another to produce additional chemicals for black or white smoke), a modern method to ensure the smoke's color is unambiguous.

At the same time, the interior of the Sistine Chapel was closed to visitors and prepared for its solemn role as the conclave hall. A table and chair for each Cardinal-elector were arranged along the frescoed walls under Michelangelo's scenes of Creation and the Last Judgment, and necessary items such as bound booklets of the conclave prayers and ballot papers were readied.

TOP *Cardinals arriving for the General Congregations.* ***BOTTOM LEFT*** *Beginning on the day after Pope Francis' death and continuing for two weeks, these twelve Congregations were closed-door sessions in which Cardinals collectively and prayerfully reflected on the Church's needs and prepared for the election.* ***BOTTOM RIGHT*** *Cardinal Robert Sarah.*

Another moving custom: During the *Sede Vacante*, the great bell of St. Peter's Basilica fell silent, only to ring out again joyously once a new Pope would be elected. During each evening of the vacancy, however, another bell—called the "cardinal's bell"—tolled to mark the end of the day's Congregations and to remind the faithful to pray for the coming conclave.

The atmosphere in Vatican City was thus one of vigilant prayer and orderly anticipation. Even beyond the Vatican walls, Catholic life took on a distinctive tone. In parish churches worldwide, special intentions, such as the following, were added to the Prayers of the Faithful: "For the Church in this time of transition, that the Holy Spirit guide the College of Cardinals to choose a Supreme Pontiff after God's own heart." Monasteries of cloistered monks and nuns—such as the Discalced Carmelite nuns in Pope Francis' native Argentina—reportedly intensified their prayers and fasting for the election of a worthy successor. This spiritual solidarity highlighted a profound truth: while the Church was without a Pope on earth, Christ the Eternal Shepherd was still guiding His flock, and the Holy Spirit was actively at work, ready to inspire the choice of the next Vicar of Christ.

The day before the conclave, the Sistine Chapel was formally sealed and checked for any recording or communication devices (modern protocol includes electronic jamming to ensure total secrecy). The cardinals prepared to celebrate a final public Mass for the upcoming election, imploring the aid of God and all of the saints. With hearts cleansed and minds focused, they stood prepared to enter the conclave—that most sacred and secret of elections—to elect the new Pope. The world waited with them in prayerful suspense.

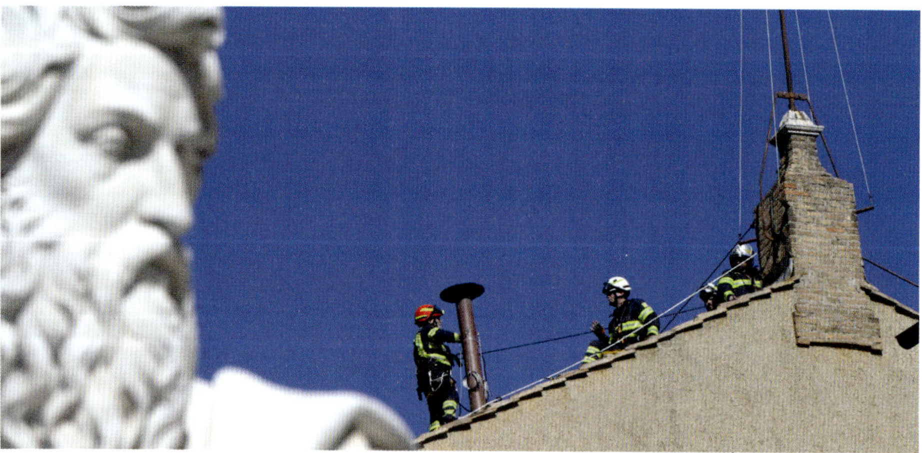

ABOVE *Workers affixing the chimney above the Sistine Chapel.* **TOP RIGHT** *Black smoke after a round of voting, signaling an inconclusive vote.* **BOTTOM RIGHT** *Pilgrims resting and praying in between rounds of voting.*

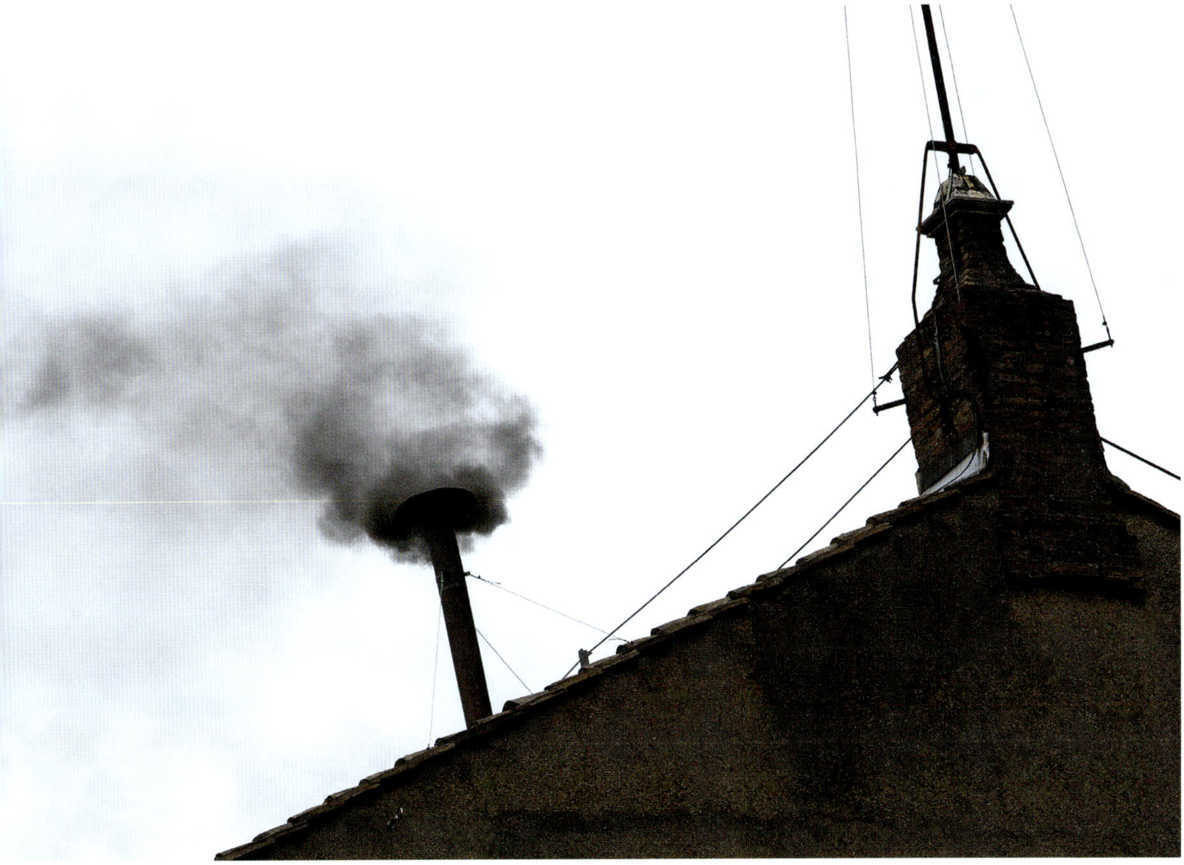

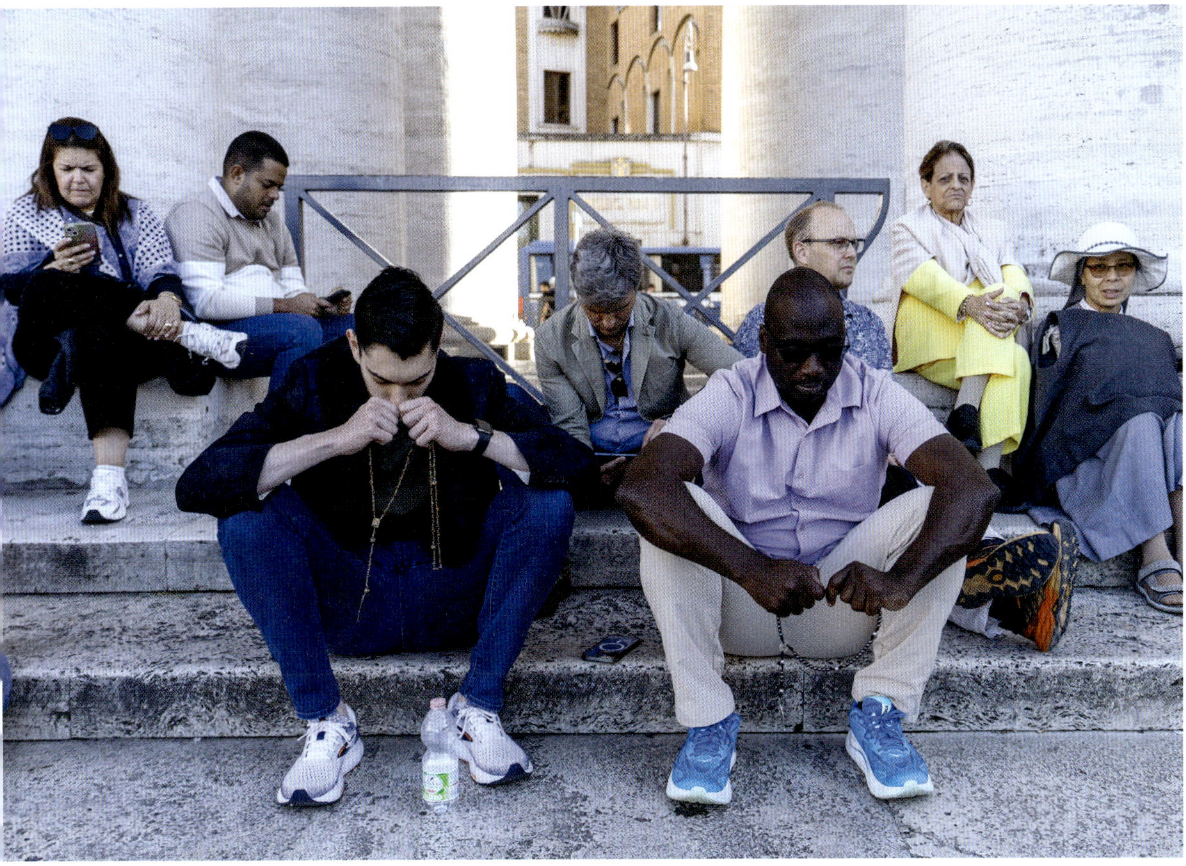

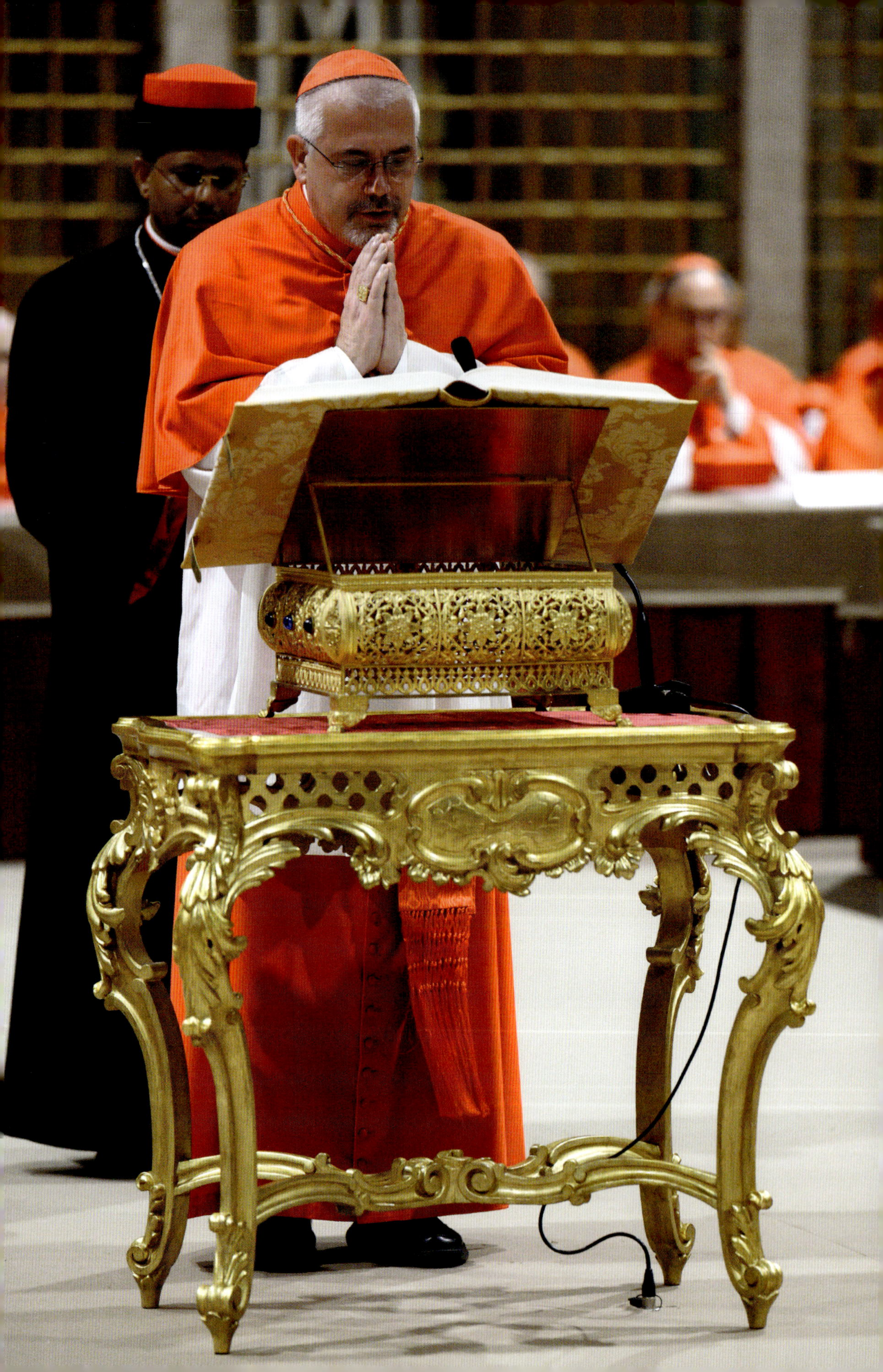

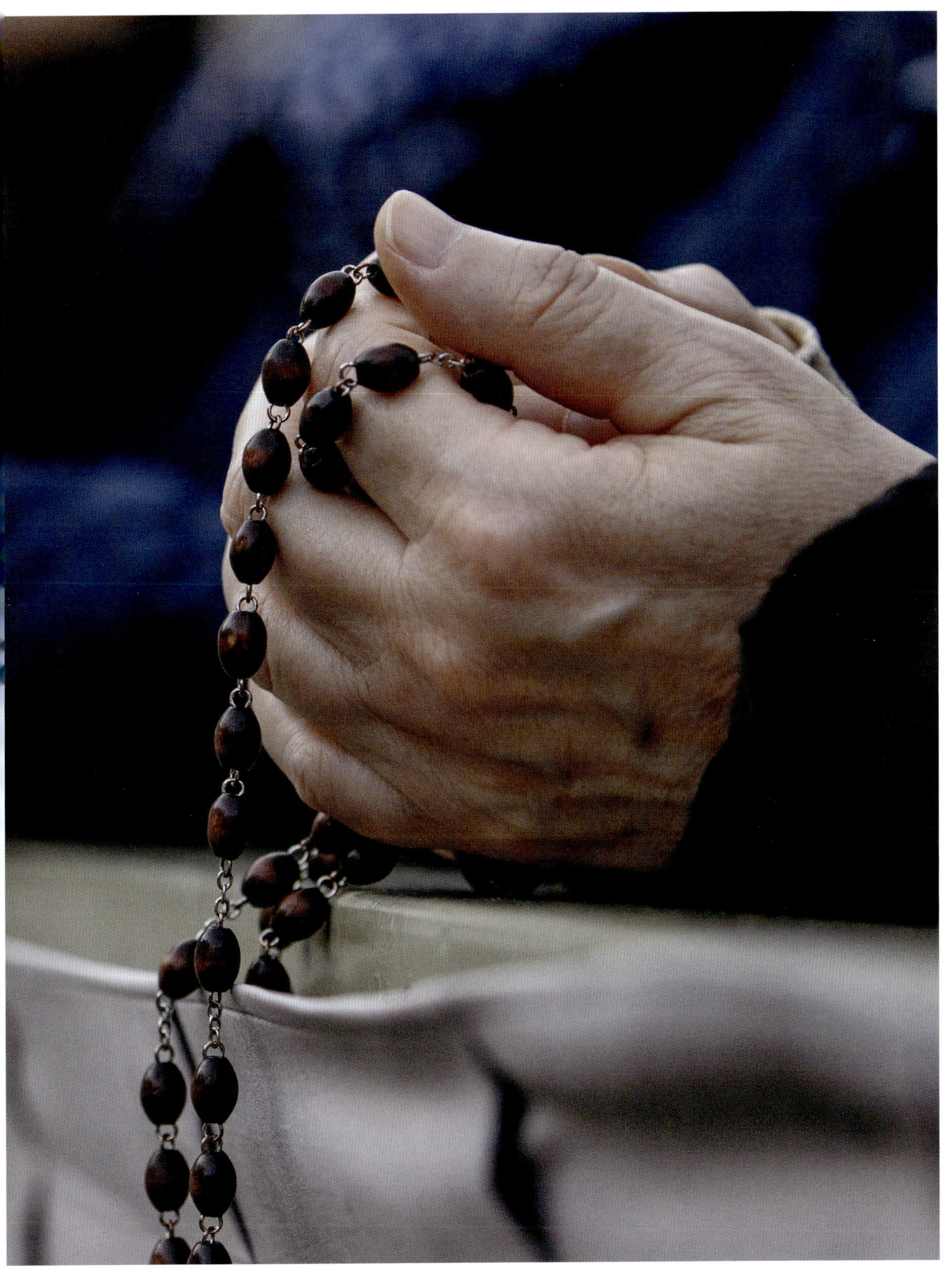

ABOVE *A pilgrim clutching rosary beads in St. Peter's Square.* **LEFT** *The voting Cardinals taking an oath of secrecy and fidelity before the conclave.*

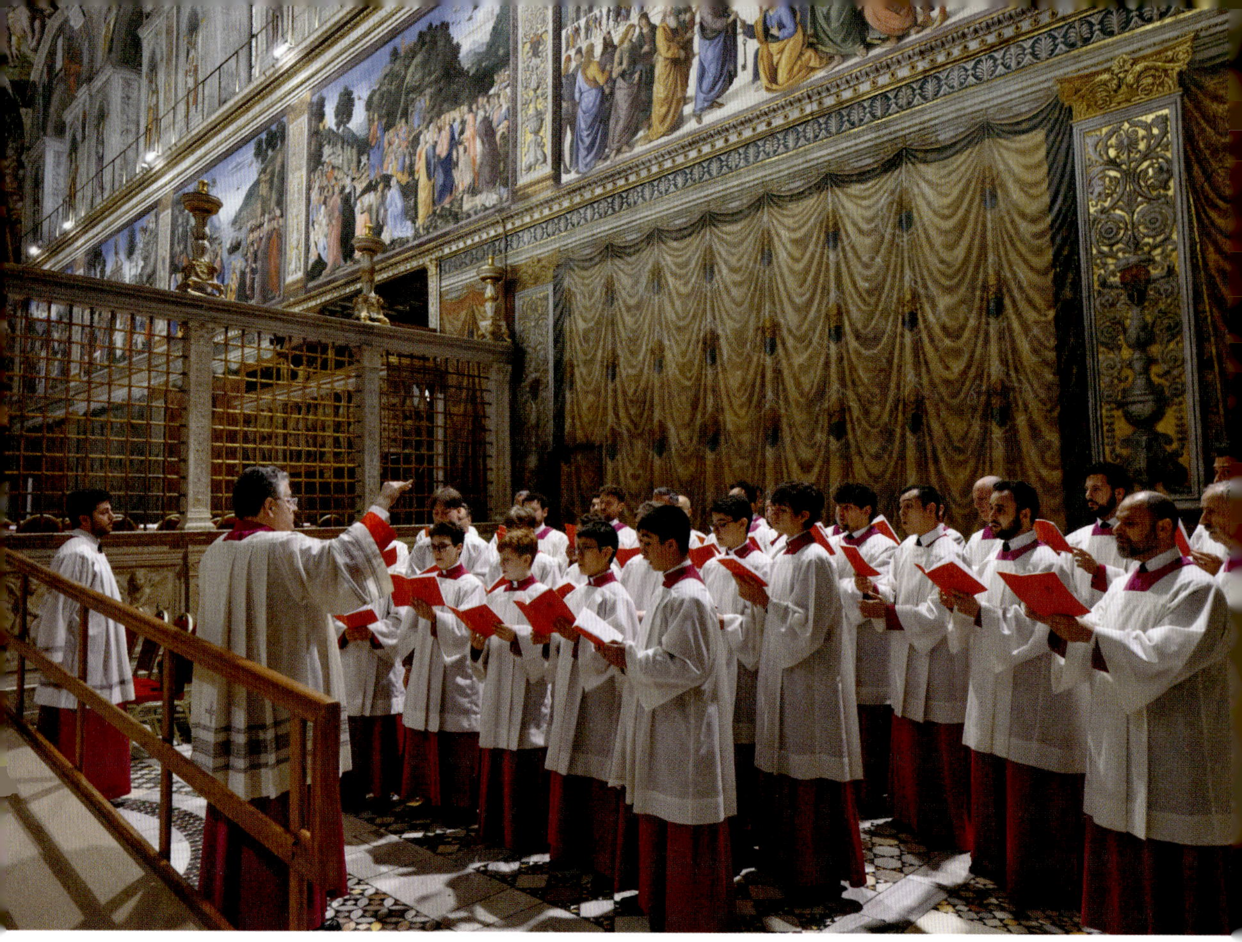

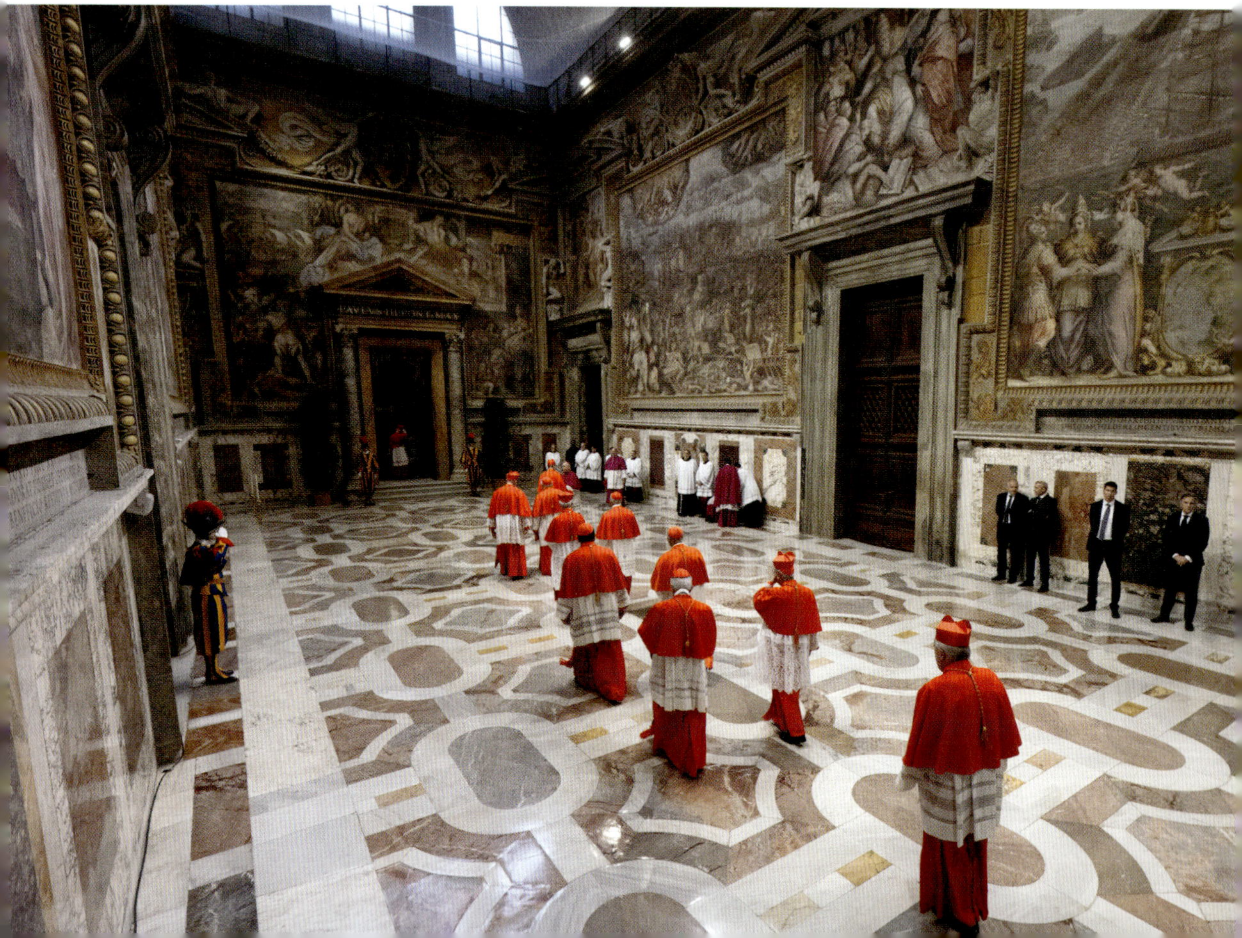

CHAPTER THREE

The Sacred Conclave

In the Sistine Chapel: *Missa pro Eligendo Pontifice* and "*Extra Omnes!*"

On the morning the conclave was to begin, the Cardinal-electors celebrated the customary *Missa pro Eligendo Pontifice*—a Mass for the Election of a Pope—at St. Peter's Basilica. The public was invited to this Liturgy, and thousands attended, knowing it was the last Mass before the Cardinals sequestered themselves. The Dean of the College, Cardinal Giovanni Battista Re, was the main celebrant; in his homily, he urged his brother Cardinals (and all the faithful) to pray intensely for the guidance of the Holy Spirit.

By late afternoon, the electors had assembled in the Pauline Chapel of the Apostolic Palace, each wearing solemn choir dress (red cassocks and lace rochets, with a mozzetta shoulder cape). Together, they chanted the *Veni Creator Spiritus*, the ancient hymn imploring the Holy Spirit to enliven their minds and hearts. In a procession steeped in centuries of tradition, the Cardinals then walked (in order of seniority) through the Sala Regia and into the Sistine Chapel, two by two, while singing the Litany of the Saints. This magnificent moment—scarlet-robed figures passing under frescoes of biblical kings and Popes—was captured by Vatican cameras and broadcast until the doors closed, allowing the world a brief glimpse of the event to come.

Inside the Sistine Chapel, each Cardinal took an oath of secrecy and fidelity, proclaiming in Latin: "I pledge and swear to observe faithfully and scrupulously the prescriptions of the Apostolic Constitution *Universi Dominici Gregis* ... and to maintain secrecy concerning all matters in any way related to the election of the Roman Pontiff." They further swore not to be influenced by secular authorities or external pressures, and that, if elected, they would carry out the Petrine office with fidelity. This oath underscored the solemn freedom from political wrangling that ought to exist within the sacredness of the conclave. After the last Cardinal swore the oath, Archbishop Diego Ravelli, the Master of Papal Liturgical Ceremonies, stood at the threshold of the Sistine

TOP LEFT *A choir chanting the* Veni Creator Spiritus *in the Sistine Chapel.*
BOTTOM LEFT *Cardinals processing into the Sistine Chapel to commence the conclave.*

Chapel and raised his voice to utter the famous command, "*Extra omnes!*—Everyone out!" All persons not immediately involved in the conclave (such as support staff and media—including Ravelli himself) exited, the heavy wooden doors swung shut, and the Cardinals were left alone, closed in and locked up *cum clave* ("with a key"). We might imagine that at that moment, with the reality of the weight of their task ahead of them, a profound silence settled among the Cardinals gathered in the Chapel. The outside world would now receive only one signal from within: smoke from the chimney.

To maintain the integrity of the conclave, the Cardinals would observe this strict enclosure. They would not depart the Vatican's secured grounds nor communicate with anyone outside until the conclave concluded. Lodging at the Domus Sanctae Marthae under similarly controlled conditions, they would be shuttled by bus to the Sistine Chapel for each voting session. All electronic devices were forbidden; the electors handed over phones and tablets prior to entering. The atmosphere within the Sistine Chapel was thus one of prayerful seclusion.

The Balloting Rituals: Scrutineers, Smoke Signals, and the Watchful World

Although the details of what went on inside the Chapel remain confidential, the basic structure of the proceedings was as follows: Once the conclave began, the Cardinals quickly moved into the first round of balloting, following procedures defined in law. On the afternoon of May 7, 2025, the first day of the conclave, one ballot was held. In subsequent days, there would be up to four ballots per day: two each morning, and two each afternoon. Each vote began with prayer and reflection. Certain Cardinals, chosen by drawing lots, were assigned special roles: three Scrutineers to count votes, three *Infirmarii* to collect votes of any electors too ill to physically cast votes themselves, and three Revisers (to verify the count). The ballots—rectangular slips bearing the Latin words "*Eligo in Summum Pontificem*—I elect as Supreme Pontiff"—were distributed, and each Cardinal, in secret, wrote the name of his choice. By custom, they are to disguise their handwriting.

One by one, in order of precedence, the Cardinals approached the altar. Holding up their folded ballot, each took a vow aloud: "I call as my witness Christ the Lord, Who will be my judge, that my vote is given to the one who, before God, I think should be elected." Then each placed his ballot into a large chalice atop the altar. This profoundly personal act—each elector casting his vote under oath before God—was done with great reverence. After all ballots were cast, the first Scrutineer shook the container to

RIGHT *Cardinals gathering in the Sistine Chapel at the beginning of the papal conclave.*

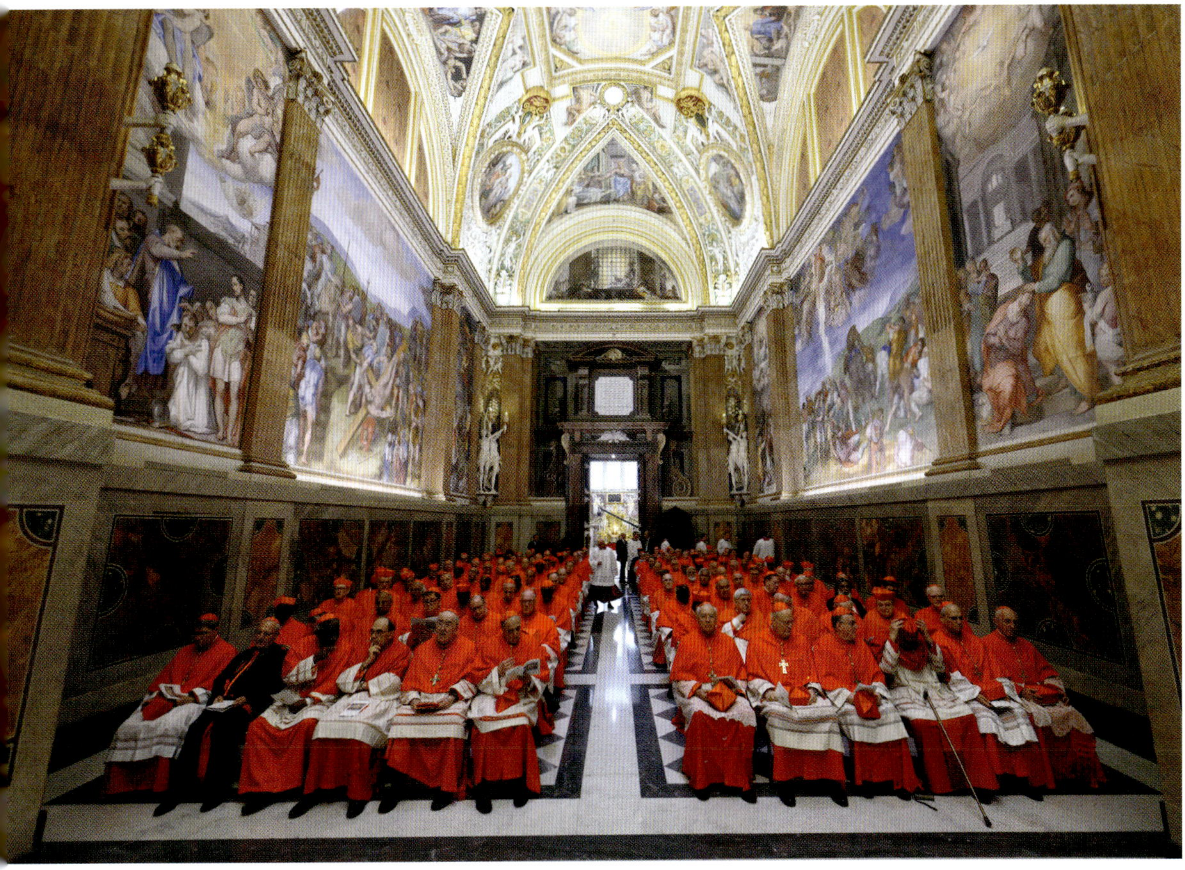

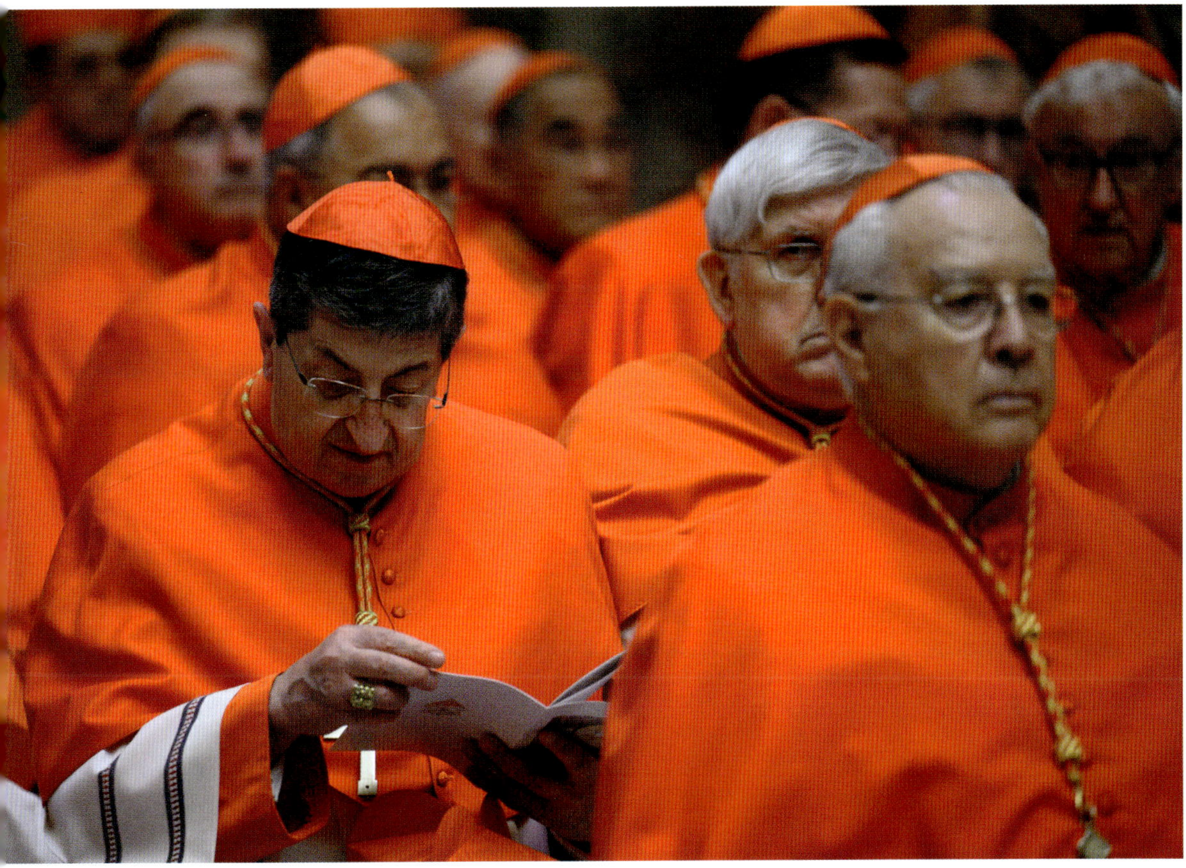

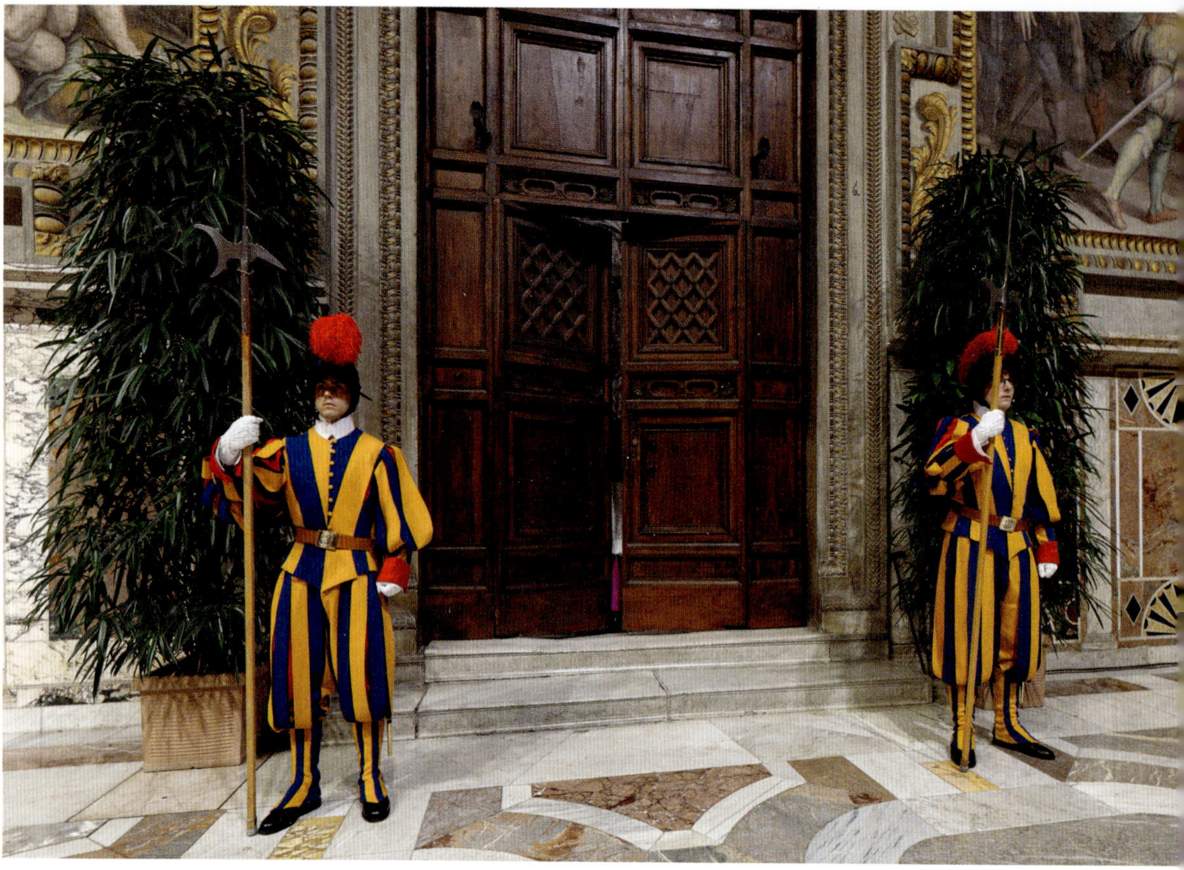

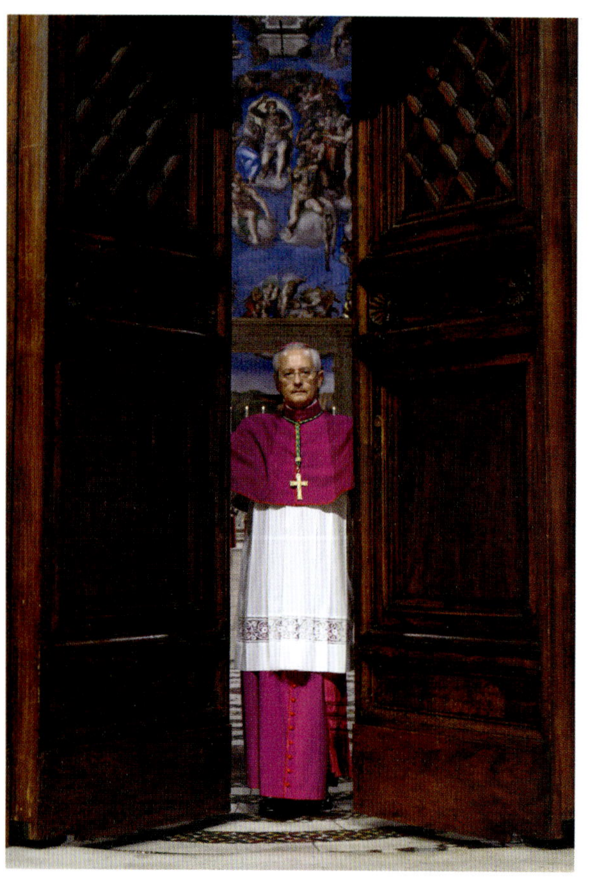

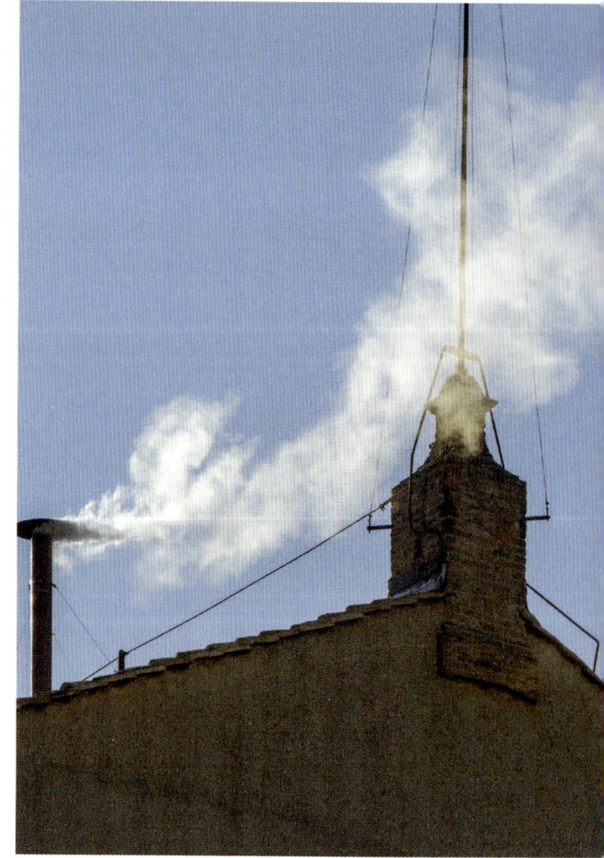

mix them, and the count began. In hushed tones, the ballots were opened one by one: one Scrutineer silently read the name on each, passed it to the next who did likewise, and the third read the name out loud for all to hear. Each name was carefully recorded on tally sheets by the Scrutineers (and by each elector privately). As each vote was announced, it was threaded onto a string; in this way, they were all tied together in the order in which they had been called, a centuries-old custom to prevent tampering.

A two-thirds majority is required to elect a new Pope. As there were 133 electors in this conclave, eighty-nine votes were needed for anyone to be elected. In any round of voting in which no Cardinal received sufficient votes, the ballots were burned in one stove while special chemicals were added to the other stove to provide the right color to the smoke; as the smoke from both stoves combined into the one chimney, the outside world saw the black smoke—the signal of an inconclusive vote. And indeed, on the first ballot that afternoon, as was expected, no clear consensus was reached; at about 9:00 p.m. that evening, the crowds in St. Peter's Square saw dark black smoke coming from the Sistine chimney. A low groan and then applause rippled through the watching crowd out in St. Peter's Square—disappointment, but also excitement for the process now truly underway. People went home or back to their hotels, clinging to rosaries and checking news alerts, knowing that the next morning would bring more ballots—and perhaps white smoke.

The Election of Pope Leo XIV

Over the next day (May 8), four more ballots could be held—two in the morning, two in the afternoon, in accordance with the set schedule. The Cardinals by now had a sense of who the leading candidates (*papabili*) were. In any conclave, however, if no one is elected after three days, a pause is taken for further prayer and discussion. But in this conclave, momentum built swiftly. By the fourth total ballot (which was on the second day of voting), a consensus emerged around an unexpected figure: the Chicago-born Cardinal Robert Prevost, an Augustinian bishop who had spent much of his ministry in Latin America and who had been made a Cardinal by Pope Francis in 2023. On that decisive ballot, as ballots were unfolded and names read, the consensus was reached. When the eighty-ninth vote for Prevost was announced, we can only imagine that a quiet gasp went through the Sistine Chapel. The Cardinals realized they had just elected a new Pope.

TOP *Swiss Guards standing outside of the Sistine Chapel after the doors are closed.* ***BOTTOM LEFT*** *Archbishop Diego Ravelli closing the doors of the Sistine Chapel after proclaiming* "Extra omnes." ***BOTTOM RIGHT*** *White smoke pouring out of the Sistine Chapel chimney, signaling a decisive ballot and a new Pope.*

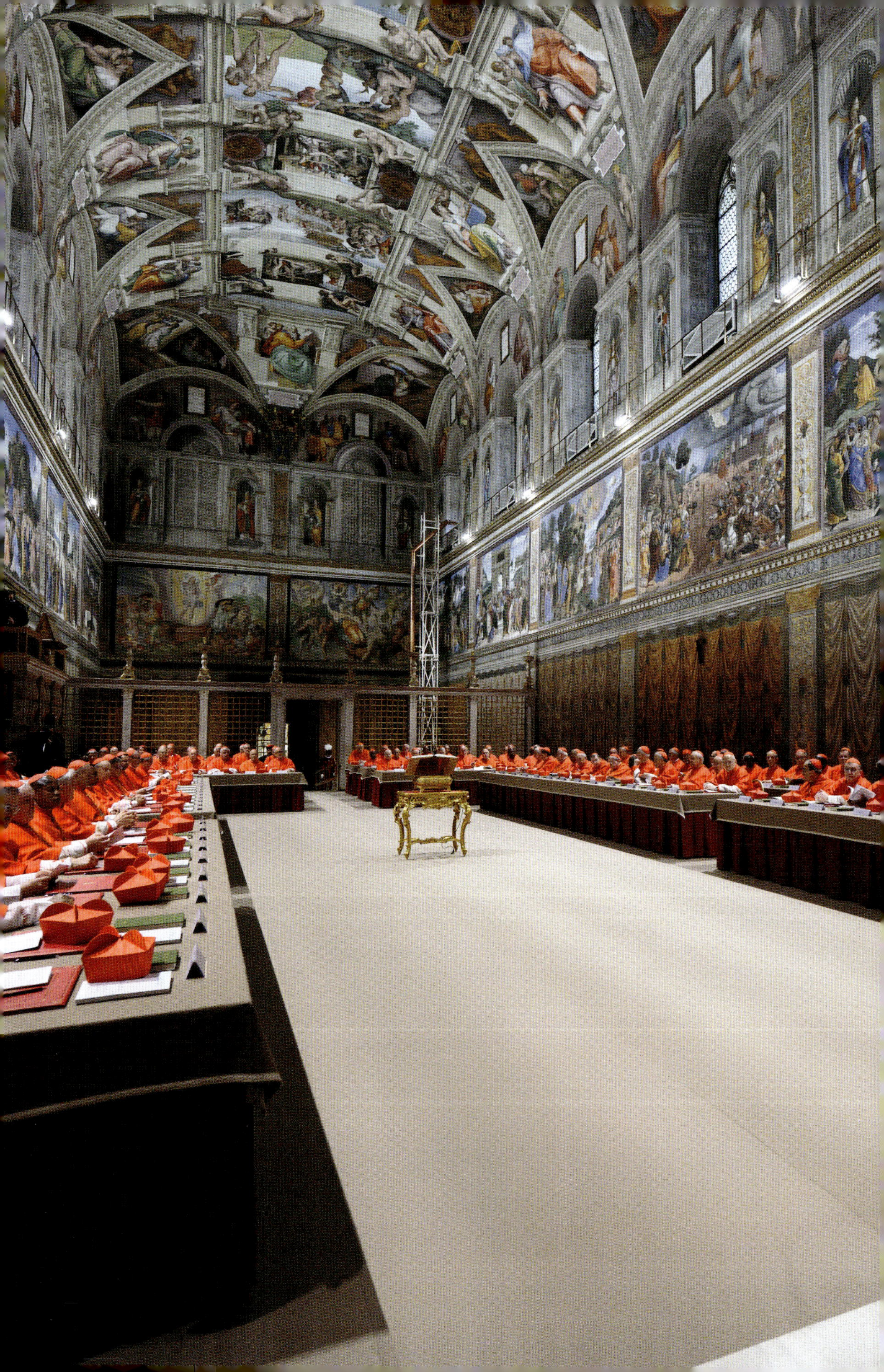

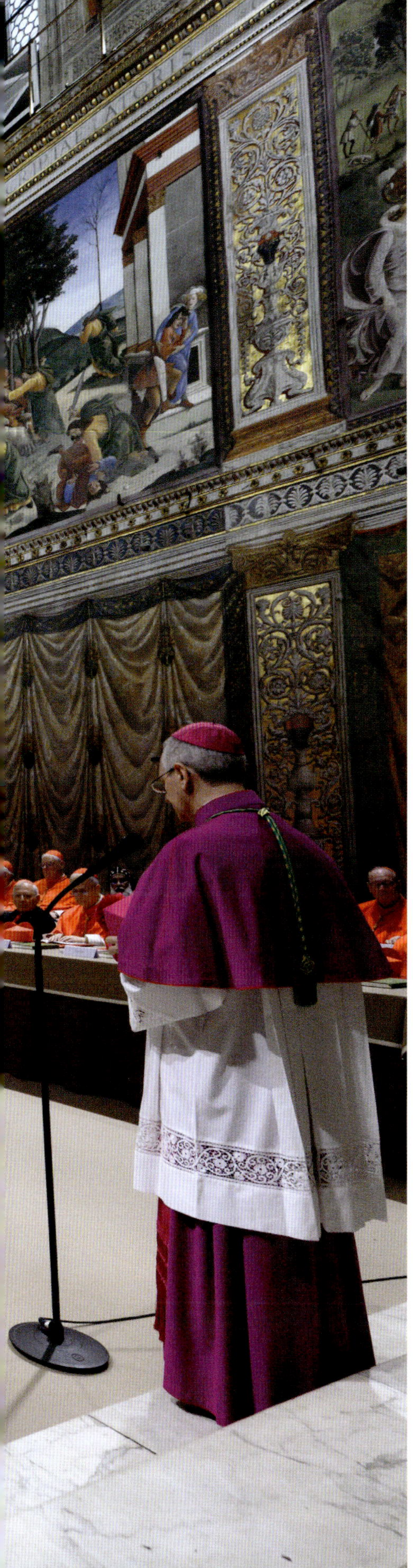

Cardinal Pietro Parolin then approached the Pope-elect. It was approximately 5:45 p.m. when he asked the formal question in Latin: "*Acceptasne electionem de te canonice factam in Summum Pontificem?*—Do you accept your canonical election as Supreme Pontiff?" The chosen Cardinal gave his assent, reportedly saying "*Accepto, in fide Domini*—I accept, in the faith of the Lord." He was then asked, "By what name shall you be called?" The Cardinal chose the name Leo XIV, honoring both St. Leo the Great from the fifth century and Pope Leo XIII of the late nineteenth century, and signaling a papacy rooted in tradition and courage. With that, Cardinal Prevost became Pope Leo XIV, the 266th Successor of St. Peter. A ripple of emotion spread through the Chapel as the Cardinals (one by one) removed their *zucchetti* in respect for the new Pontiff.

The Room of Tears

The Master of Ceremonies then led Pope Leo XIV to a small room adjacent to the main Chapel, known as the "Room of Tears." There, sets of white papal vestments in three sizes awaited him. After a brief private prayer—surely a moment of intense gravity for the new Holy Father—he donned the white cassock of the Pope for the first time, quickly pinned to fit him. When he emerged, clothed in white, the Cardinals greeted him with applause and approached in turn to offer a gesture of

LEFT *Archbishop Diego Ravelli declaring* "Extra omnes."

obedience and homage. Meanwhile, outside, the view of the watching world was still colored only by the black smoke from earlier ballots. But that was about to change.

Habemus Papam!

At approximately 6:06 p.m. on May 8, 2025, white smoke suddenly billowed from the Sistine Chapel chimney. Immediately, the bells of St. Peter's Basilica began ringing wildly in confirmation that a new Pope had indeed been chosen (a practice introduced to avoid any confusion about the smoke's color). A tremendous cheer erupted from the thousands gathered in the square below, many shouting *"Viva il Papa!"* even though they did not yet know who the Pope was. Some people wept openly with joy, waving flags of their home countries, realizing they were witnessing history. The jubilant scene was transmitted across the globe: from Manila to Nairobi to São Paulo, Catholics cried out in elation at the news: "*Habemus Papam!*—We have a Pope!"

Inside the Sistine Chapel, Pope Leo XIV, now dressed in the papal white soutane and his pectoral cross (a gift that had been given to him by one of his fellow Augustinians), a cross that contains relics of St. Augustine and his mother, St. Monica, among others, took a moment to pray with the Cardinals. Together, they sang the *Te Deum*, an ancient hymn of thanksgiving, the chant echoing off the frescoed walls. Then, the new Pope made his way back out to prepare for his first appearance. Meanwhile, Cardinal Protodeacon Dominique Mamberti stepped onto the central loggia, or balcony, of St. Peter's Basilica, facing the ecstatic and expectant crowd. At 7:12 p.m. local time, he raised his hands for silence and then pronounced the traditional Latin announcement to the city and the world:

> ***"Annuntio vobis gaudium magnum: Habemus Papam! Eminentissimum ac Reverendissimum Dominum, Dominum Robertum Franciscum Sanctae Romanae Ecclesiae Cardinalem Prevost, qui sibi nomen imposuit Leonem Decimum Quartum."*** **("I announce to you a great joy: We have a Pope! The Most Eminent and Most Reverend Lord, Lord Robert Cardinal Prevost of the Holy Roman Church, who has taken for himself the name Leo the Fourteenth.")**

RIGHT Habemus Papam! *Following the decisive round of voting, Cardinal Dominique Mamberti announces to the world that a new Pope has been elected.*

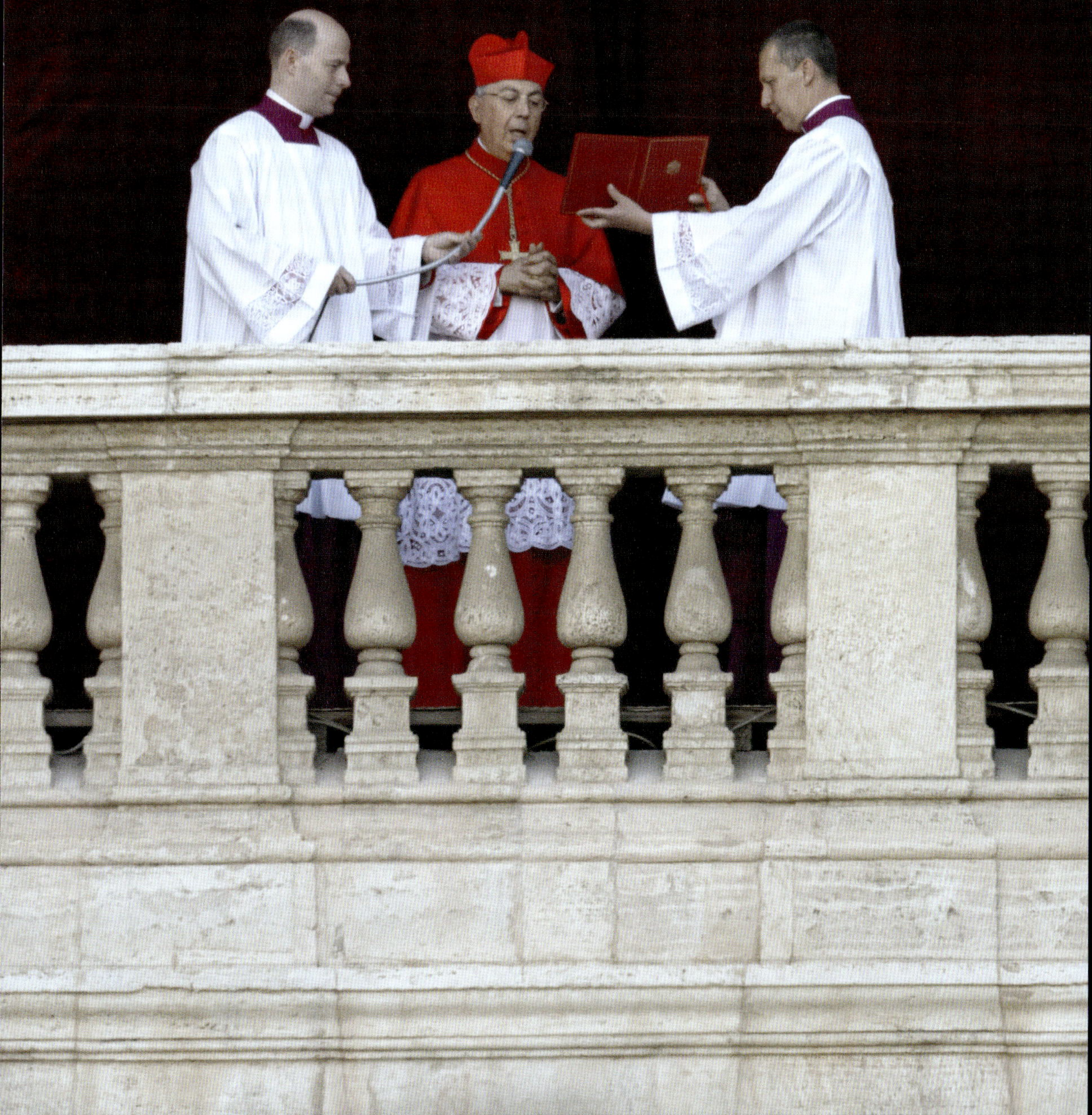

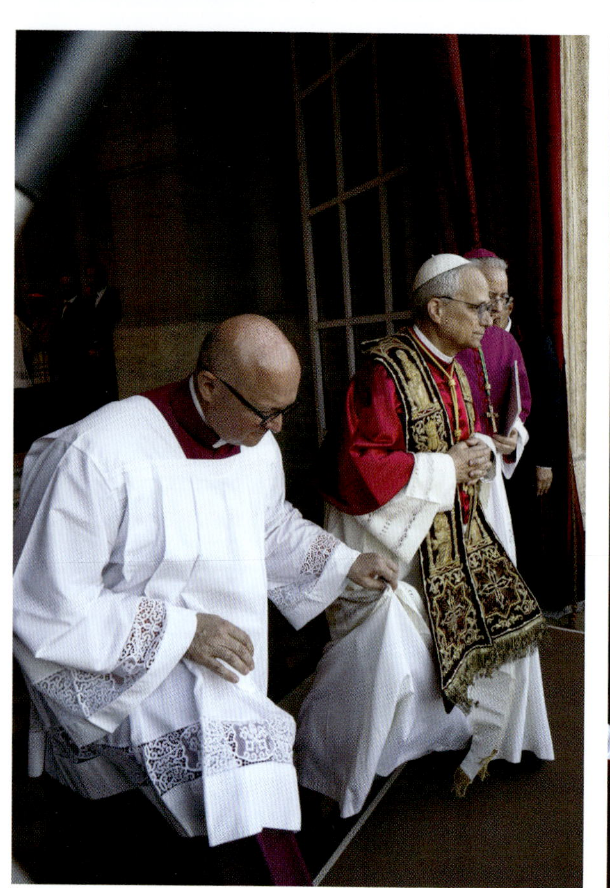

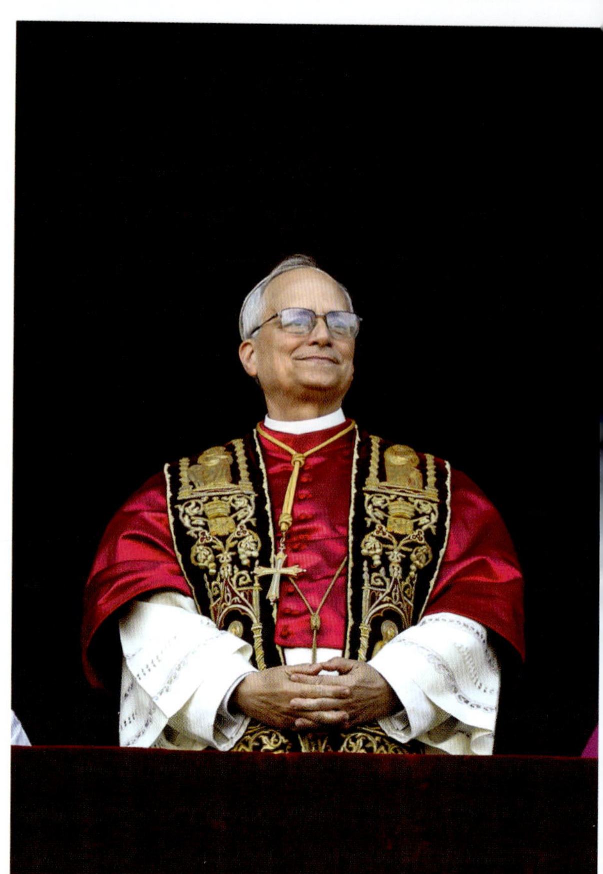

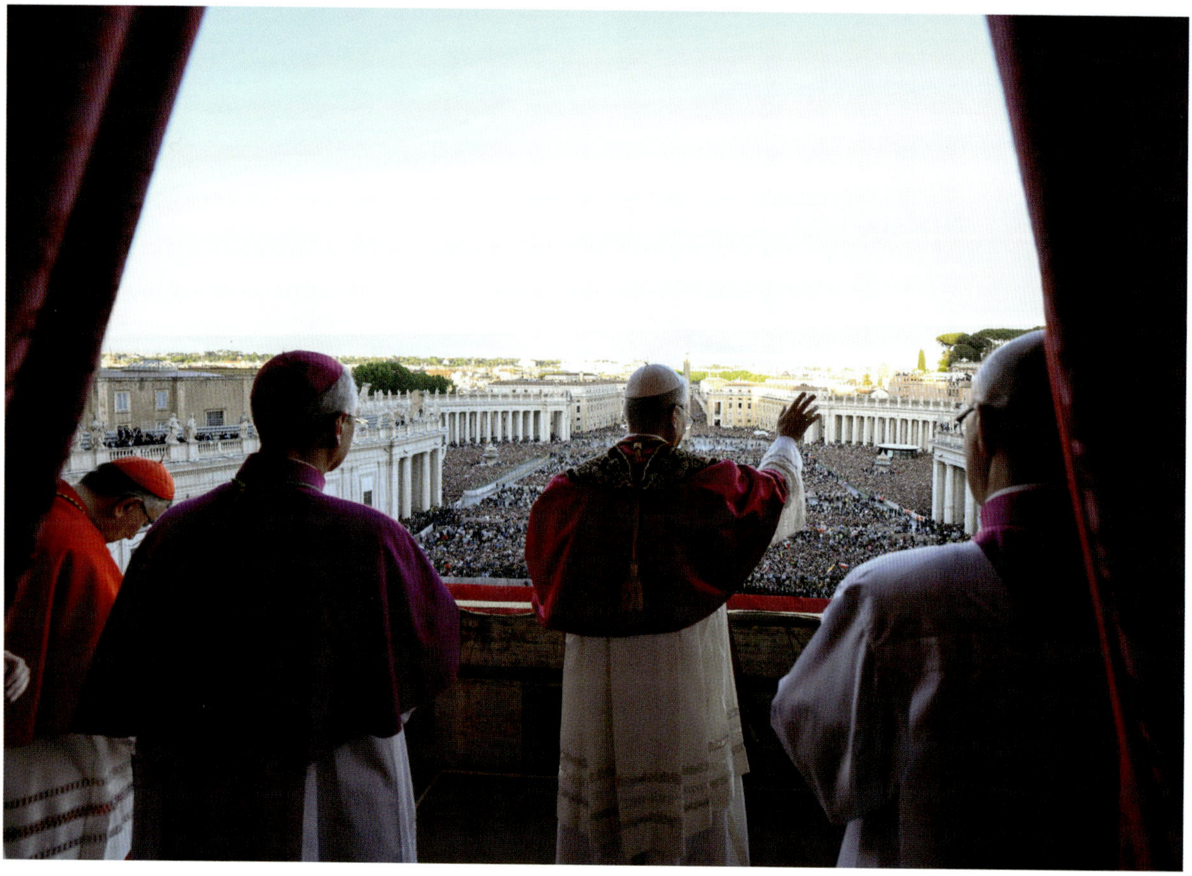

The Piazza broke into thunderous applause and cheers at these words. History had been made: the U.S.-born Cardinal Robert Prevost was now Pope Leo XIV. Many in the crowd waved American flags alongside Vatican flags in astonishment and pride at what had always before seemed an unlikely scenario: an American Pope. But more important than that, he was now the Universal Shepherd of 1.4 billion Catholics all over the world. As cameras flashed and broadcasters repeated his name, the red velvet drapes on the balcony parted. Pope Leo XIV stepped forward into view, greeted by a roar of joy from the faithful. He looked slightly overwhelmed by the newfound weight of the world on his shoulders, and yet he also appeared serene and touched with joy by the sight of so many of his flock cheering for him already; at 69 years old, he smiled gently, and he raised both hands repeatedly in a warm and benevolent greeting.

The First Papal Blessing: *Urbi et Orbi*

After the applause subsided, Pope Leo gave his *Urbi et Orbi* blessing—his first blessing "to the City [of Rome] and to the World" as Pope. Pope Leo expressed thanks to his brother Cardinals for the trust they placed in him and led everyone in praying the Hail Mary in supplication to the Blessed Mother for Her guidance. Then he imparted the Apostolic Blessing, to which a plenary indulgence was attached. The sight of the new Pope extending his hands in blessing over the crowd—against the backdrop of the summer early evening sky and iconic Basilica—was a moving testament to the continuity of the Church. Here was Peter's Successor, blessing the crowds just as so many Popes had done for so many centuries before him.

As Pope Leo XIV disappeared back behind the loggia curtains, the people lingered in the square, buzzing with excitement. Pilgrims danced and sang, on fire with the joy of being in Rome for such a historic moment. Around the world, the news had already spread rapidly: *Habemus Papam, Leo XIV!* In countless churches, bells rang out to mark the election. Many Catholics (even those who had gone to sleep in distant time zones) woke to alerts on their phones, eagerly texted and called each other, and offered prayers for their new Holy Father. *Sede Vacante* was over: the Church had a Pope again, and joy filled the air.

TOP LEFT *Pope Leo XIV walking out onto the loggia for the* Urbi et Orbi *blessing.* **TOP RIGHT** *The 266th successor of St. Peter—Pope Leo XIV.* **BOTTOM** *Pope Leo XIV greeting his flock for the first time.*

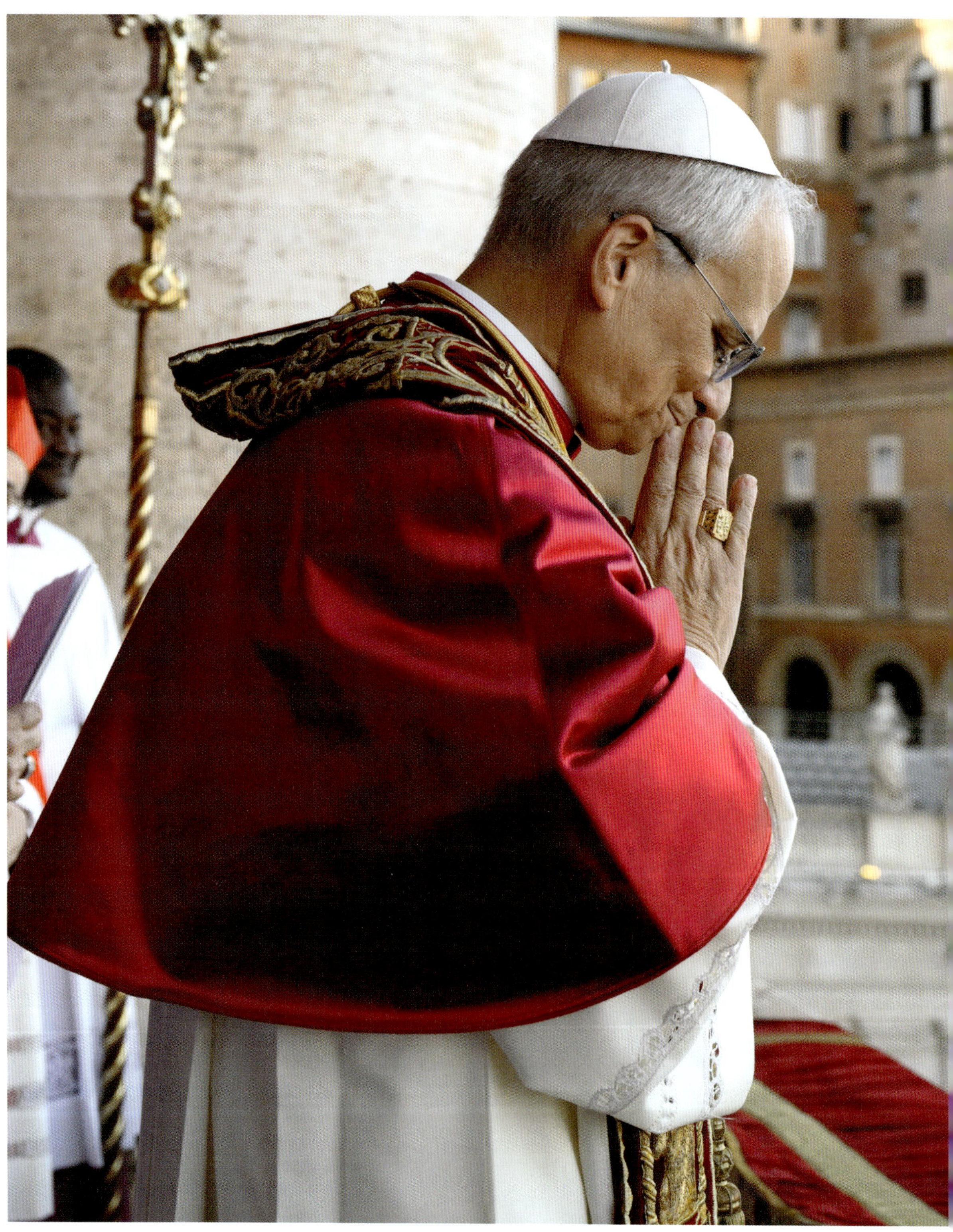

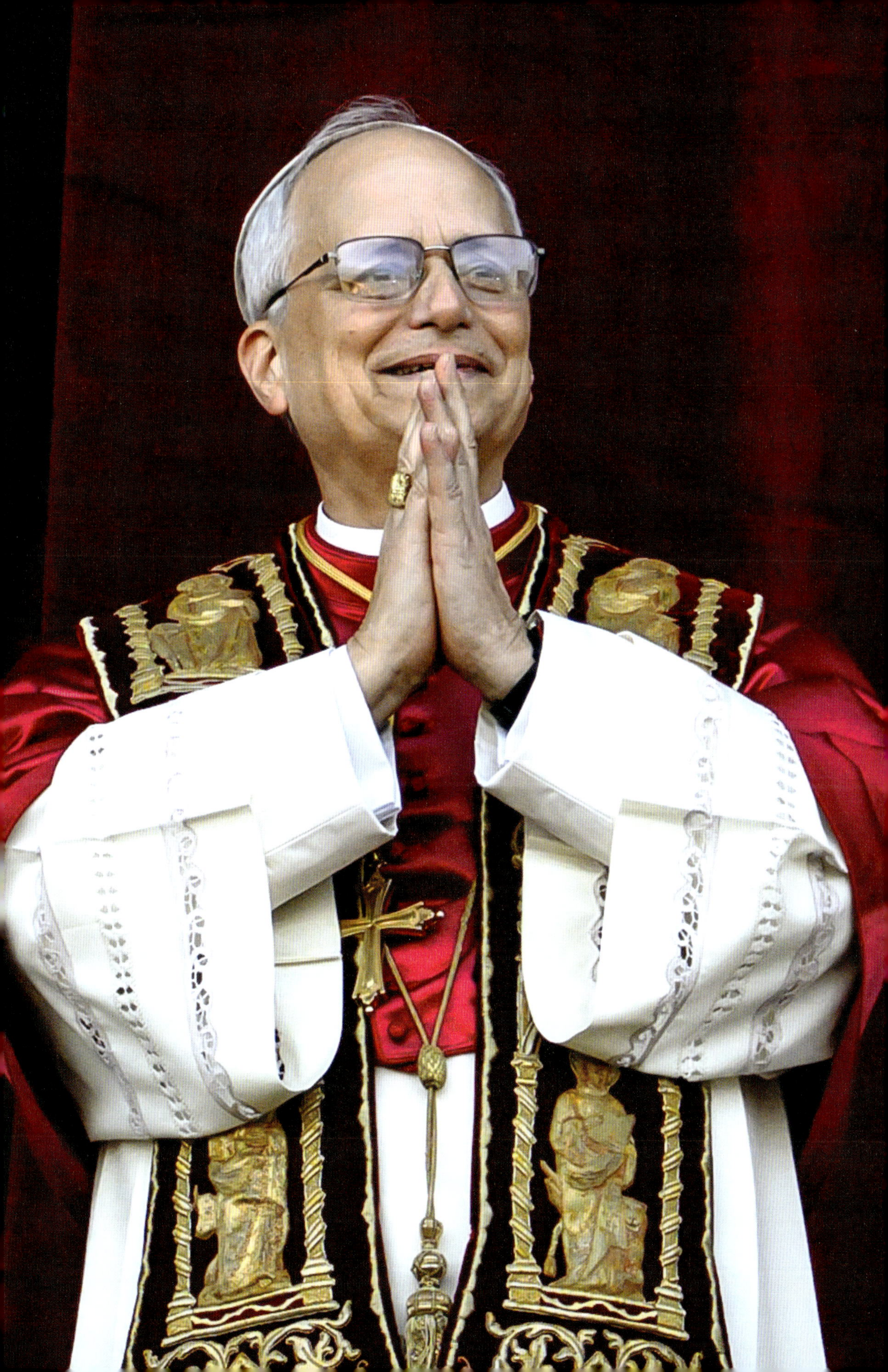

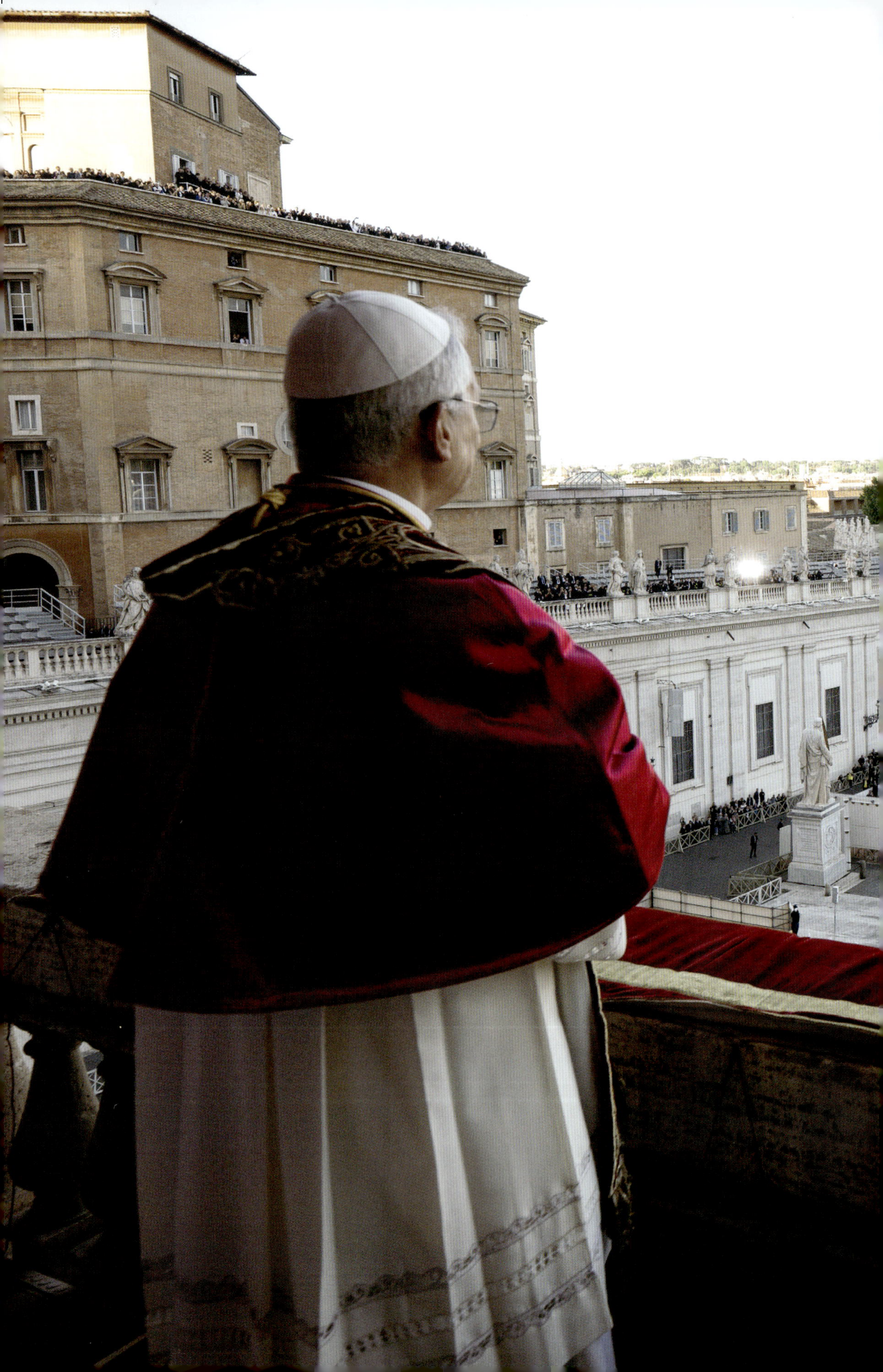

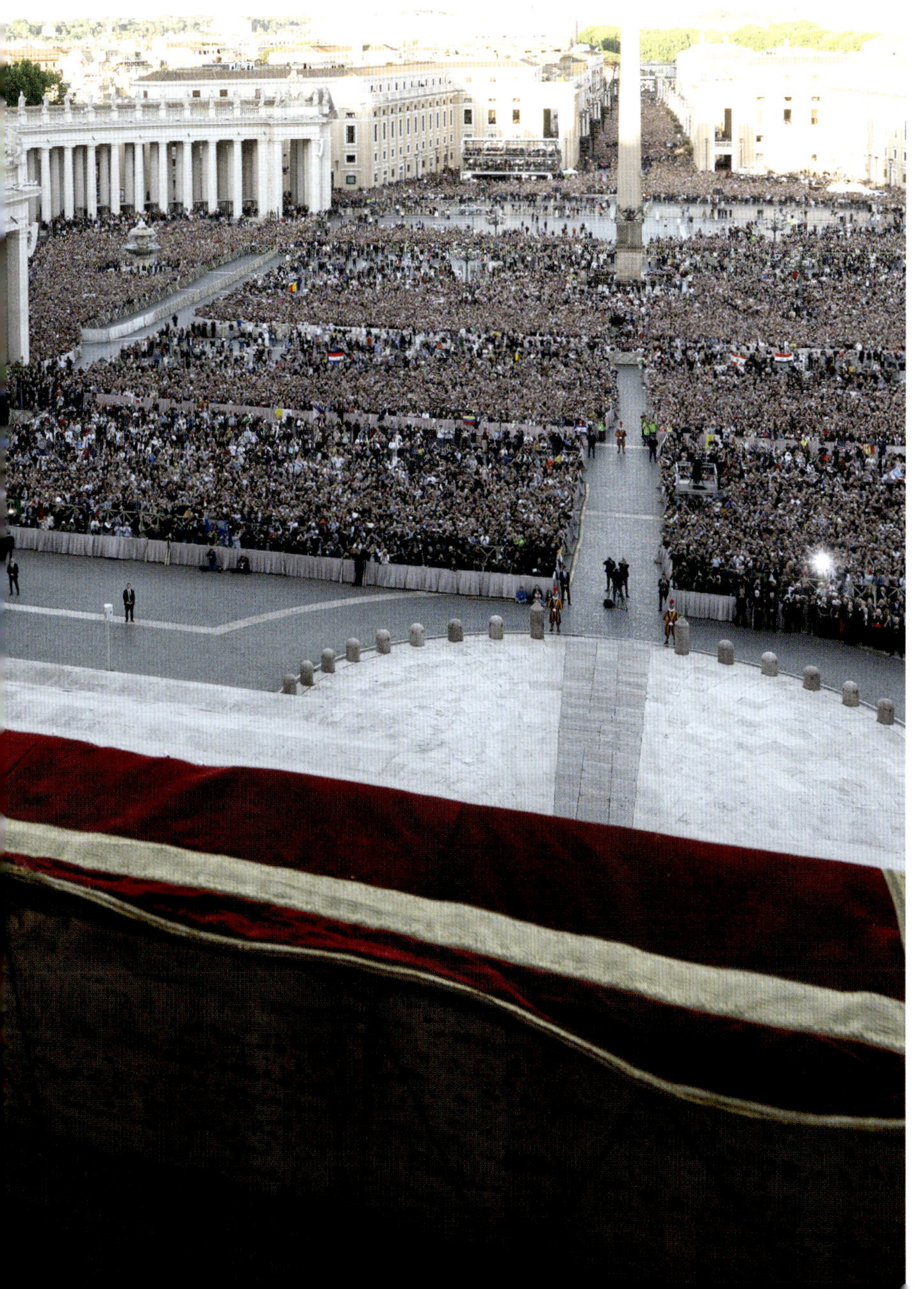

LEFT *The* Sede Vacante *period was over: the Church had a Pope again, and cries of joy filled the air.*

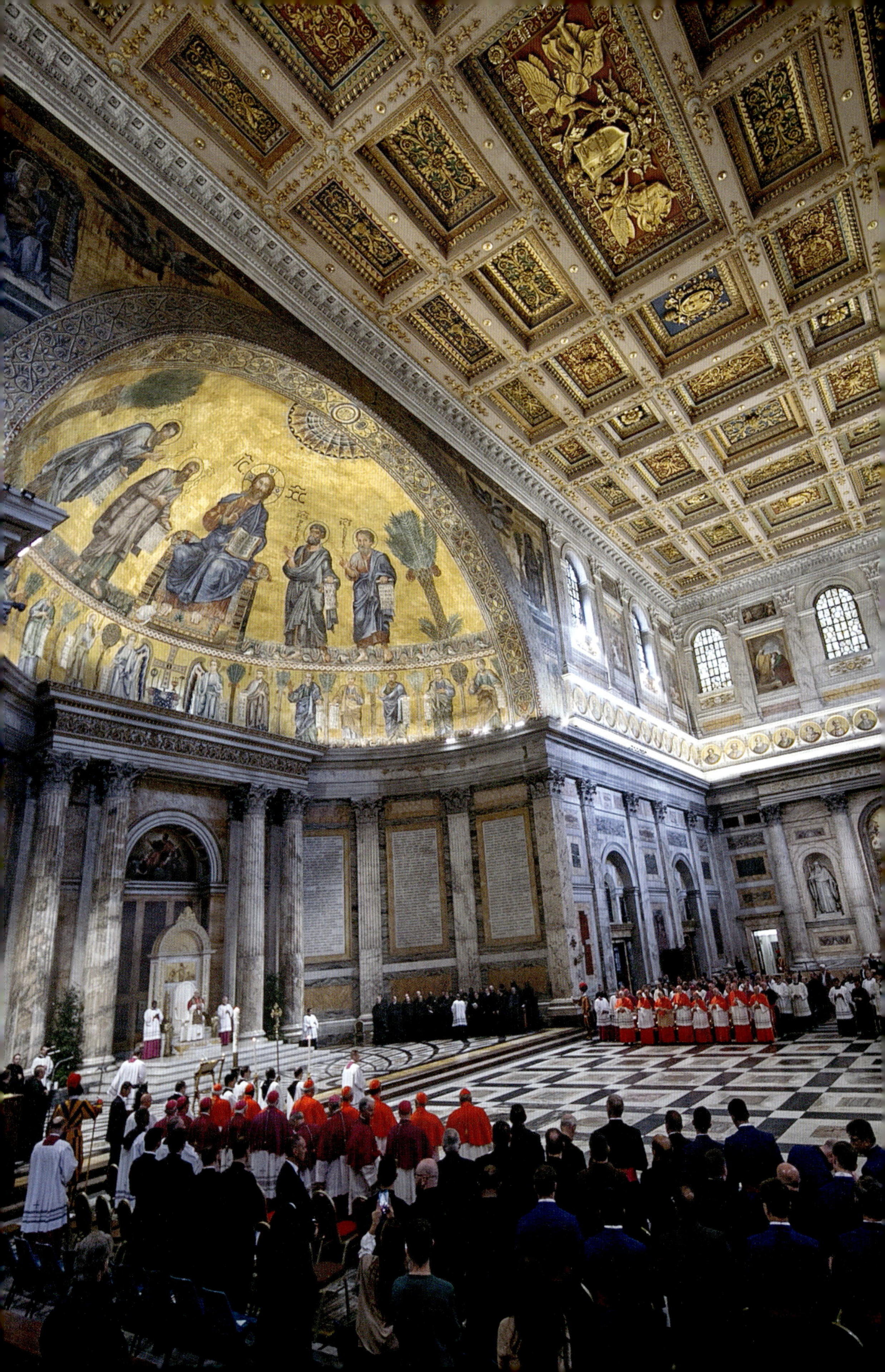

CHAPTER FOUR

The First Days of Pope Leo XIV

Mass and Meeting with the College of Cardinals

In the days following the conclave, Pope Leo XIV began his pontificate with both humility and energy. At 11:00 a.m. on his very first morning as Pope—May 9, 2025—Leo XIV returned to the Sistine Chapel—not to vote, but to pray and celebrate Mass together with the Cardinals who elected him. Michelangelo's frescoes, witness to the drama of the days before, looked down on the new Pope, vested in white and gold, a striking contrast to the scarlet of the Cardinals. In his brief homily, he began by noting the mission given to him by the electors, and urged them to walk with him as a united Church, announcing the Gospel together. He then discussed how we come to know Christ through St. Peter and the Petrine ministry established by Christ from the beginning. As the Successor of Peter, Pope Leo recognized that it is now his duty to proclaim Christ to the world at this time in history.

On May 10, the following day, Pope Leo met with all of the Cardinals in Paul VI Hall and focused on a number of issues: "I would like to highlight several fundamental points: the return to the primacy of Christ in proclamation; the missionary conversion of the entire Christian community; growth in collegiality and synodality; attention to the *sensus fidei*, especially in its most authentic and inclusive forms, such as popular piety; loving care for the least and the rejected; courageous and trusting dialogue with the contemporary world in its various components and realities." Many observers felt that Pope Leo's first interactions showed his personality: scholarly yet simple, firm in faith yet approachable—not unlike his namesake, Pope St. Leo the Great, known for combining courage with compassion.

Pope Leo XIV's First Public *Regina Caeli* and Messages

That first Sunday after his election, May 11, Pope Leo XIV appeared on the balcony of St. Peter's Basilica at noon to lead the *Regina Caeli* prayer (the Marian antiphon said during the Easter season in place of the *Angelus*). It was his first public address to the faithful of Rome and the world.

LEFT *Leo XIV celebrating his first Mass as Pontiff with the College of Cardinals, May 9, 2025.*

St. Peter's Square was again packed—this time with cheers of welcome rather than pilgrims on the edge of their collective seat, awaiting the outcome of the conclave. The bells tolled joyfully as he was greeted by roaring applause and the waving flags of countries from all over the world. Pope Leo smiled and gave a cheerful "*Buona domenica a tutti!*—Happy Sunday to you all!" He then remarked how blessed he felt that his first address to the public was on Good Shepherd Sunday, a reminder to him of his duties as Bishop of Rome, but also to all of us, to care for each other, especially for young people.

After singing the *Regina Caeli* prayer with the faithful, Pope Leo XIV spoke briefly again, this time focusing on the need for peace and reconciliation around the world. He talked specifically about the ongoing conflicts between Israel and Hamas in Gaza and between Ukraine and Russia. He added, "But how many other conflicts there are in the world! I entrust this heartfelt appeal to the Queen of Peace, so that She may present it to the Lord Jesus to obtain for us the miracle of peace." These early words signaled that Pope Leo would also carry forward Pope Francis' heartfelt concern for the marginalized.

Before withdrawing, he took the time to greet individual groups of pilgrims from around the world and wished a happy Mother's Day to all mothers around the

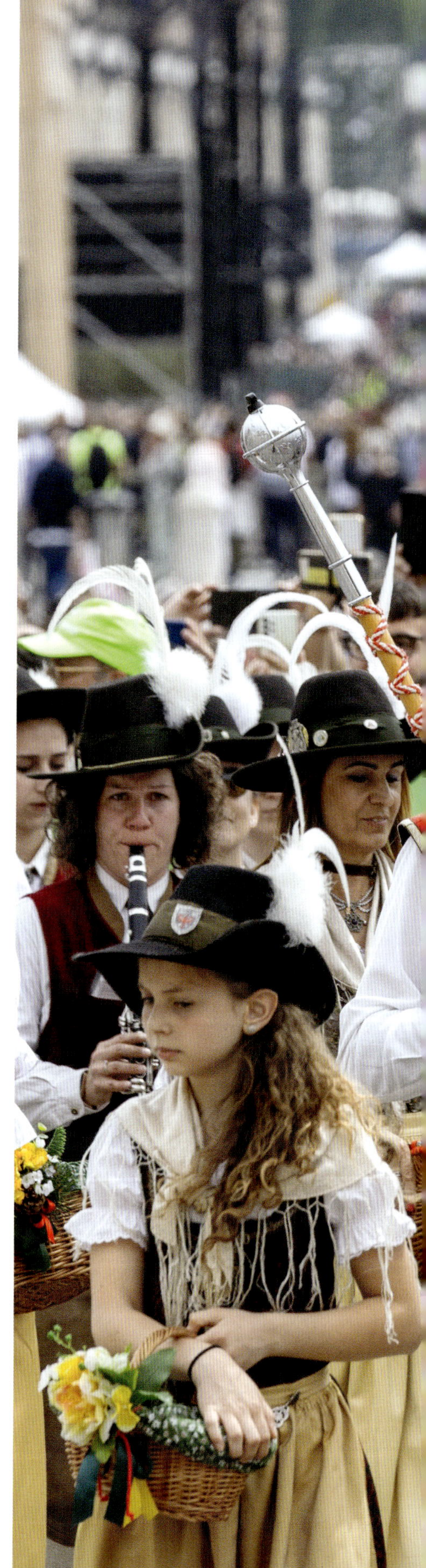

RIGHT *A group of pilgrims gathering for Leo XIV's first* Regina Caeli *prayer, which the Pope sang, May 11, 2025.*

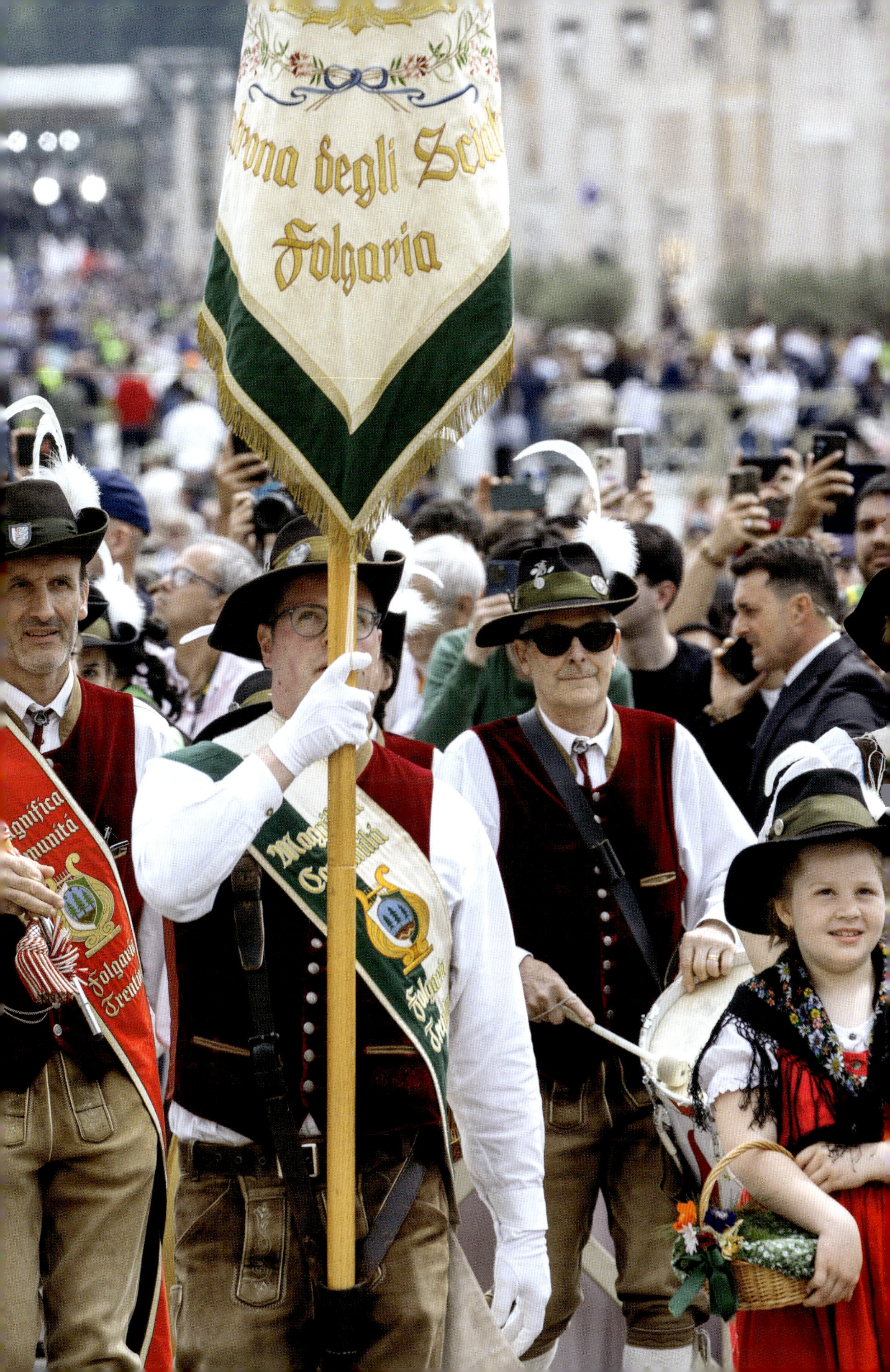
Folgaria

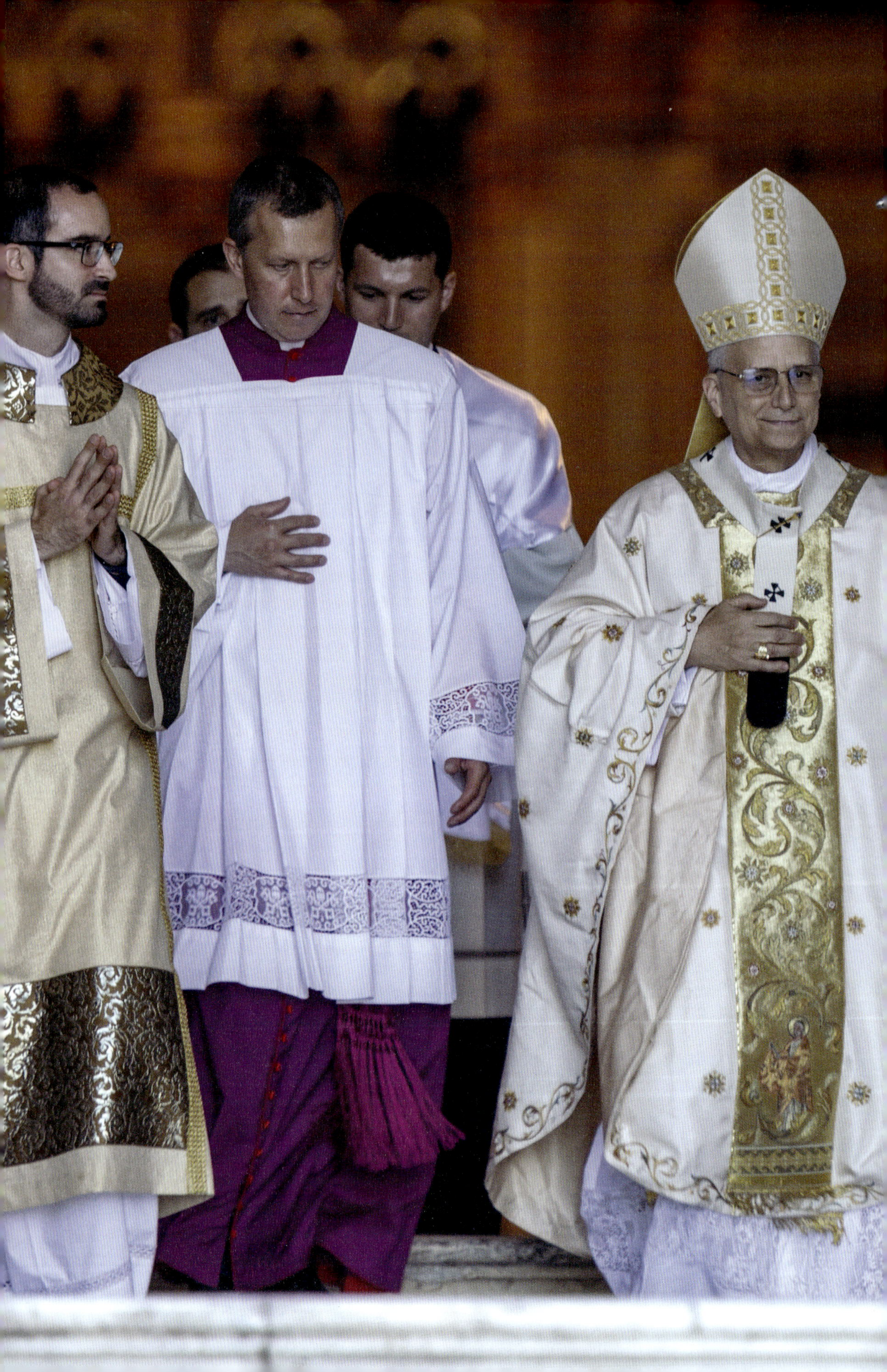

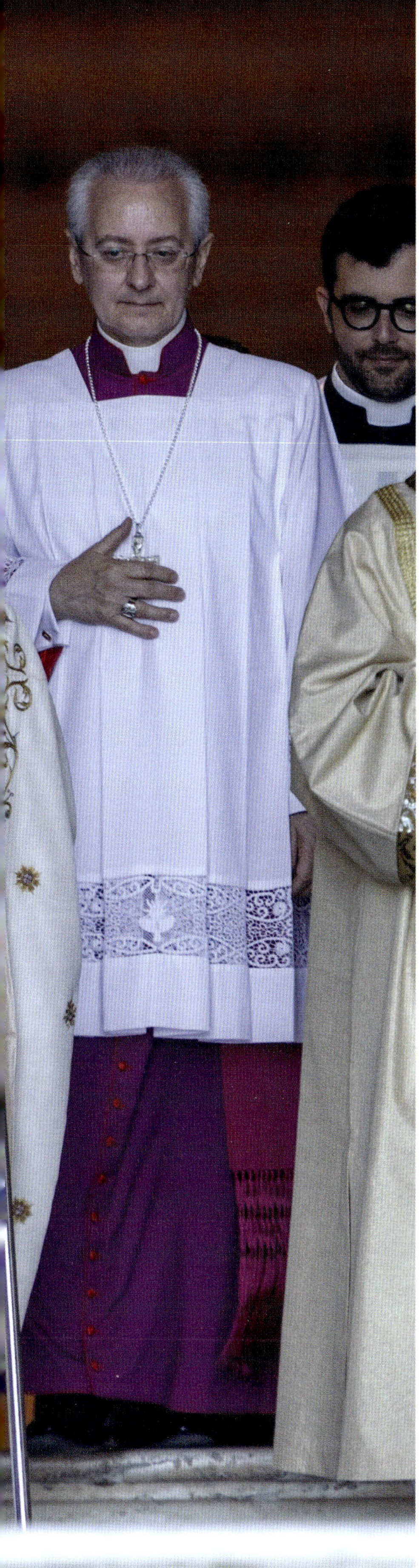

world. As he left, the crowd erupted in clapping and a spontaneous chant of "Leo! Leo! Leo!" cheering their affection for him just days into his reign.

In the following week, Pope Leo began reaching out in various ways. On May 12, he held a special audience with hundreds of international journalists and media workers who had covered the conclave. In the Paul VI Audience Hall, he thanked them for their work, especially for their coverage of the papal conclave. He noted the peril that many dedicated journalists face in their pursuit of communicating the truth. And he thanked all of the press in the audience for their coverage of the many life-changing moments in the Vatican during these important and historic events. The Vatican Press Office noted that Leo XIV emphasized truth and compassion in journalism, hinting at an open, engaging papacy ahead.

Pope Leo's early messages were consistently reverent in tone, while also relevant and accessible. He frequently mentioned our reliance on God's grace and the guidance of the Virgin Mary. In fact, on one of his very first evenings as Pope, he visited the icon *Salus Populi Romani* (Protector of the Roman People) in the Basilica of St. Mary Major. There he laid a bouquet of flowers and prayed silently for Our Lady's help in his new Office. Vatican photogra-

LEFT *Pope Leo exiting the Basilica of St. John Lateran after his formal inauguration as the Bishop of Rome.*

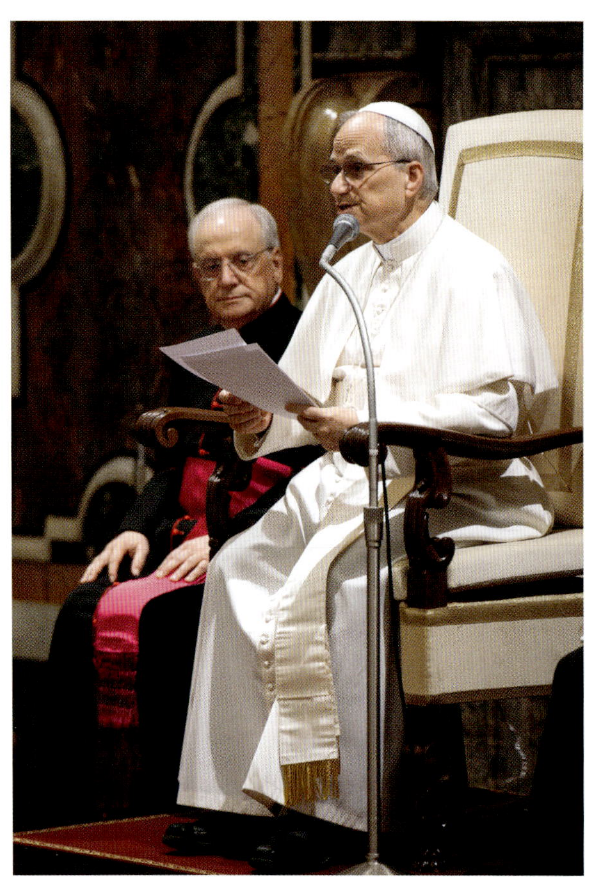
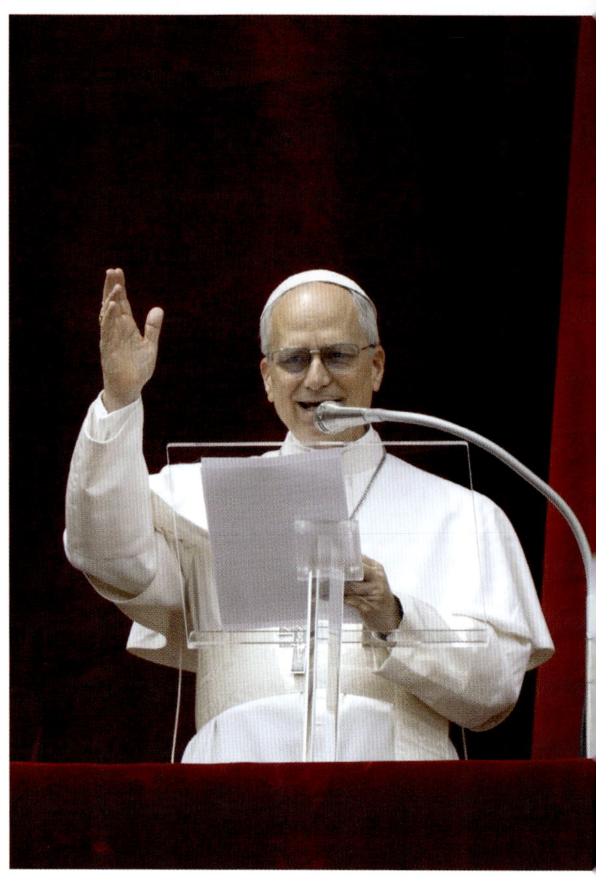
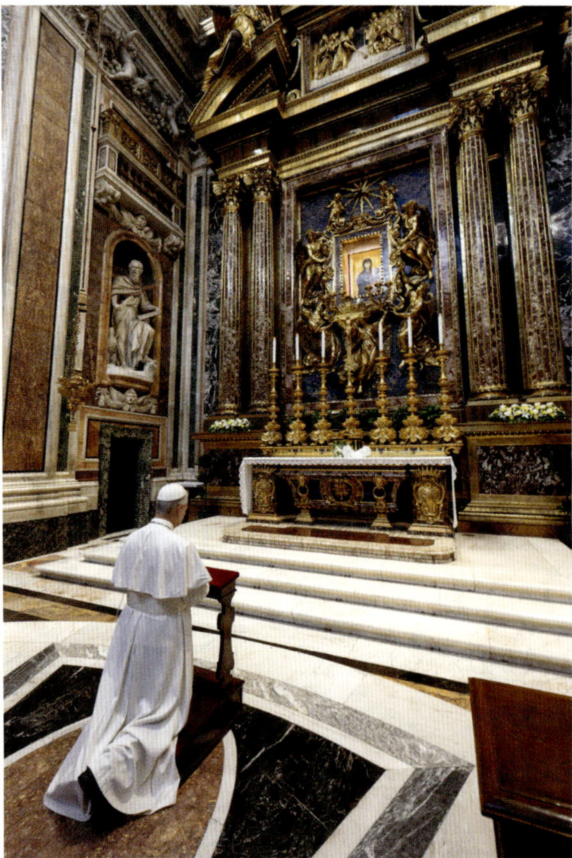
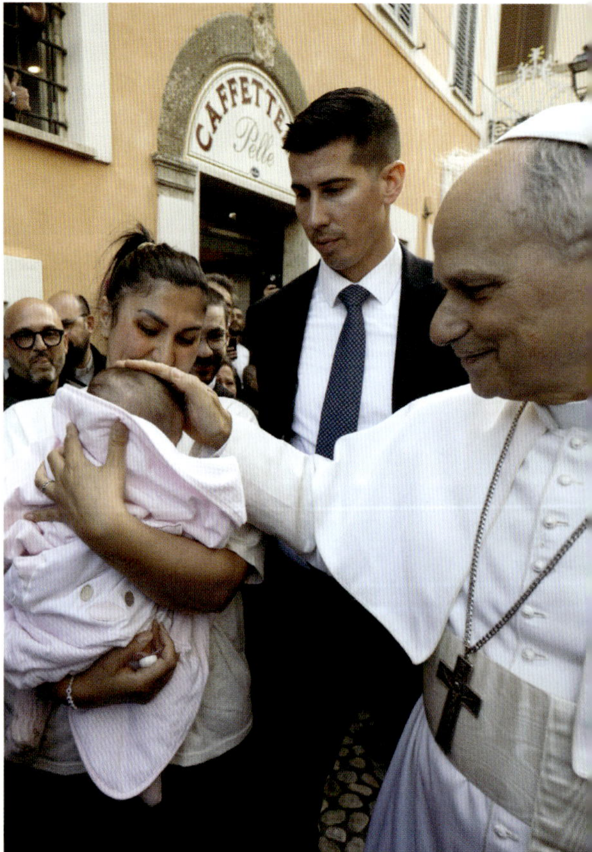
Pelle

phers captured him kneeling before the icon, a poignant image of humility and devotion at the start of his ministry.

Engaging the World: First Acts and Outreach

In the early days of his papacy, Pope Leo XIV, just as Pope Francis had done, exhorted his audiences and assemblies to care for the poor and needy of the world.

He also quickly established a rapport with civil and religious leaders worldwide. On May 16, he met with the entire Diplomatic Corps accredited to the Holy See—ambassadors from more than 180 countries—in the Clementine Hall of the Vatican's Apostolic Palace. In his address, Leo XIV told them that peace, justice, and truth are three essential words, "that represent the Church's missionary activity and the aim of the Holy See's diplomacy." He highlighted that his papal namesake, Leo XIII, was a champion of workers' rights and dialogue with the modern world, signaling that he too would prioritize social justice and engagement. The diplomats who were present were witness to the Pope's scholarly precision in his natural quoting of erudite texts and the genuine warmth of his personal greetings and manner.

Ecumenical and interfaith outreach were also prominent during these first days. Letters of goodwill poured into the Vatican: the Ecumenical Patriarch of Constantinople, the Archbishop of Canterbury, and leaders of Jewish and Muslim communities all sent greetings to the new Pope, to which he graciously responded. In one notable gesture, Pope Leo called the Chief Rabbi of Rome to extend wishes for peace, continuing a tradition of friendship between the Vatican and the Jewish community.

By the end of his first week, Pope Leo XIV had not only met Heads of State but also visited people who were "like family" to him. On May 11, he made a surprise visit to an Augustinian Shrine on the outskirts of Rome, a place he had visited as a Cardinal. The locals were overjoyed to see the Pope enter, bless them, pray with them, and spend time with them. Images of his visit reinforced the sense that the new Pope is committed to personal, "on-the-ground" ministry.

TOP LEFT *Leo XIV welcoming pilgrims from Denmark, Ireland, England, Wales, and Scotland, July 5, 2025.* ***TOP RIGHT*** *Leo XIV intoning the* Regina Caeli*, May 11, 2025.* ***BOTTOM LEFT*** *Pope Leo visiting the Basilica of St. Mary Major and praying before the Salus Populi Romani icon.* ***BOTTOM RIGHT*** *Pope Leo blessing a child.*

Continuity and New Beginnings

Throughout these early days, the faithful witnessed a beautiful blending of continuity and newness. Pope Leo XIV made a point to affirm the work of Pope Francis, frequently referencing his priorities in his speeches. During a meeting with the Roman Curia officials on May 24, he praised his predecessor's emphasis on the missionary dimension of the Church and indicated he would carry that work forward. As his address concluded, he exhorted the Curia, "Each person can be a builder of unity with his attitudes towards colleagues, overcoming inevitable misunderstandings with patience, with humility, putting himself in the shoes of others, avoiding prejudices, and also with a good dose of humor, as Pope Francis taught us." His returning to the works and words of Pope Francis provided reassurance that the change in leadership would not derail the pastoral momentum in the Church.

At the same time, Leo XIV's unique emphases began to emerge. As a trained canon lawyer with a background in mathematics, he spoke in a few addresses about the harmony of faith and reason. This earned him the playful moniker "the mathematician Pope." More substantively, this love for the precision of logic underscores Pope Leo XIV's strong dedication to doctrinal clarity. He also demonstrated a great care for evangelization. Together with his name, these two emphases invoke the spirit of Pope St. Leo I, who was a great defender of the importance and centrality of the Church. Also, his revival of the Church's traditional greeting in many speeches ("Peace be with you") signaled a respect and love for the ancient beauties of the Church.

Crucially, Pope Leo's first days set a tone of reverence for tradition with an openness of heart. He also insisted on keeping his first audience with the poor of Rome, a longstanding Monday tradition of the Papal Almoner, on the calendar just days after his election. Thus, even amid all the formalities and global attention, Leo XIV remained "grounded" in his pastoral mission.

By the eve of his formal installation, Pope Leo had already made a strong positive impression on practicing Catholics worldwide. Parishes held prayer vigils in thanksgiving for the new Pope. Social media was abuzz with clips of his first homilies and appearances, often tagged with #HabemusPapamLeo. The Church, while grieving the loss of Pope Francis, was filled with renewed hope and pride in the

TOP LEFT *Pope Leo kneeling before the tomb of St. Paul in the Basilica of St. Paul Outside the Walls, May 20, 2025.* ***TOP RIGHT*** *Pope Leo blessing a child from the popemobile, May 21, 2025.* ***BOTTOM LEFT*** *Pope Leo addressing members of the media, May 12, 2025.* ***BOTTOM RIGHT*** *Pope Leo greets a child during his audience with the Brothers of the Christian Schools, a Catholic lay community dedicated to education, May 15, 2025.*

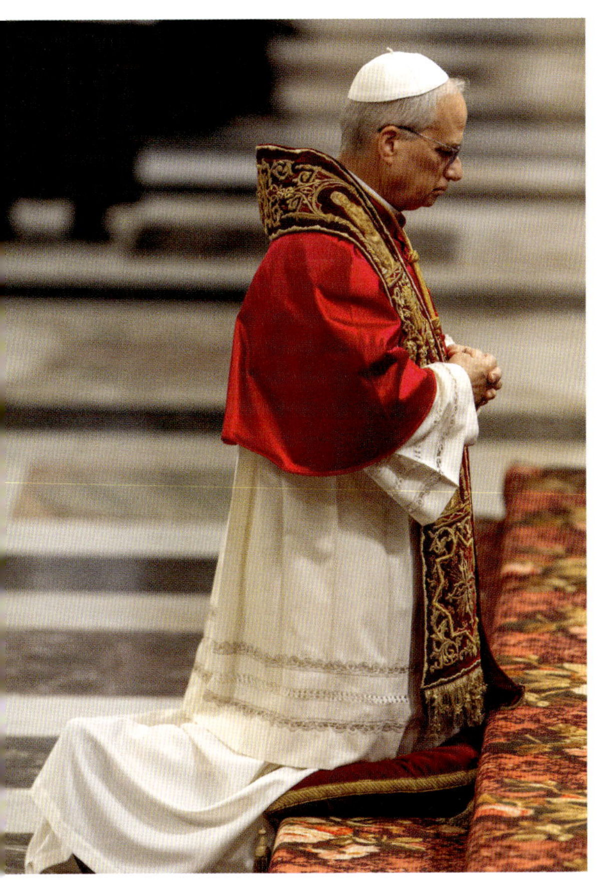
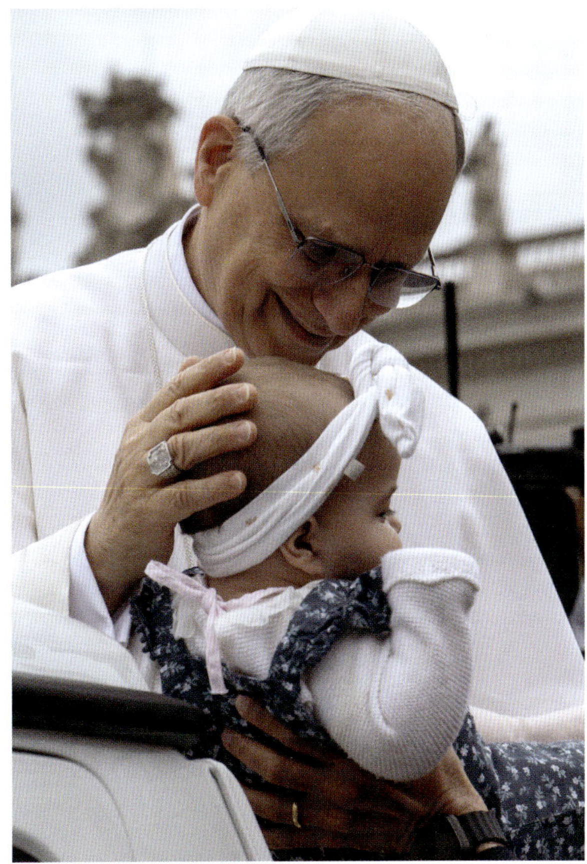
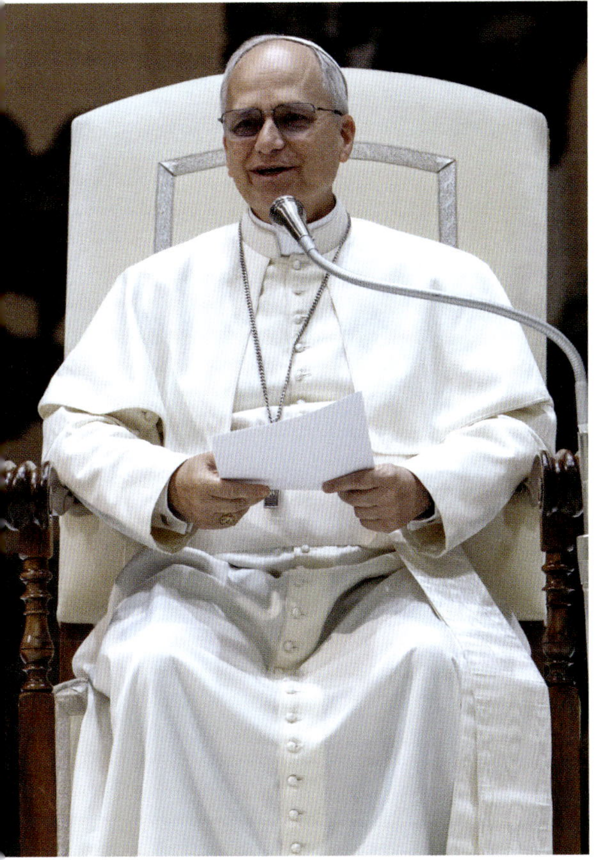
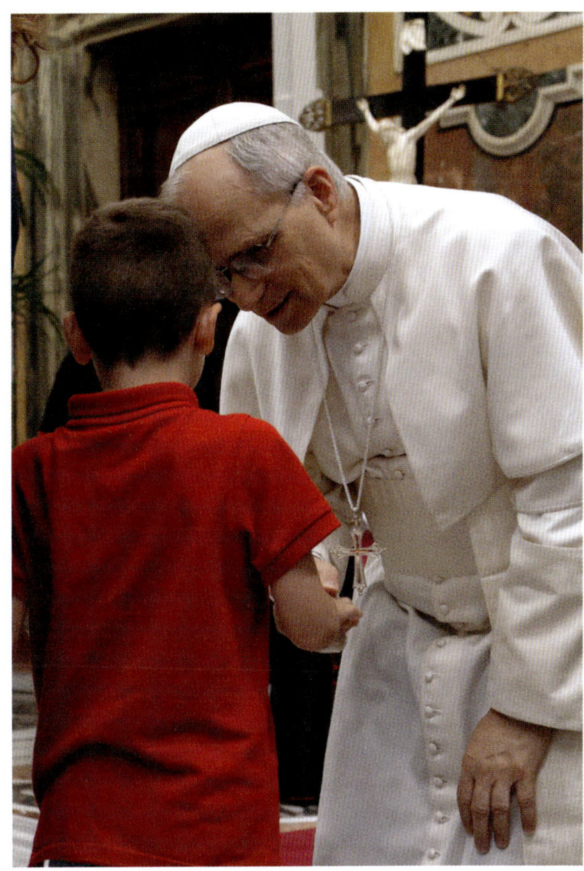

seamless passing of the torch. The transition felt a bit like a family grieving a grandfather, while joyously welcoming a new father—sorrow and joy intermingled, all bonded by faith.

With the stage thus set, all attention turned to the upcoming Sunday, May 18, when the grand Installation Mass of Pope Leo XIV would take place and officially inaugurate his Petrine ministry.

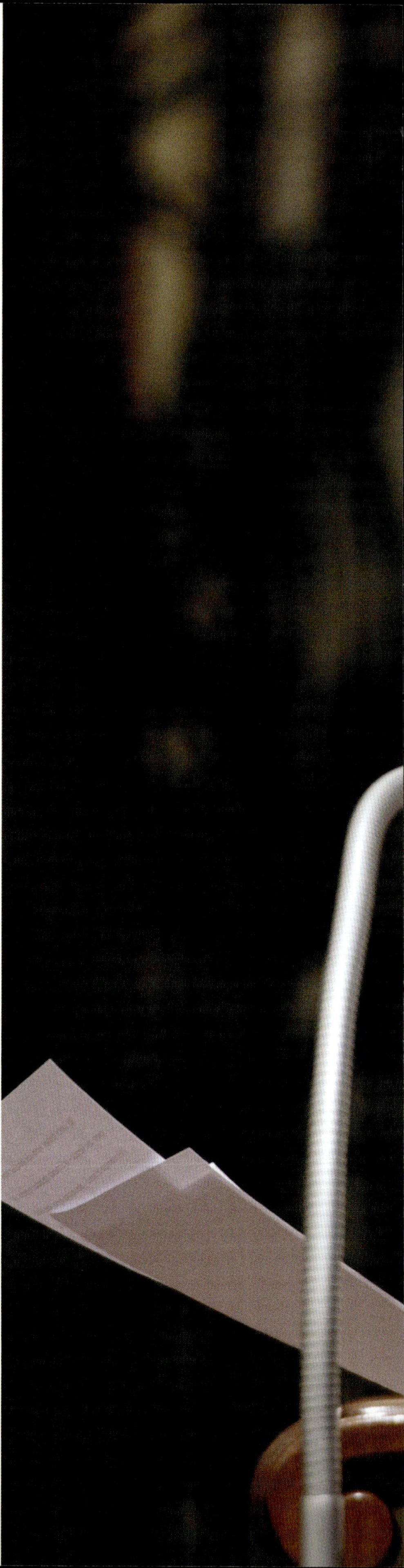

RIGHT *Pope Leo speaks to representatives of the media in the Paul VI Audience Hall.*

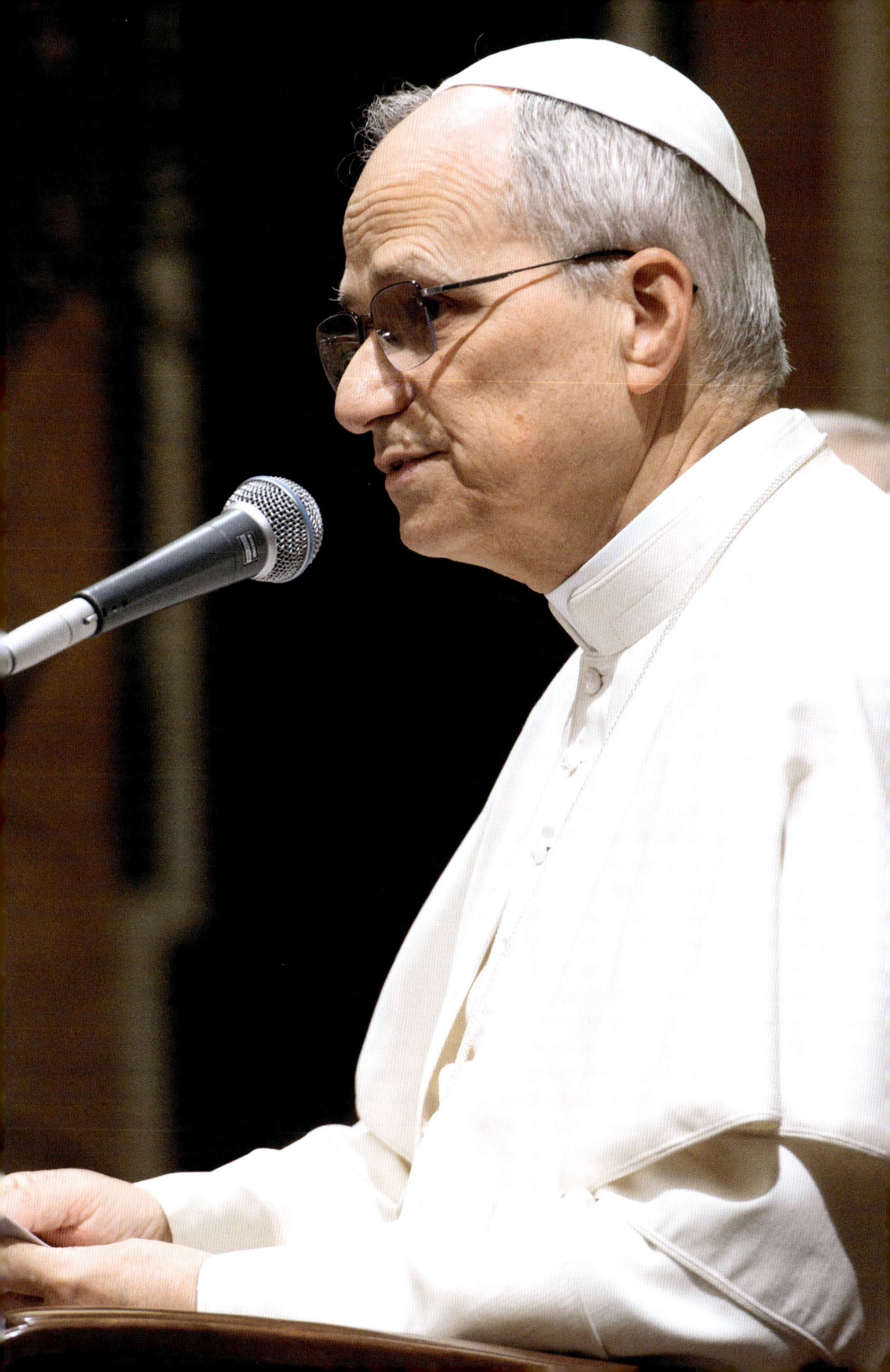

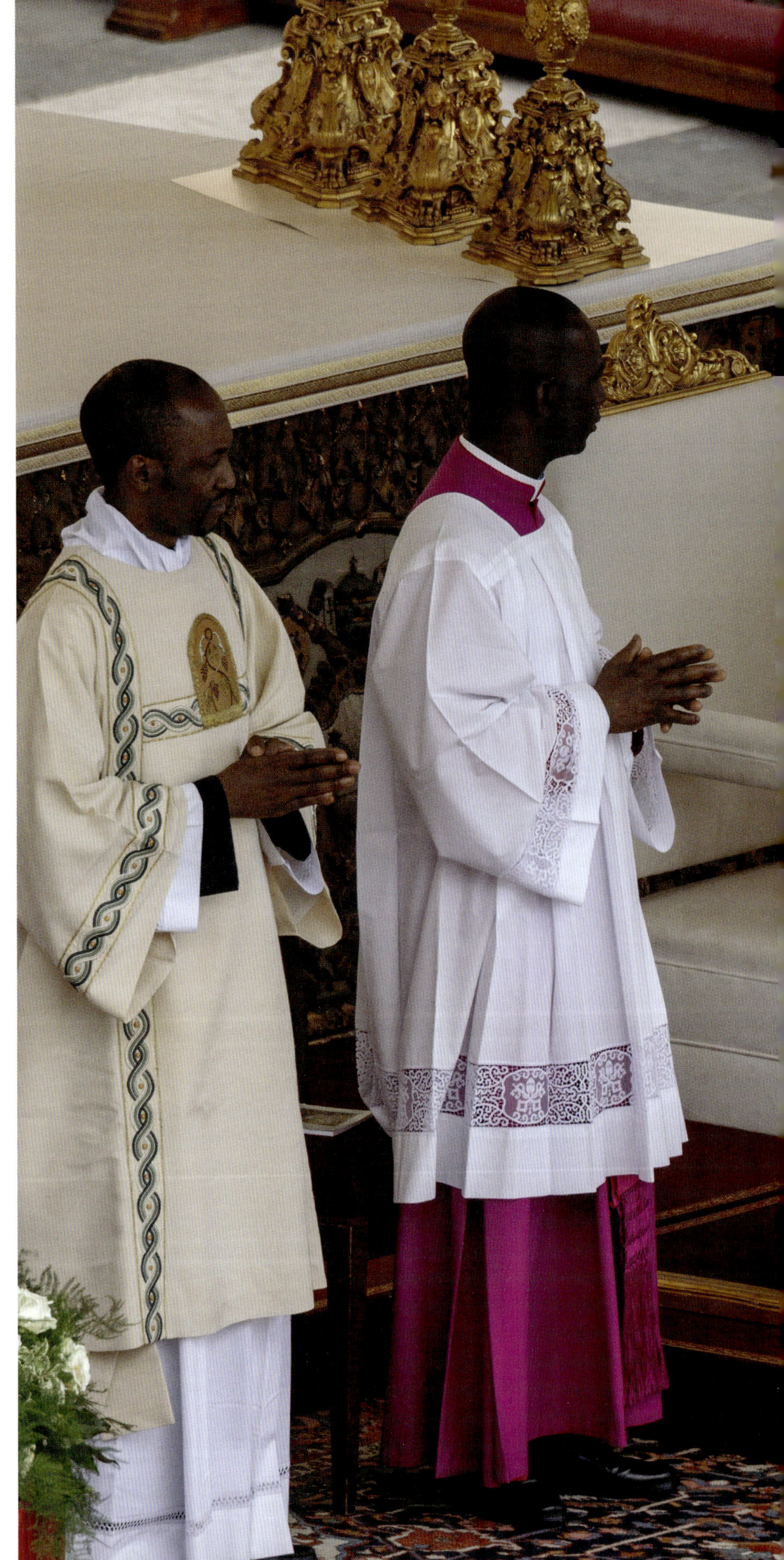

RIGHT *Cardinal Mario Zenari draping the pallium over Pope Leo's shoulders, signifying the Pope's role as Shepherd of Rome and the Universal Church.*

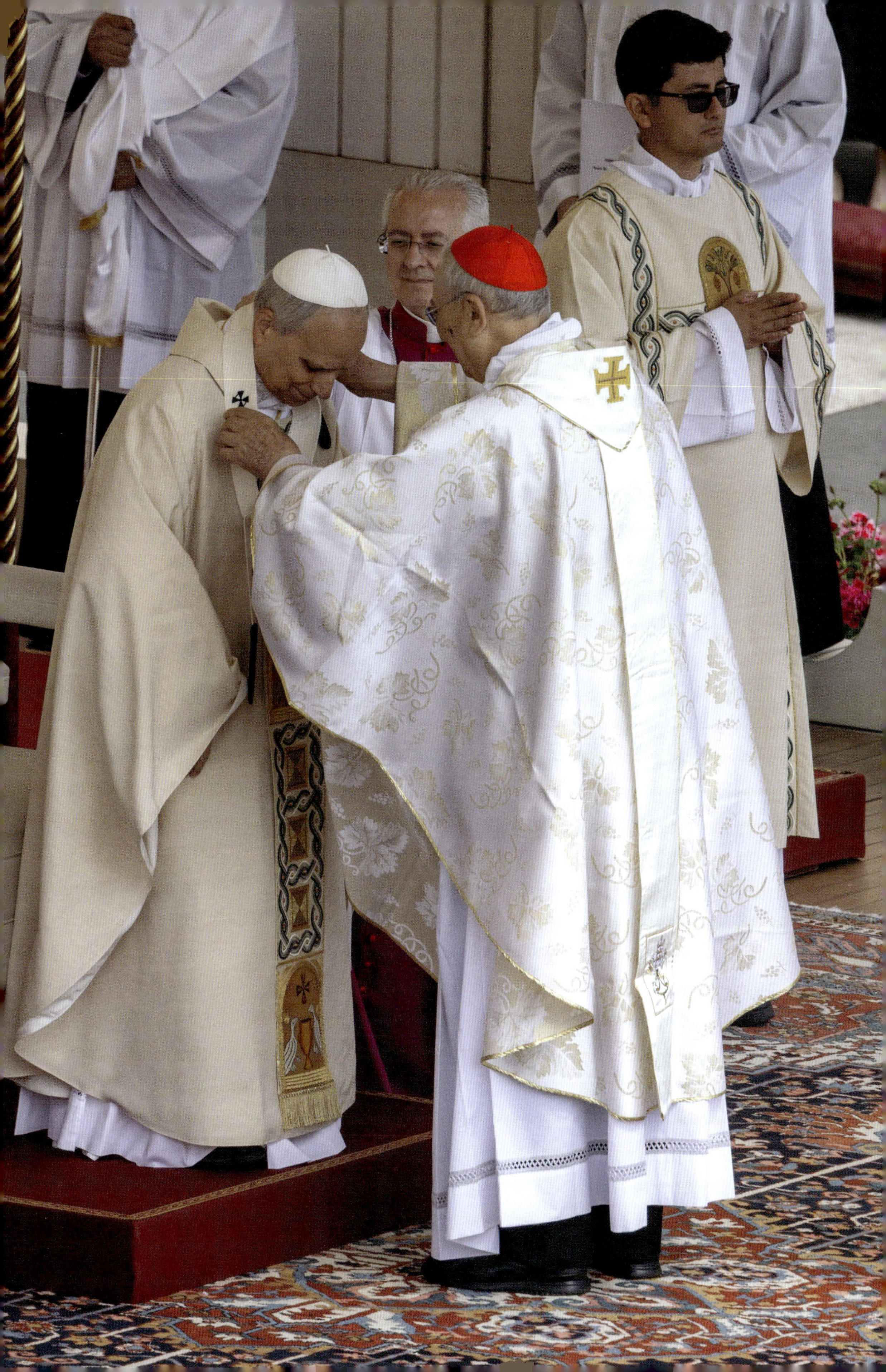

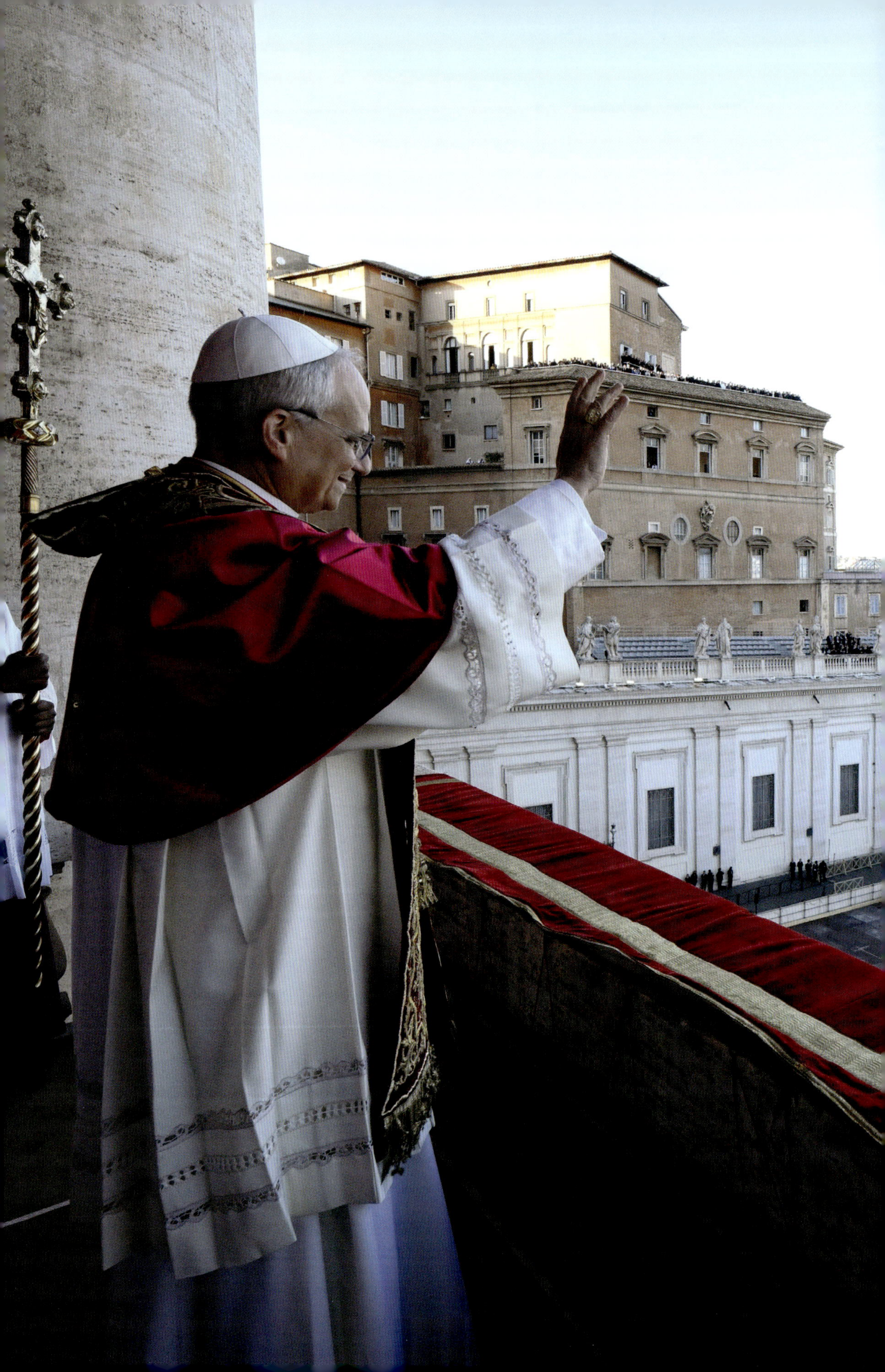

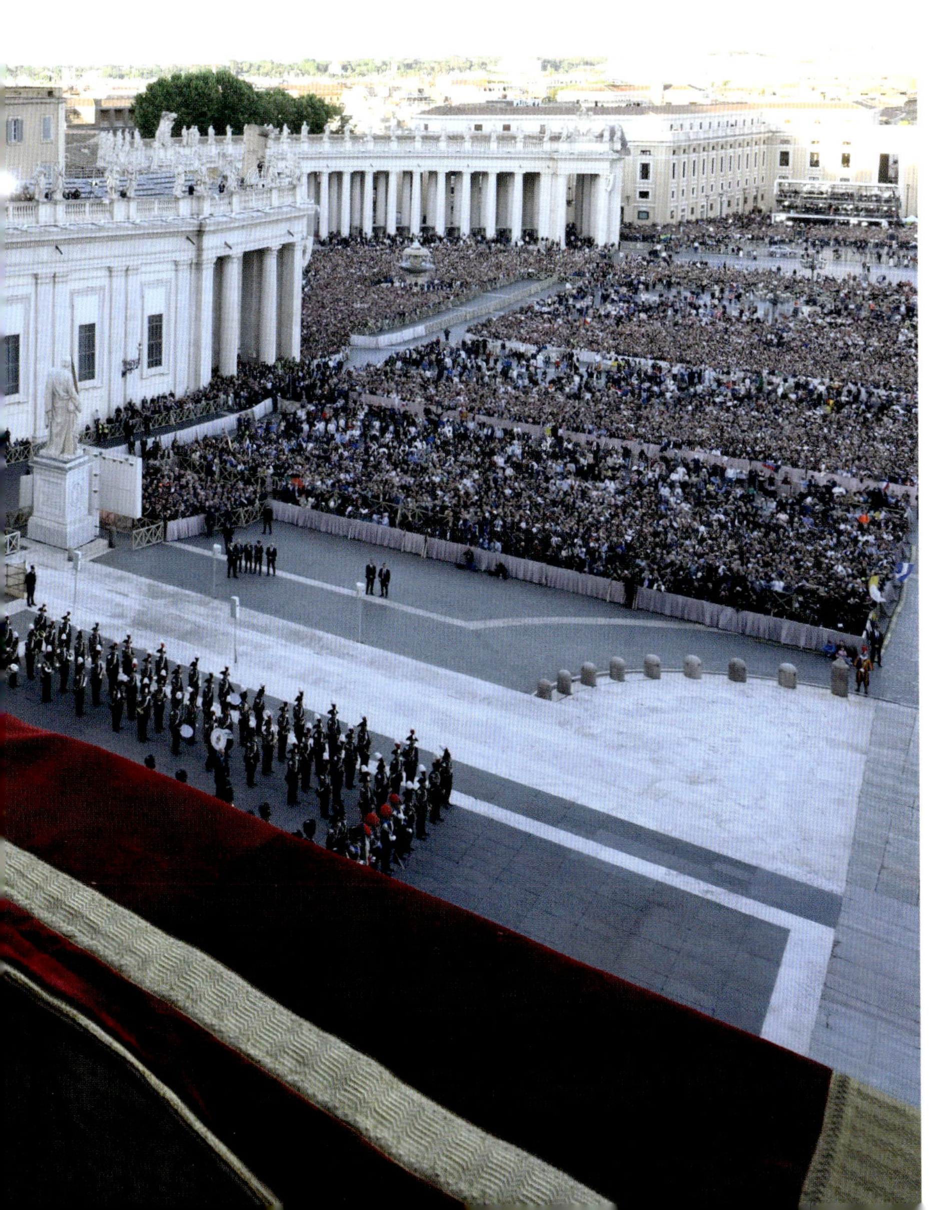

LEFT *Pope Leo XIV addresses his flock for the first time, May 8, 2025.*

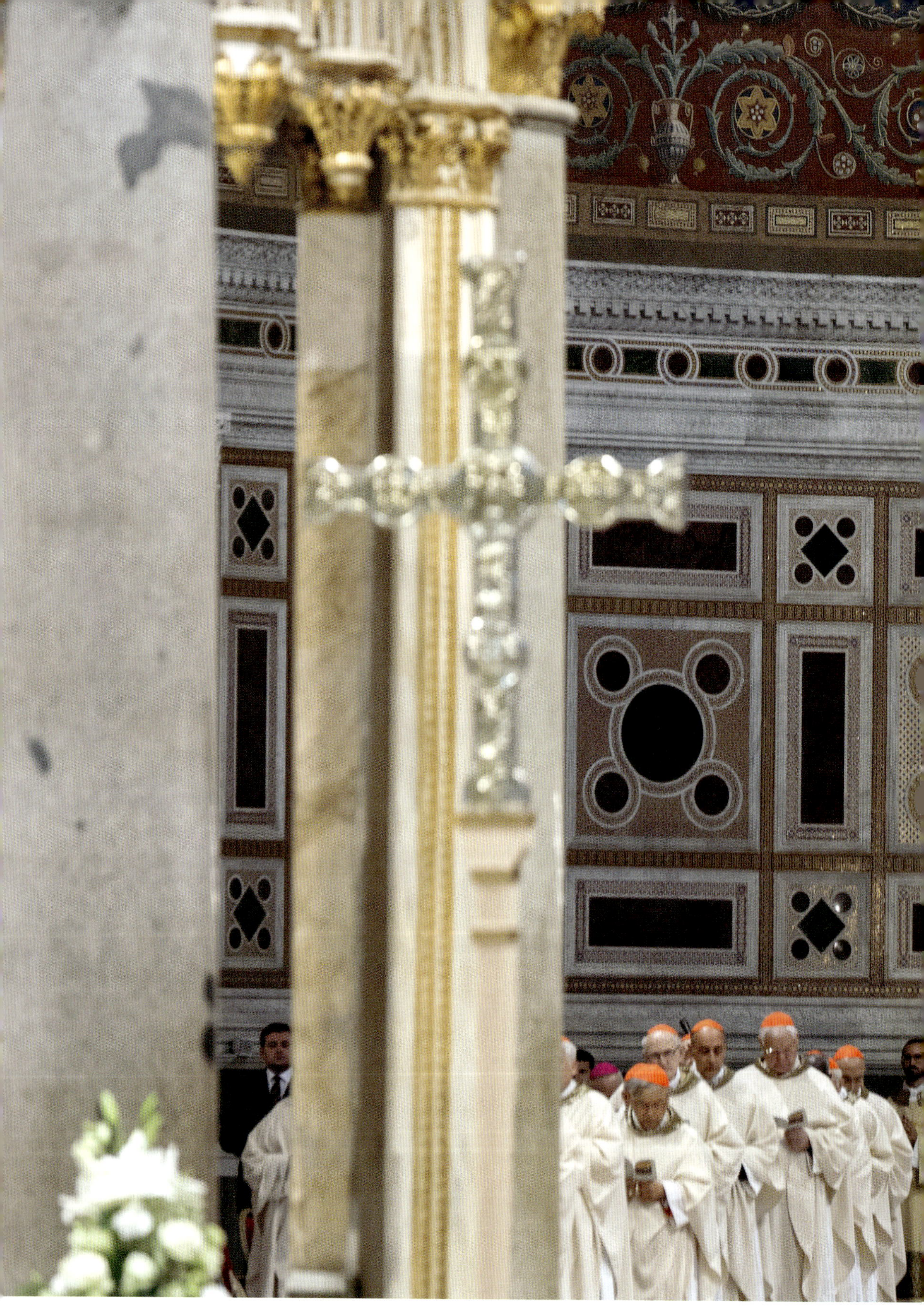

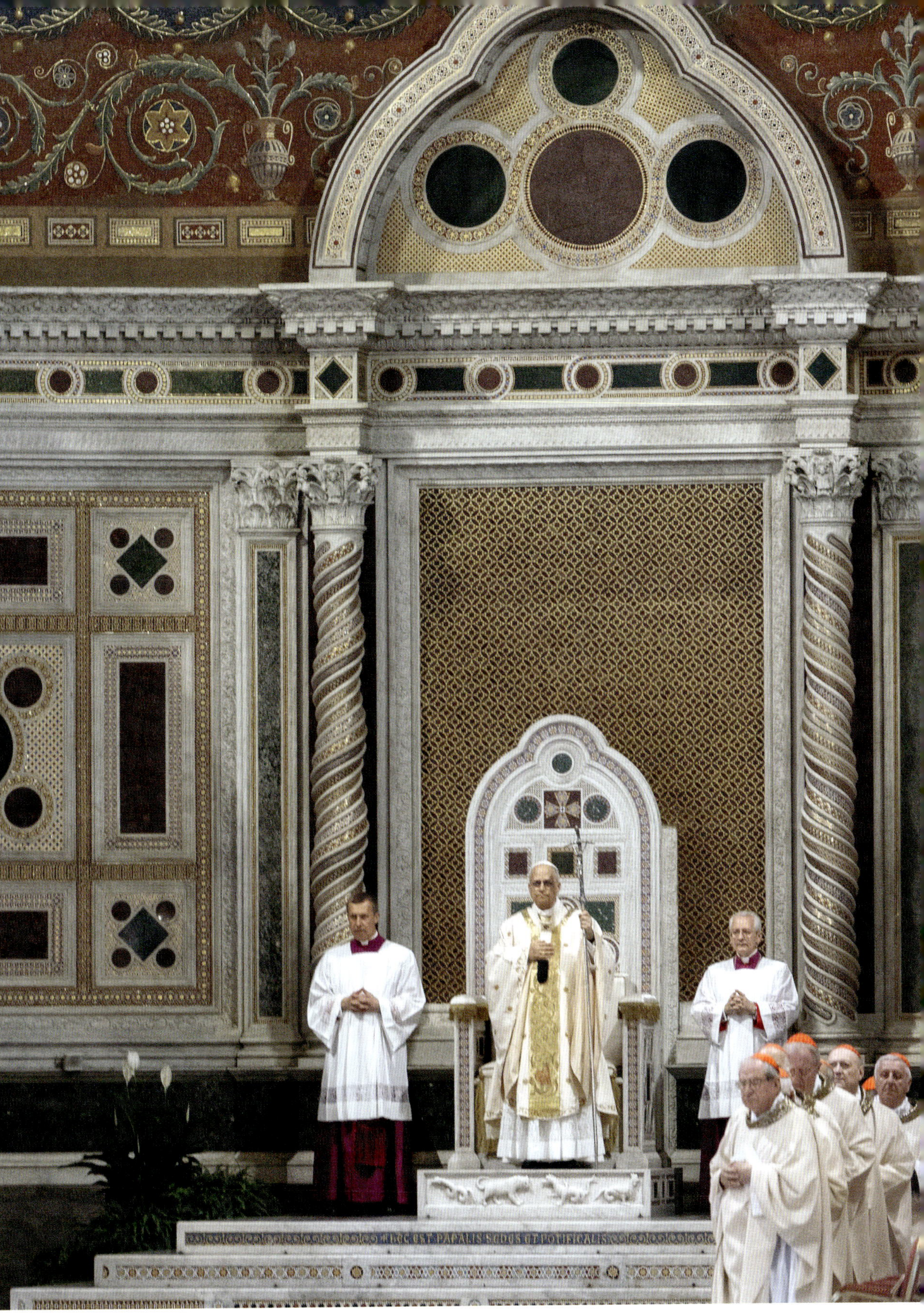

ABOVE *Pope Leo at the Basilica of St. John Lateran—the Seat of the Bishop of Rome.*

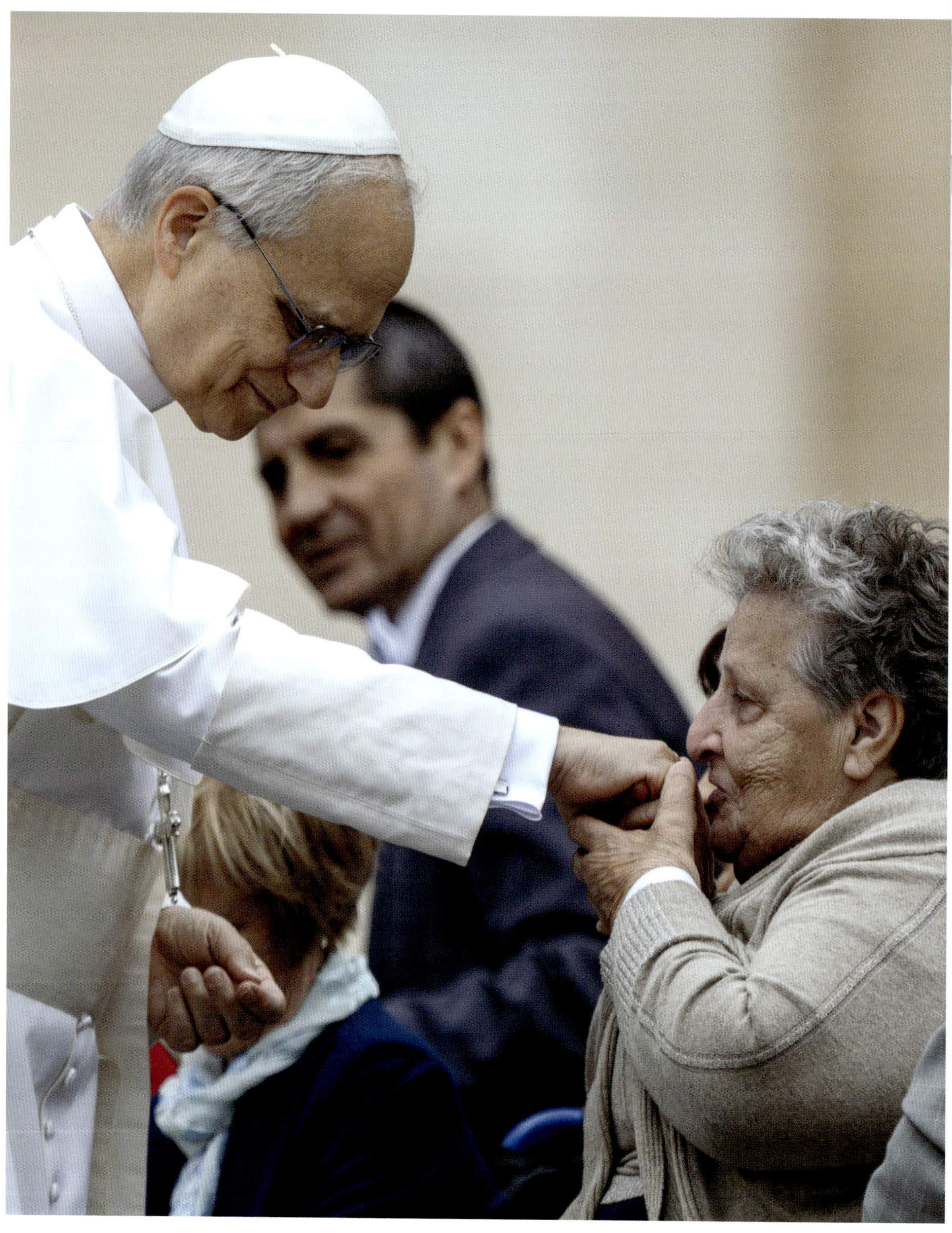

ABOVE *Kissing the Pope's ring is an indulgenced act and a traditional sign of respect for the Office of the Papacy.* ***RIGHT*** *Pope Leo raising the chalice during Mass at the Basilica of St. John Lateran, May 25, 2025.*

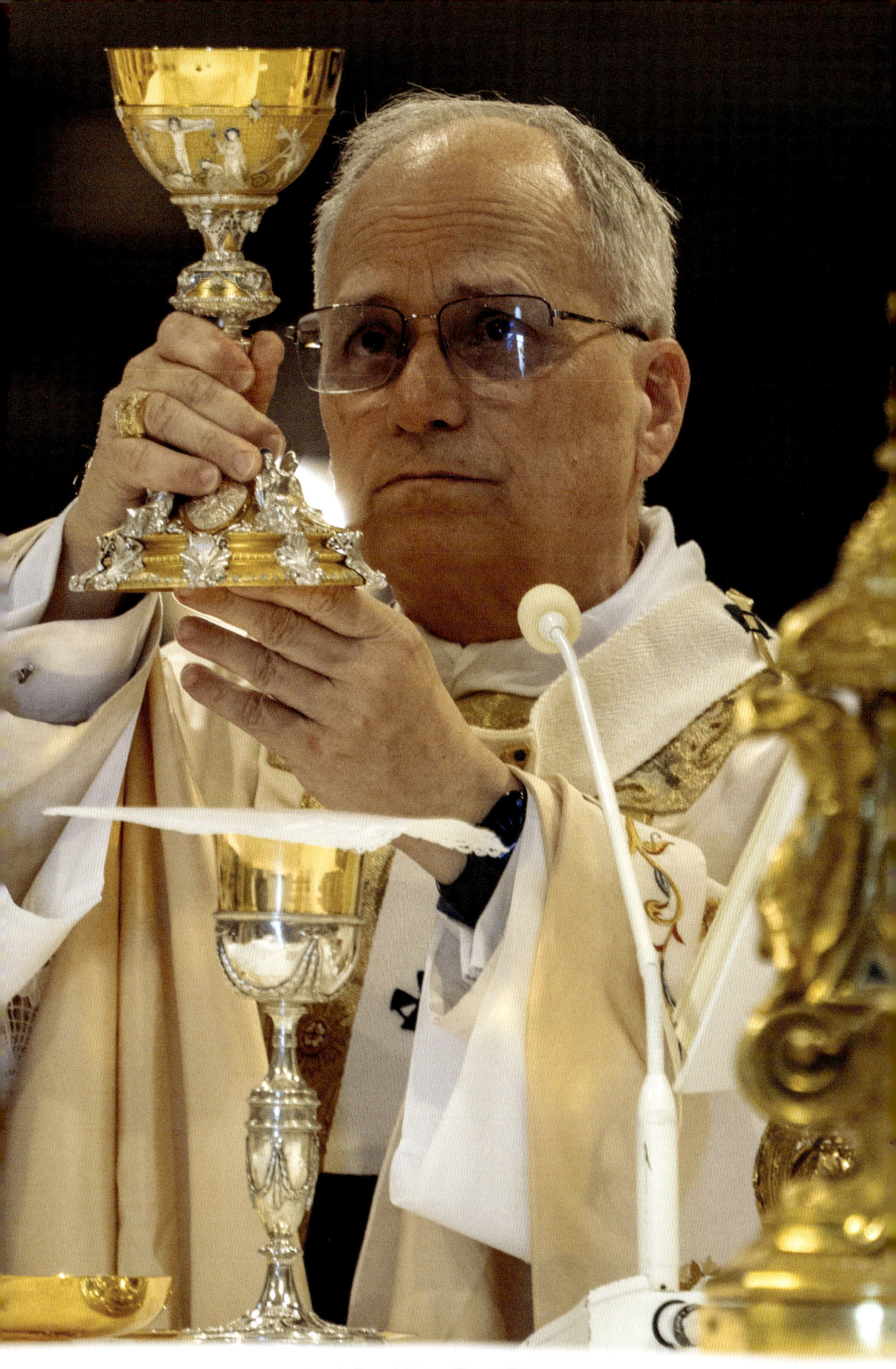

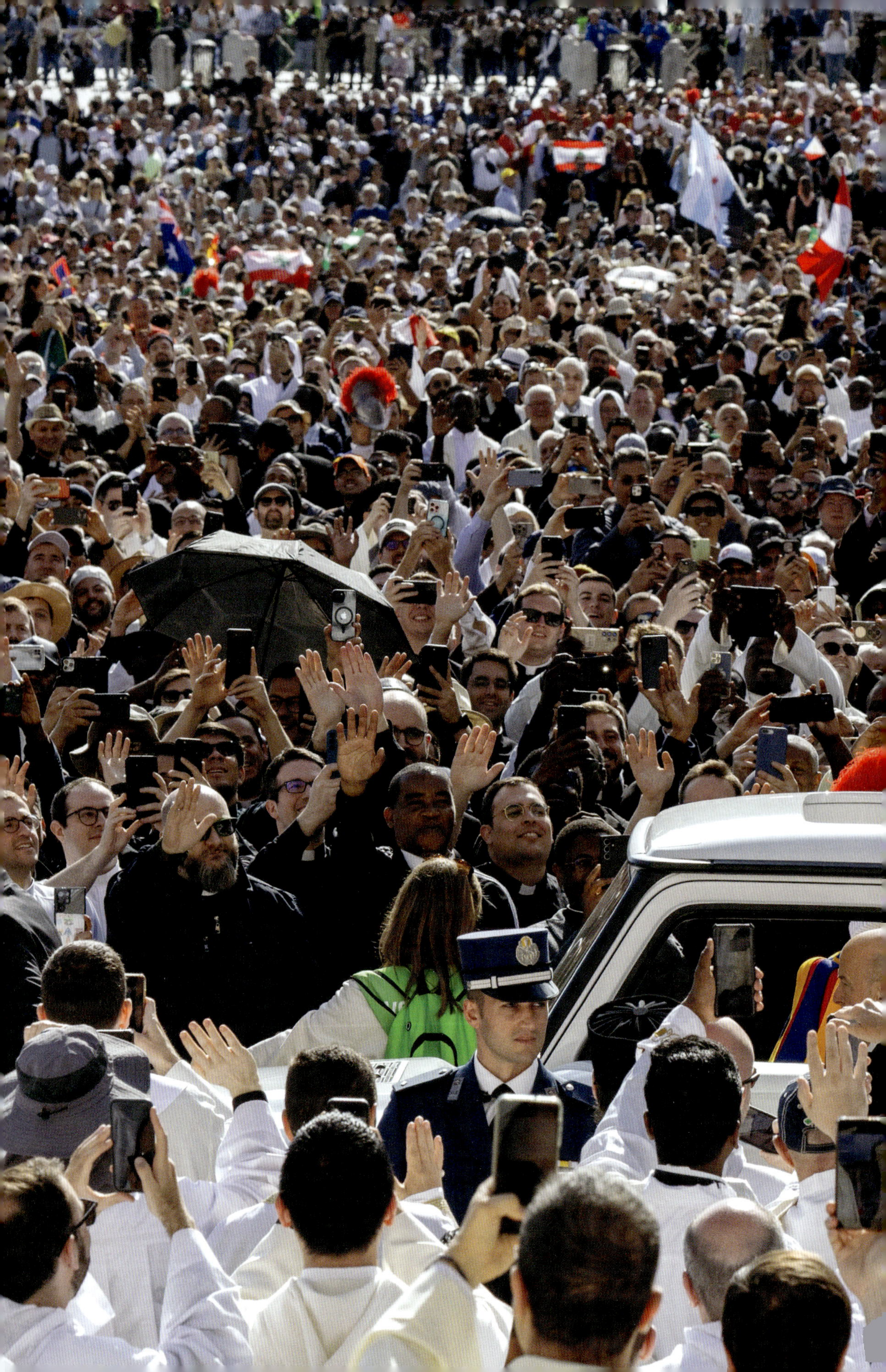

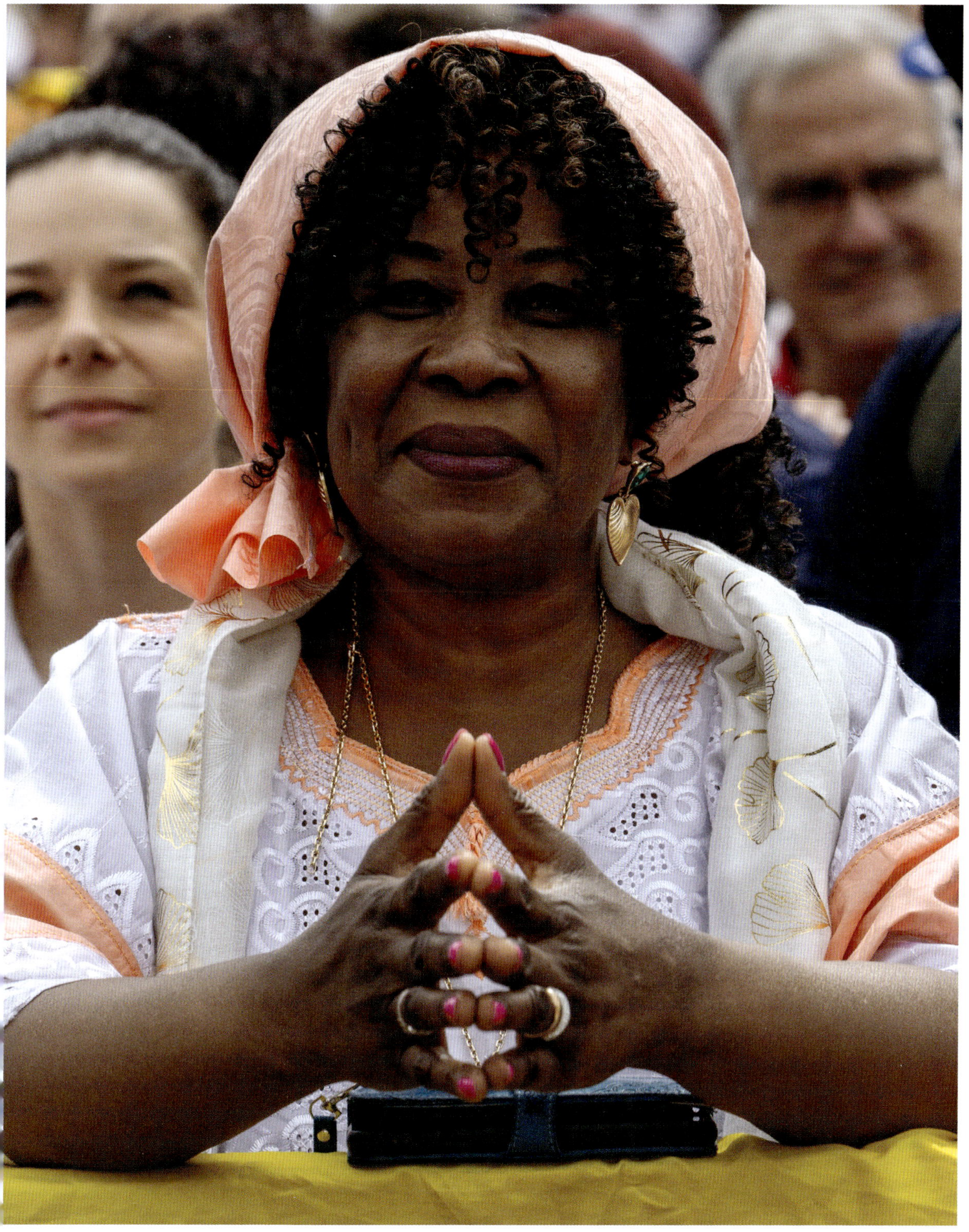

ABOVE *A woman prays during Pope Leo XIV's first* Regina Caeli. **LEFT** *People gathered in St. Peter's Square after Pope Leo's inaugural Mass.*

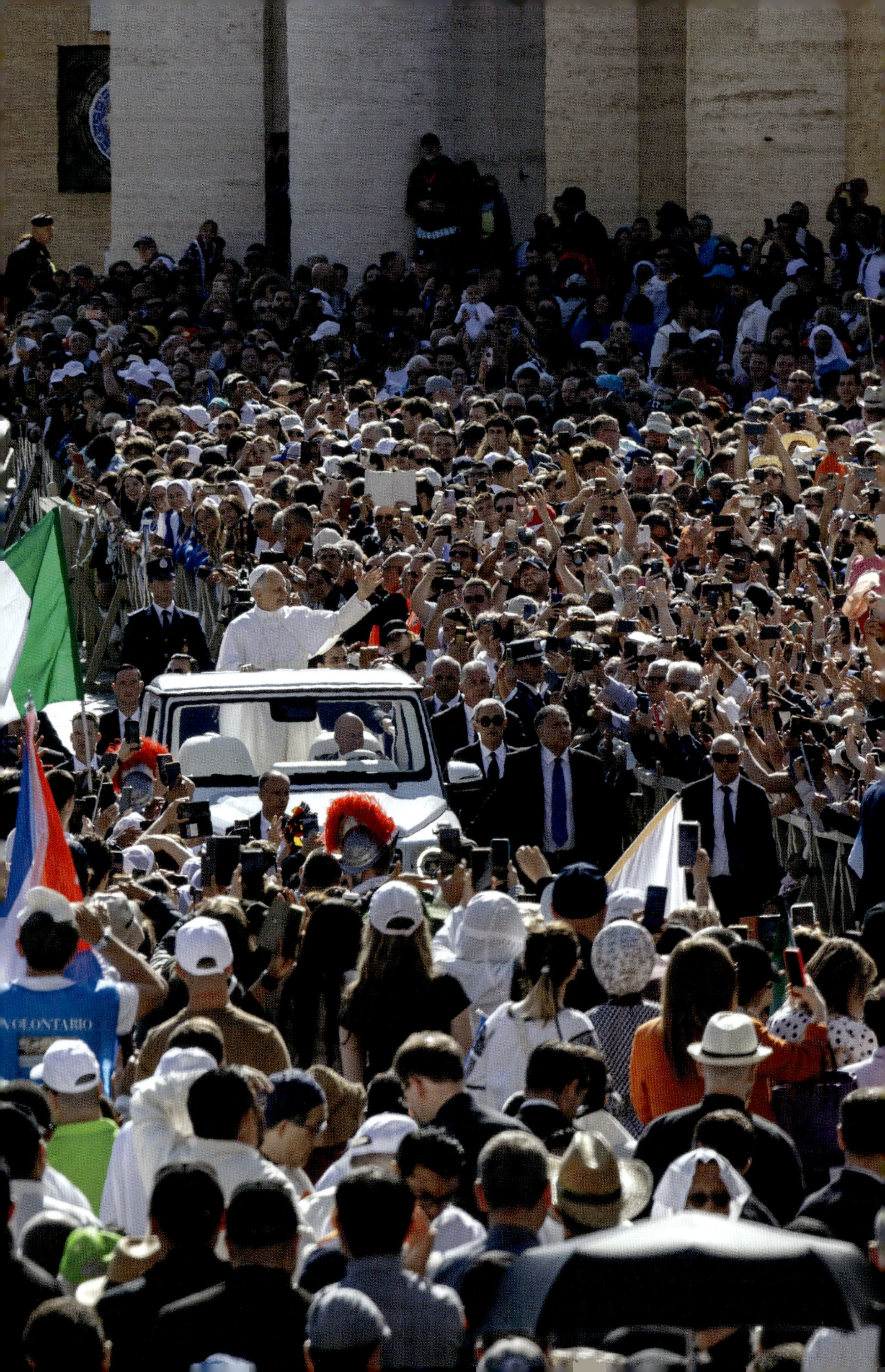
VOLONTARIO

CHAPTER FIVE

Installation of the New Pope

The Inauguration Mass: A New Pontificate Begins

On Sunday, May 18, 2025, the Vatican resounded with celebration as Pope Leo XIV was formally inaugurated as Bishop of Rome and Supreme Pontiff of the Catholic Church. The Mass for the Inauguration of the Petrine Ministry took place in St. Peter's Square at 10:00 a.m., transforming the vast plaza into an "open-air Cathedral." An estimated two hundred thousand pilgrims and dignitaries gathered under a pleasant spring sun, many having arrived before dawn to secure a place. The Square was adorned with splendid flower arrangements in yellow, red, white, and pink, and a massive tapestry bearing Pope Leo's coat of arms hung from the central loggia.

Before Mass began, Pope Leo XIV joyfully greeted the crowds in St. Peter's Square and in the nearby streets, making the circuit in the popemobile. He waved and smiled as cheers of *"Viva il Papa!"* rang out, even stopping the vehicle to kiss and bless babies passed to him—a longstanding and beloved papal custom. Then, rather than going straight to the altar at the front of the Square, he first entered St. Peter's Basilica and descended to the crypt, to the tomb of St. Peter, accompanied by the choir singing Palestrina's timeless *Tu Es Petrus*. Standing alongside the Eastern Catholic Patriarchs in their ornate liturgical robes, he prayed at the Apostle's tomb, asking for the fisherman's intercession as he took up the Office. On the tomb were placed principal symbols of the papacy—the pallium and the Fisherman's Ring—beautiful symbolic links between St. Peter and his 266th successor. After a moment of profound prayer, these items were carried out, and the Pope and Patriarchs processed out into the Square to begin the Mass.

The Mass was rich with tradition at every turn. The entrance procession included the chanting of the *Laudes Regiae*, an ancient litany invoking Christ's protection and the intercession of saints for the new Pope—names of Apostles, Martyrs, Holy Popes, and many other Saints echoed across the Square. The sight of Eastern Catholic Patriarchs walking alongside Roman Rite Cardinals emphasized the univer-

LEFT *Pope Leo blessing the crowd in St. Peter's Square from the popemobile.*

sality and unity of the Church. Pope Leo, vested in a gold-embroidered white chasuble and miter, took his place at a raised altar on the steps of the Basilica.

The Liturgy of the Word featured readings specially chosen for a papal inauguration. The first was from the Acts of the Apostles, in which Peter, the first Pope, proclaims Jesus Christ as the only name "by which we are to be saved" (4:12). The second was from 1 Peter 5, in which Peter exhorts pastors to tend their flocks willingly and selflessly. Finally, the Gospel, from John 21, was the poignant account of the Risen Christ speaking to Peter, admonishing him: "Feed my sheep" (v. 17). This Gospel was proclaimed in both Latin and Greek, a tradition symbolizing the universality of the Church.

Immediately after the Gospel came the specific Rites of Installation—all done in full view of the faithful, emphasizing that the Papal Office is a public ministry of service. First, a Cardinal Deacon, Mario Zenari, approached with the pallium. The pallium is a woolen white stole adorned with black crosses, woven from the wool of lambs blessed on St. Agnes' Feast—symbolizing jurisdiction and the lost sheep carried by the Good Shepherd. In a gesture rich in symbolism, the protodeacon draped the pallium over Pope Leo's shoulders, signifying his role as Shepherd of Rome and the Universal Church. A second element of the installation included a solemn prayer offered by a Cardinal Priest, Fridolin Ambongo Besungu, invoking the Holy Spirit's strength and wisdom upon the Pope's ministry. Pope Leo listened with head bowed as this prayer echoed through the Square, reminding him of the generations of predecessors who had stood in that same place before him.

Next, it was time to present him with the Fisherman's Ring. This gold ring, unique to each Pope, depicts St. Peter casting his net—a sign of the Pope's duty to spread the Gospel as "fisher of men." Cardinal Luis Antonio Tagle of the Philippines, a Cardinal Bishop, had the honor of placing it on Pope Leo's right ring finger. As the Pope's face betrayed the emotion he felt at the enormity of what he was accepting, the faithful in the Square cheered. The new Pope now wore the very badges of Office that once belonged to Peter—the yoke of pastoral love (the pallium) and the authority to bind and loose (the ring with the keys and the net of St. Peter).

Following these rites, a beautiful act underscored the Pope's connection with the people of God: representatives of the Church—clergy, religious, and laity—approached to offer obedience. Twelve people were chosen to represent the whole

TOP LEFT *Pilgrims gathering in St. Peter's Square to participate in Pope Leo's inaugural Mass.* ***TOP RIGHT*** *Cardinal Mario Zenari placing the pallium on Pope Leo's shoulders.* ***BOTTOM*** *Pope Leo during his inaugural Mass, May 18, 2025.*

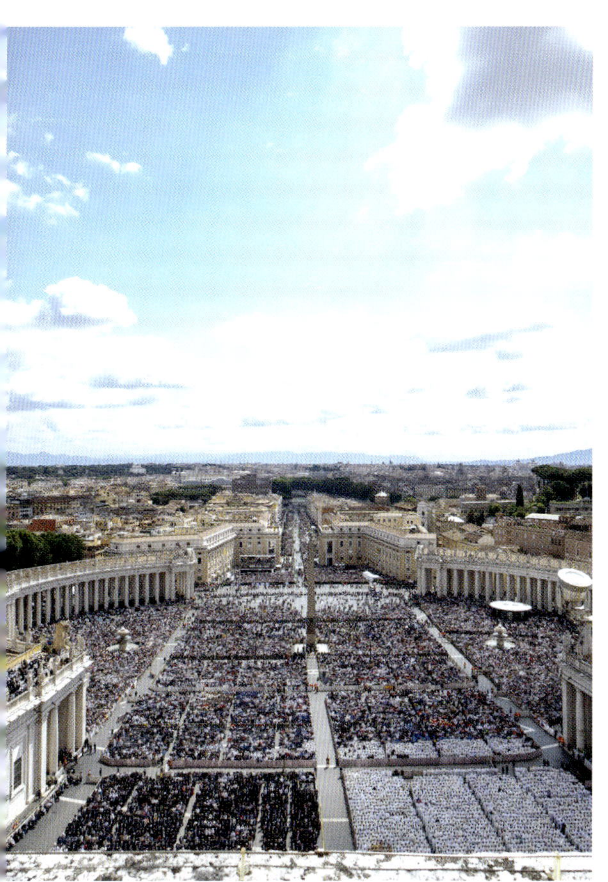

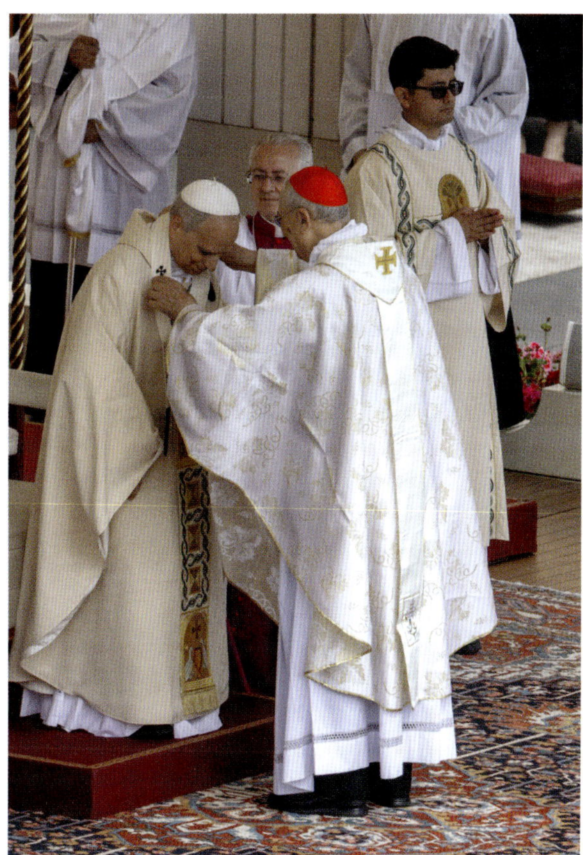

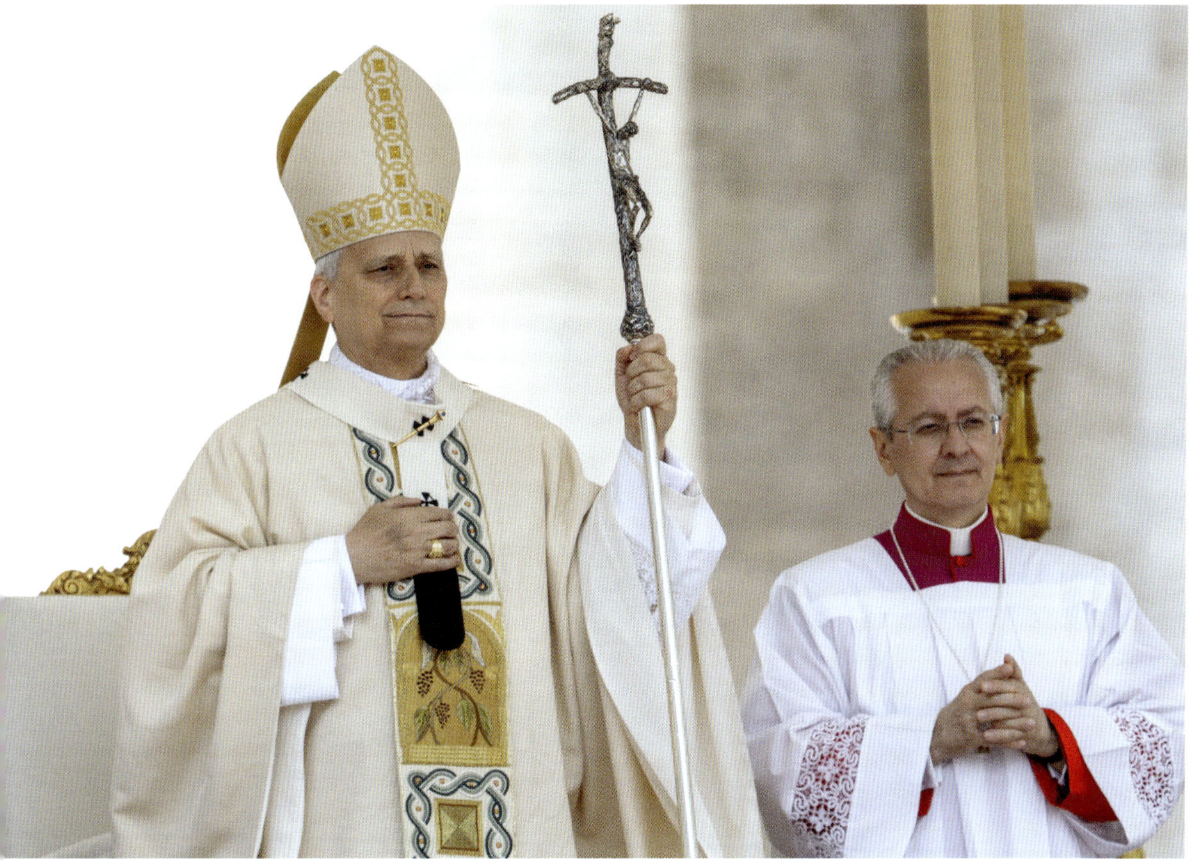

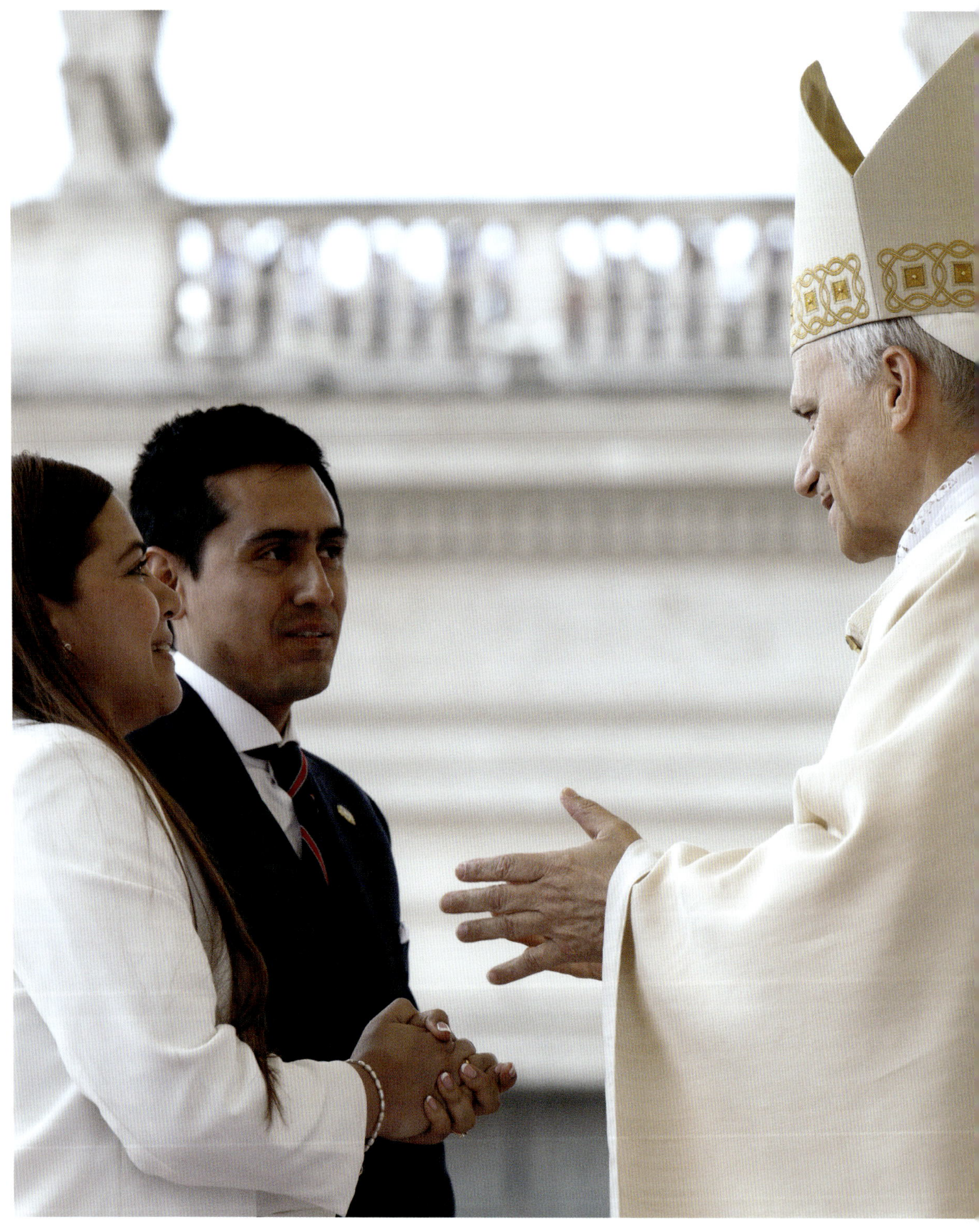

Representative members of the Church offer gestures of obedience and respect during the Pope's inaugural Mass, May 18, 2025. **ABOVE** *A young couple.* **RIGHT** *A member of the clergy.*

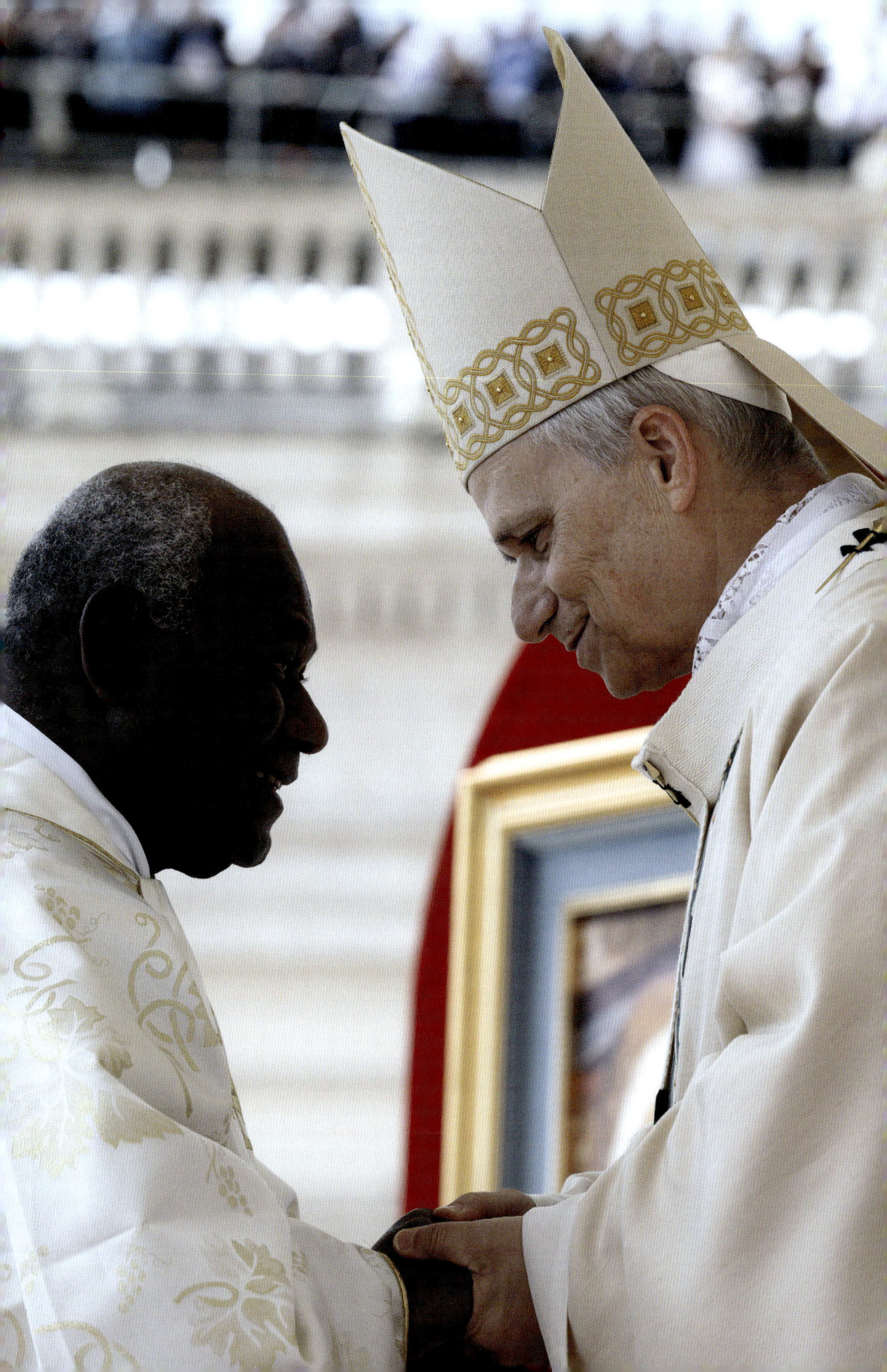

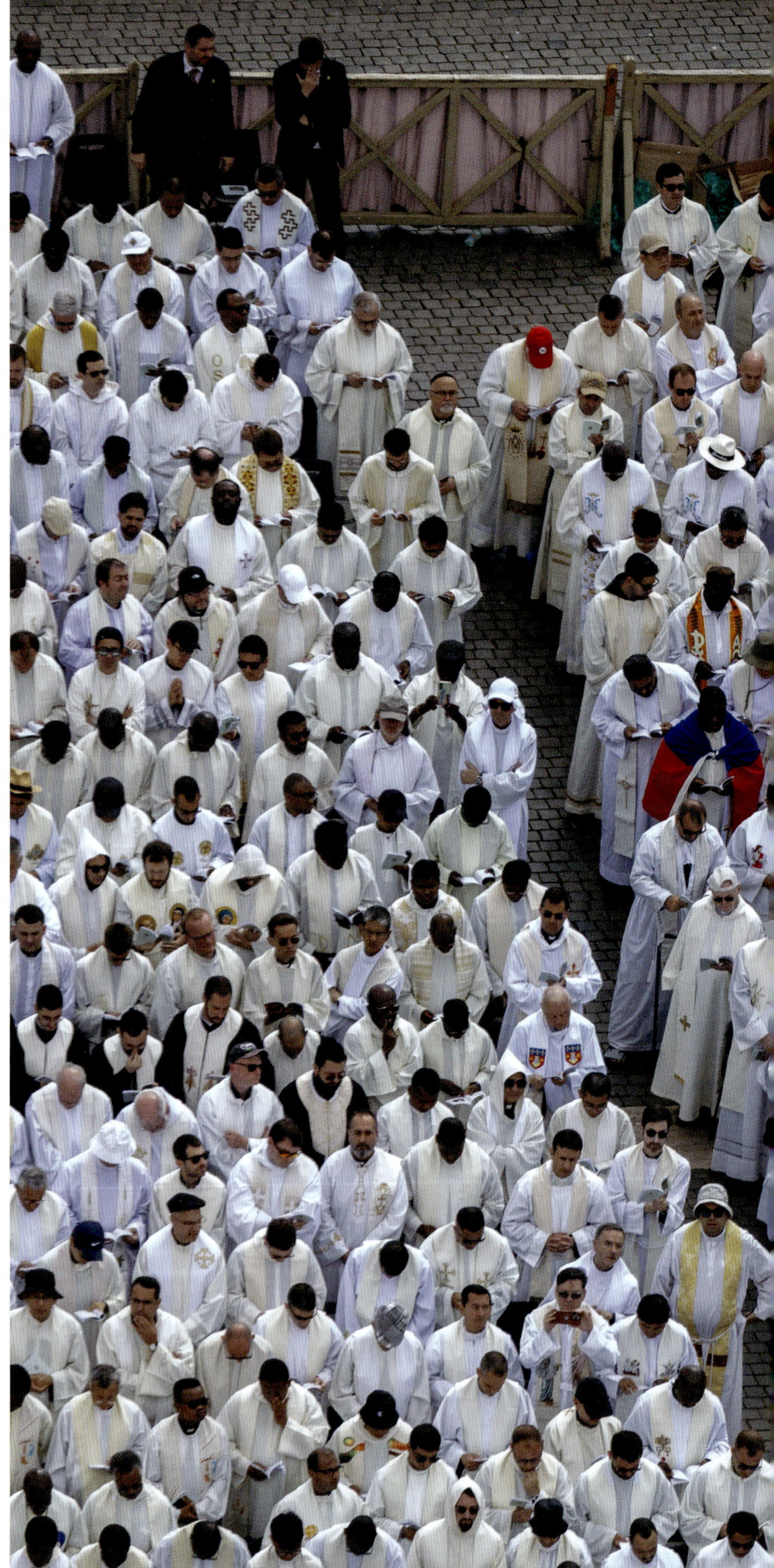

RIGHT *Priests participating in Pope Leo's inaugural Mass, May 18, 2025.*

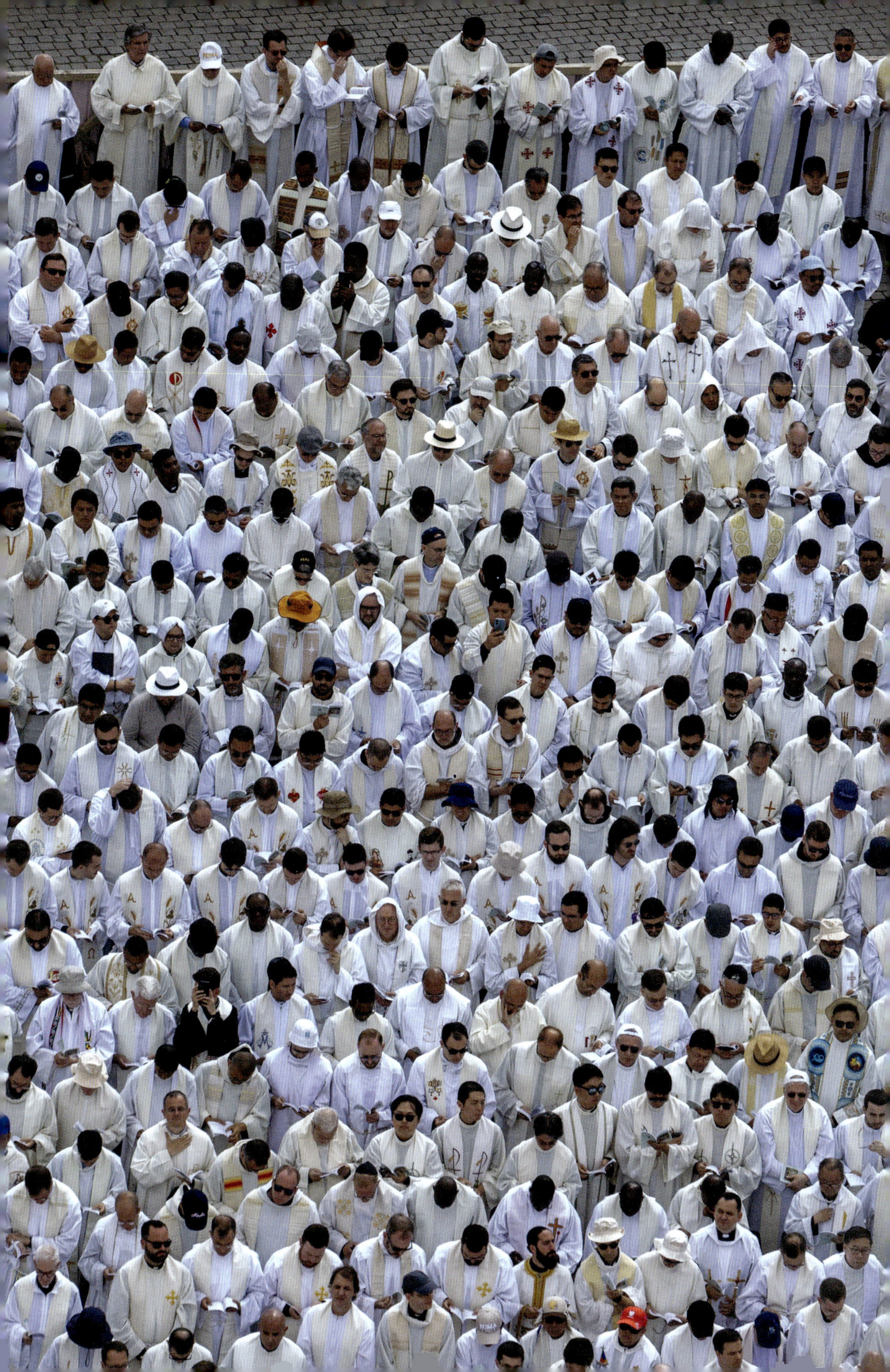

Church, reflecting its diversity. They included a bishop, a priest, a deacon, a religious brother and sister, a married couple, a young man and woman, and others from various continents. Each came up to Pope Leo, knelt or bowed, and clasped his hand or kissed his ring in a sign of respect and obedience. He, in turn, greeted each with a few words and a smile. In addition to being a demonstration of the respect and obedience that every Catholic owes to the Holy Father, this moment also showed that Pope Leo will serve as a caring father for all believers.

With the installation rites concluded, the Mass ended with the Liturgy of the Eucharist. Pope Leo XIV stood at the altar as the main celebrant, surrounded by Cardinals and Patriarchs concelebrating. At the Sign of Peace, he exchanged a warm embrace with several of the concelebrants and guests, including the Ecumenical Patriarch of Constantinople, who was present—a significant ecumenical gesture that has become tradition since Vatican II, symbolizing hopes for Christian unity. Mass continued with clergy distributing Holy Communion throughout the immense crowd.

Finally, after Communion, the Pope imparted the final blessing. Before doing so, he led the assembly in the singing of the Easter-season Marian hymn *Regina Caeli*, since it was a Sunday in Eastertide. This joyful prayer to Our Lady seemed a fitting capstone to the Mass, entrusting the new pontificate to the motherly care of the Blessed Mother.

After the Mass concluded, the Pope undertook one more act of both pastoral and diplomatic significance: he returned into St. Peter's Basilica to greet briefly the various Heads of State and religious delegations. There was a vast line of presidents, prime ministers, and representatives of other Christian communities assembled to meet him. Pope Leo spent a moment with each, offering individual respectful nods, handshakes, and a few words of conversation. Notably, among the clerical leaders, the presence of the Orthodox delegation and a representative of the Protestant communities served as a sign of hope for ecumenical dialogue; Pope Leo's gracious attention to them did not go unnoticed. And from his own country, he had a brief exchange with the American vice president and secretary of state and their wives. As the new Pope retired, the crowds began to disperse, many singing hymns or songs of joy. The Church had formally received Her new Shepherd.

TOP *Cardinal Luis Antonio Tagle places the Fisherman's Ring on Pope Leo's right hand.*
BOTTOM *A religious sister greeting the Pope during his inaugural Mass, May 18, 2025.*

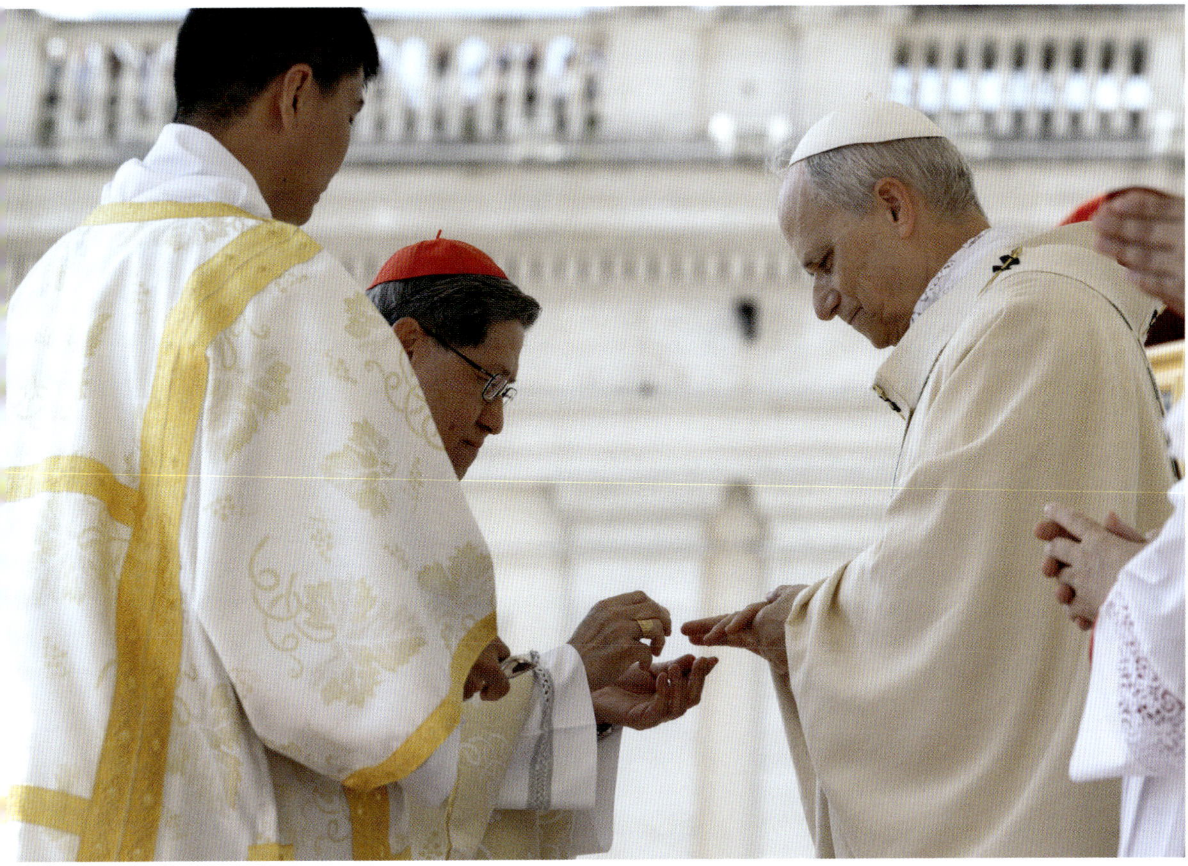

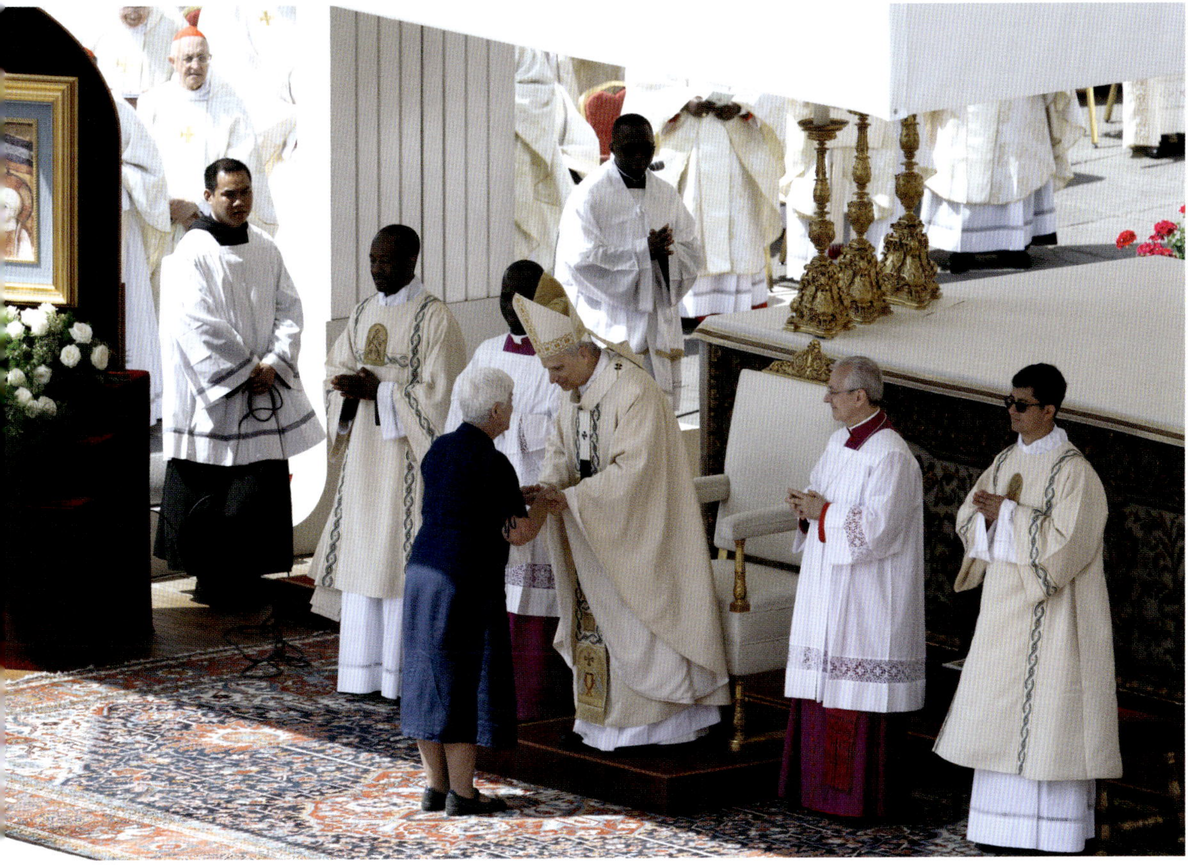

The Chair of Peter and the City of Rome

With the Installation Mass complete, Pope Leo XIV fully assumed all facets of the Papal Office. In the following days, he carried out a few additional ancient ceremonies linking him to his role as Bishop of Rome. Notably, on May 25, just a week after the inauguration, Pope Leo went to the Papal Basilica of St. John Lateran—the official Cathedral of the Bishop of Rome—to take formal possession of his *cathedra*. This event, sometimes called the Enthronement at the Lateran, was slightly more low-key than the installation, but no less significant spiritually. Amid prayer and the presence of Rome's diocesan clergy, the Pope seated himself in the ancient marble bishop's throne in St. John Lateran, symbolically marking him as the new Bishop of Rome in the eyes of the diocesan faithful. The Lateran Basilica's bells rang out and local Roman faithful cheered "*Benvenuto!*" as their new Bishop greeted them. Pope Leo's choice to schedule this and his taking possession of the other major Papal Basilicas (St. Paul's Outside the Walls on May 20 and St. Mary Major on May 25) within the first week of his pontificate demonstrated his desire to root his service firmly in the soil of Rome.

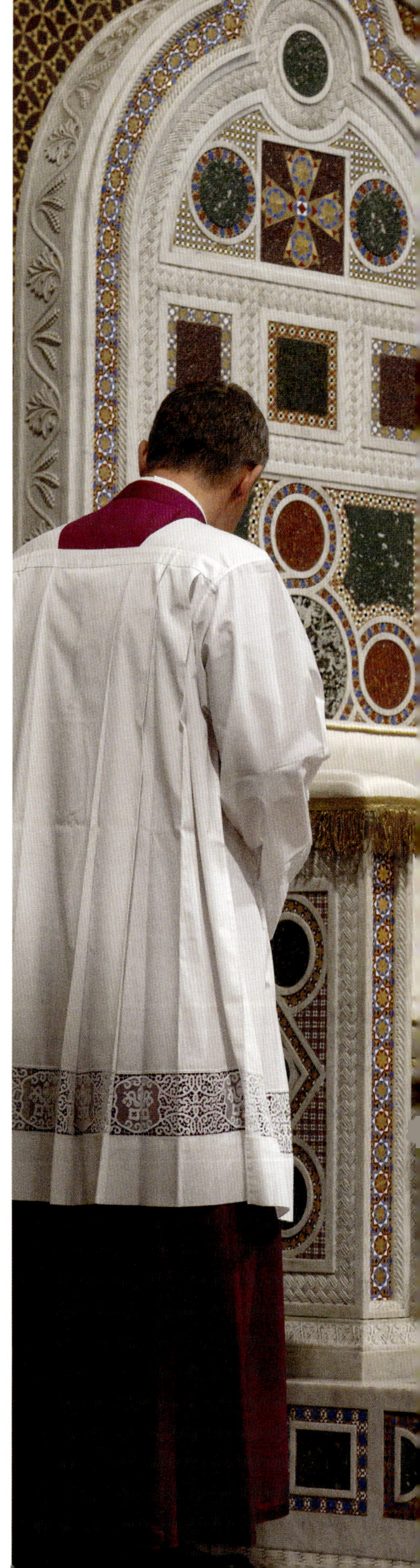

RIGHT *Pope Leo officially taking possession of the Basilica of St. John Lateran—the Seat of the Diocese of Rome.*

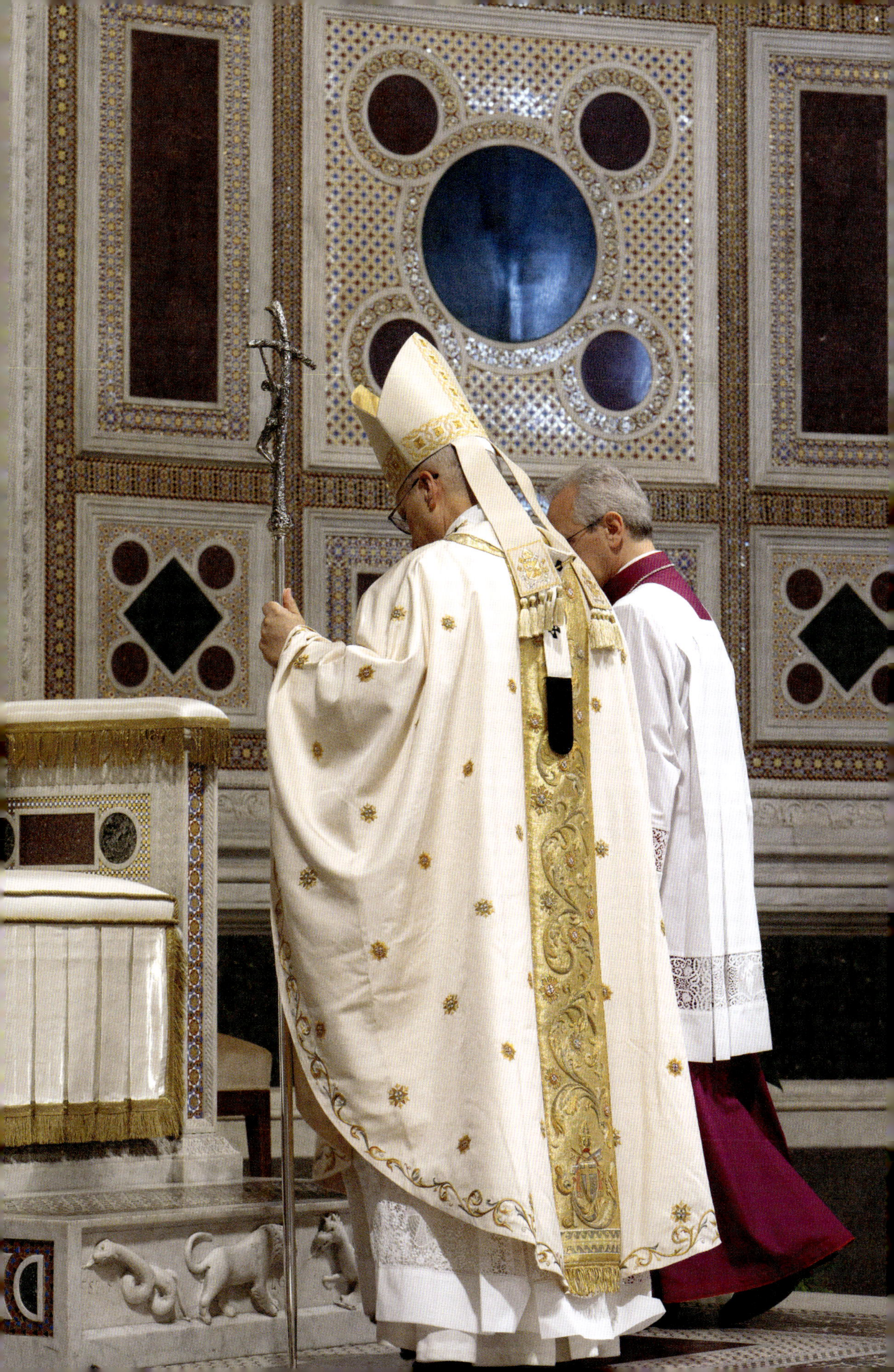

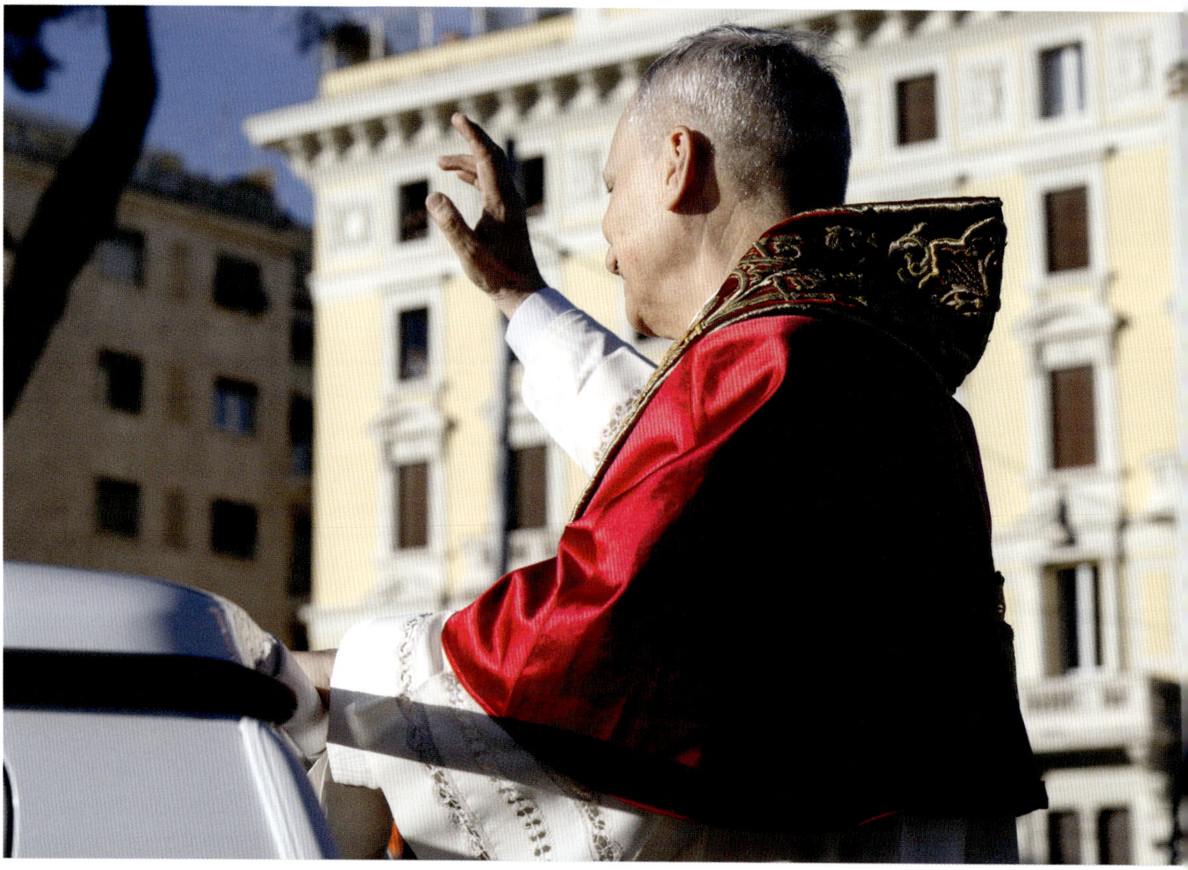

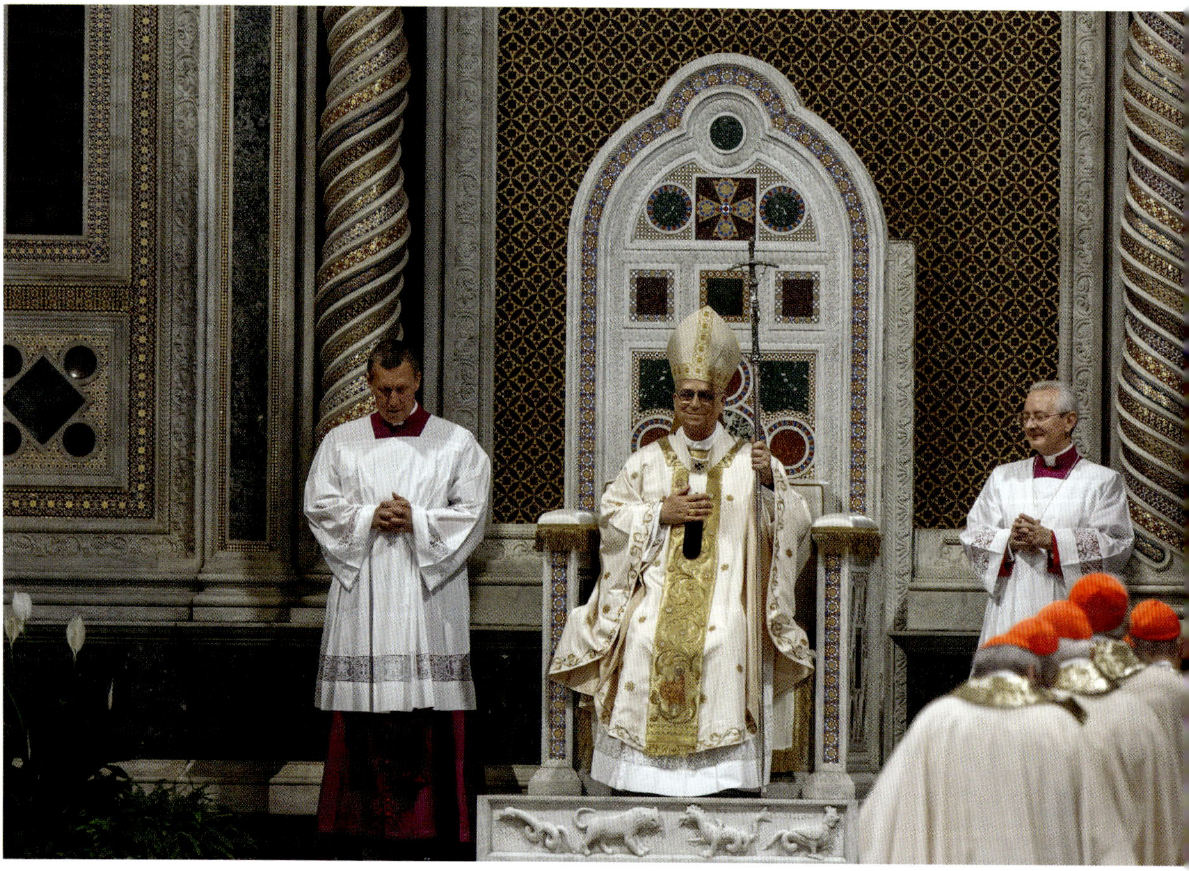

At the Lateran, during his homily, he spoke of his love for this particularly Roman church: "The Church of Rome is heir to a great history, grounded in the witness of Peter, Paul and countless martyrs, and it has a unique mission, as we see from the inscription on the façade of this Cathedral: to be *Mater omnium Ecclesiarum*, Mother of all the Churches." Harking back to Pope Francis, he recalled how his predecessor encouraged the faithful to think of the Church as a Mother, full of tenderness, self-sacrifice, and the ability to listen. Through such qualities, the people of God can meet and anticipate the needs of humanity and so bring the light of God into the presence of the whole world.

Meanwhile, outside of the Lateran and in the corners of the world far removed from Rome, Catholics the world over were still savoring the images and messages of the installation. The sight of Pope Leo XIV with the pallium and ring, and his thoughtful yet smiling countenance, was on the cover of diocesan newspapers and secular magazines alike. Many commented on how seamlessly the Church's ancient ceremonies had once again translated to a modern audience: from the *fumata* (smoke) to the *Habemus Papam* to the installation Mass, all were moments of shared Catholic heritage that also captivated the general public.

Now installed, Pope Leo XIV set out to continue the mission of his predecessors with his own charism. Notably, he has chosen to live in the traditional papal apartment with fellow Augustinians. Other key early actions included signing his first apostolic blessing certificates and sending his personal greetings and thanks to the Church in Peru, thanking them for nurturing his vocation during his years spent there as a missionary and bishop. These last two actions in particular showed that, even as the world looked to him as the Supreme Pontiff, he did not forget the origins and stages of his own journey.

The city of Rome, for its part, also celebrated having a new "Papa." The Sunday of the installation, the atmosphere was festive—vendors sold papal flags and memorabilia with Leo XIV's image, and spontaneous prayers of thanksgiving were held at churches. The Roman sky was filled with the sound of church bells not just at the Vatican but in parishes around the city, ringing in chorus at the hour of the inauguration and again when the Pope sat at the Lateran *cathedra*.

And beyond Rome, a renewed sense of hope spread. Bishops from around the world offered loyalty and prayers to the Vatican. Social media saw Catholic youth

TOP *Pope Leo blessing the crowd from the popemobile.* ***BOTTOM*** *Pope Leo seated at the Basilica of St. John Lateran, demonstrating his authority as the bishop of Rome.*

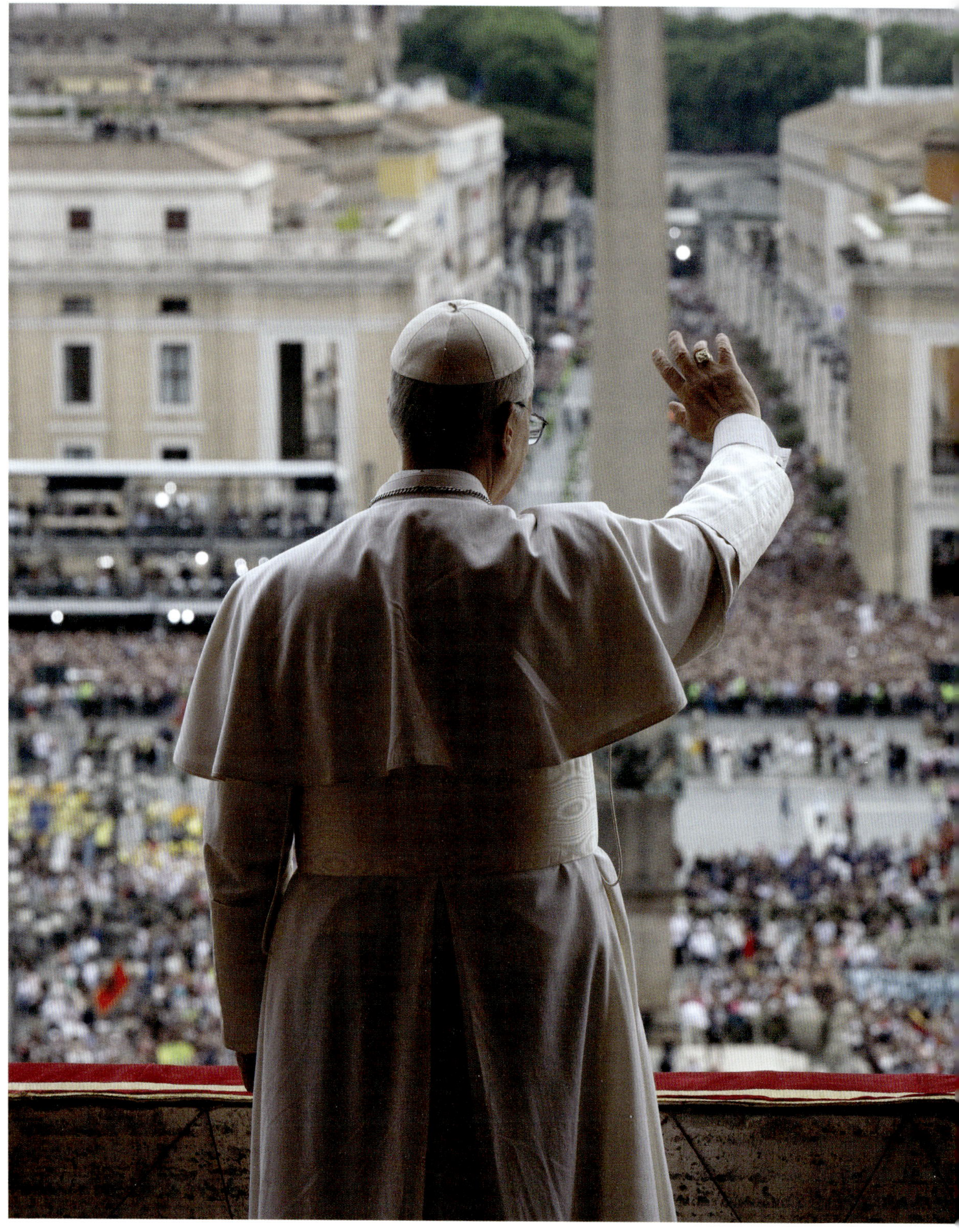

ABOVE *Pope Leo waving to the crowd from a balcony in St. Peter's Square.* **RIGHT** *Pope Leo praying at the Shrine of Our Lady of Good Counsel, Genazzano, Italy.*

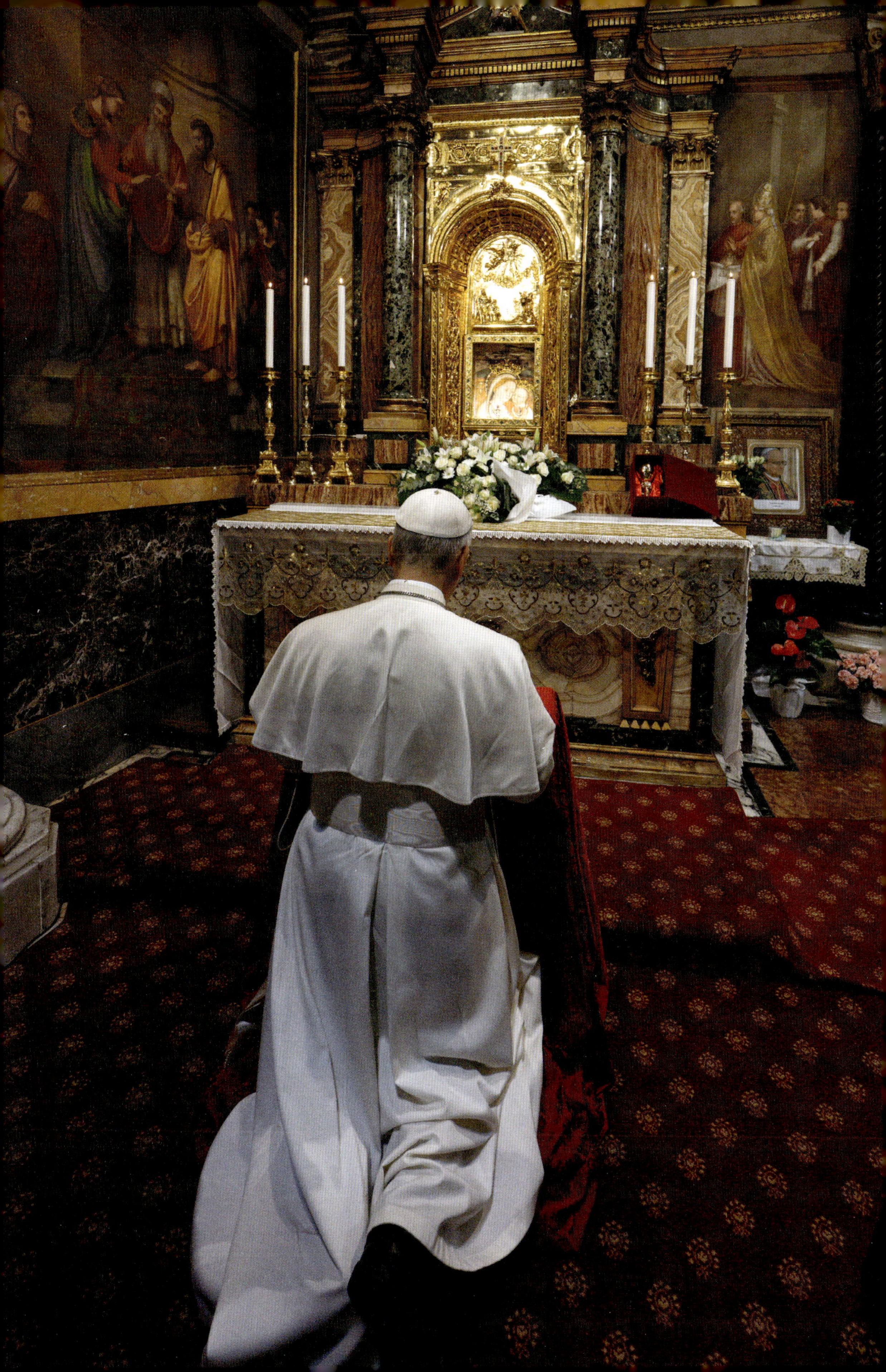

proudly post quotes from Leo XIV's first homily. It was clear that the faithful took pride in the Church's ability to honor its centuries of tradition while moving forward under new leadership. The papal transition from Francis to Leo was complete: an end and a beginning woven seamlessly together, a testament to the enduring guidance of the Holy Spirit.

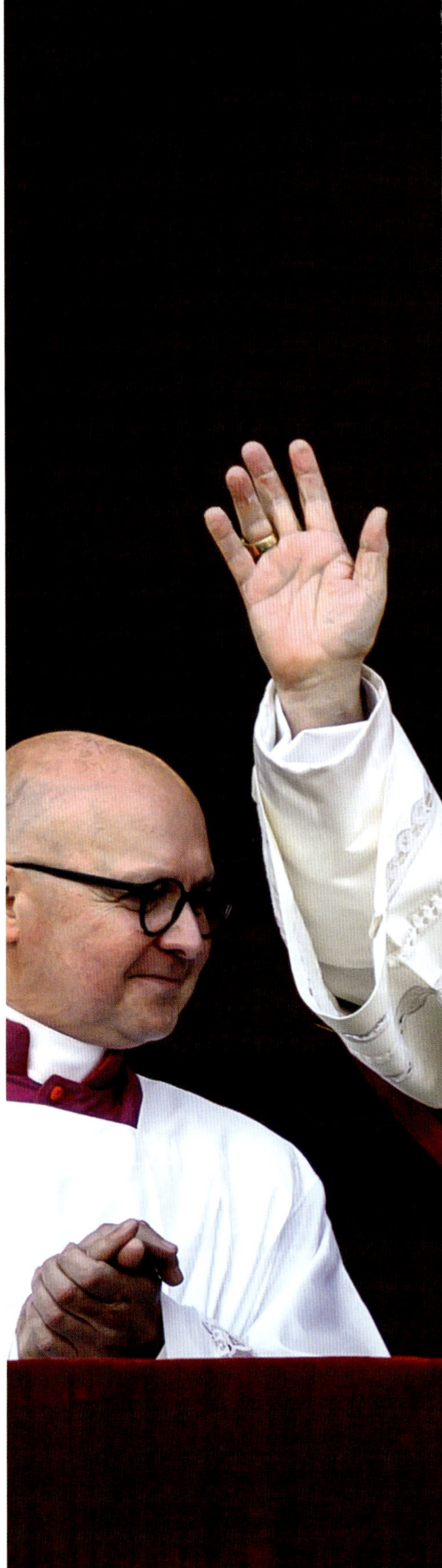

RIGHT *The papal transition from Francis to Leo was complete, an end and a beginning.*

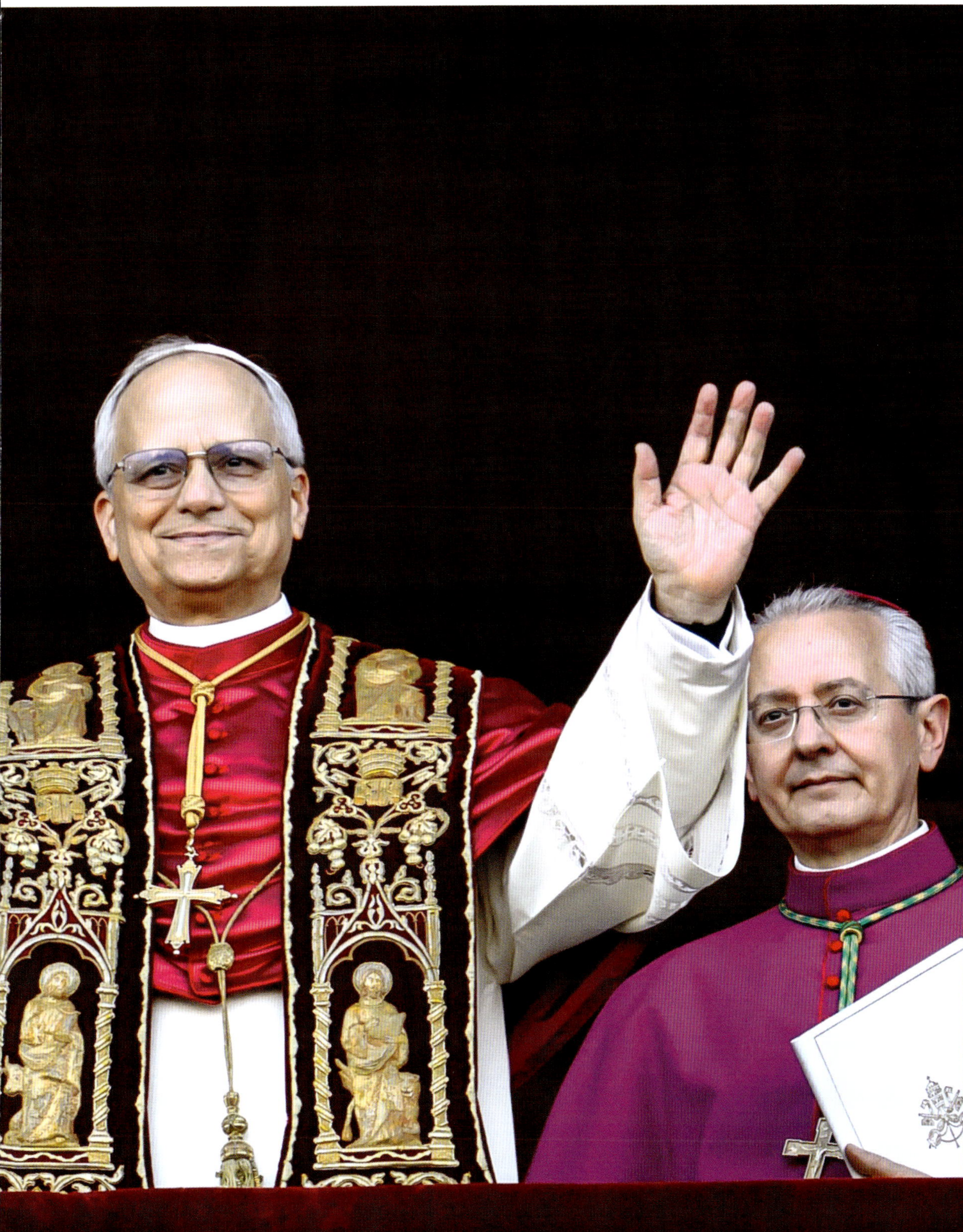

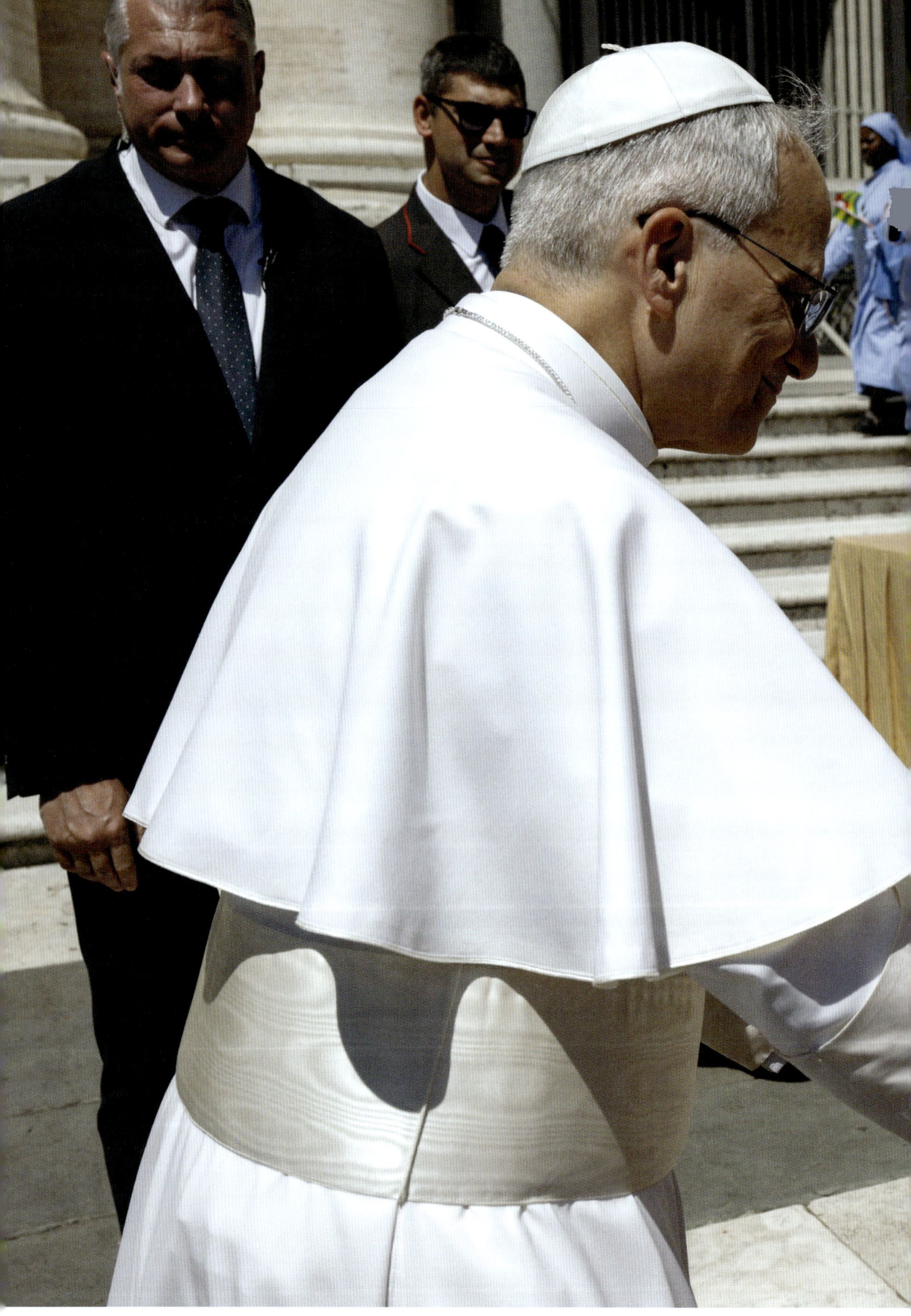

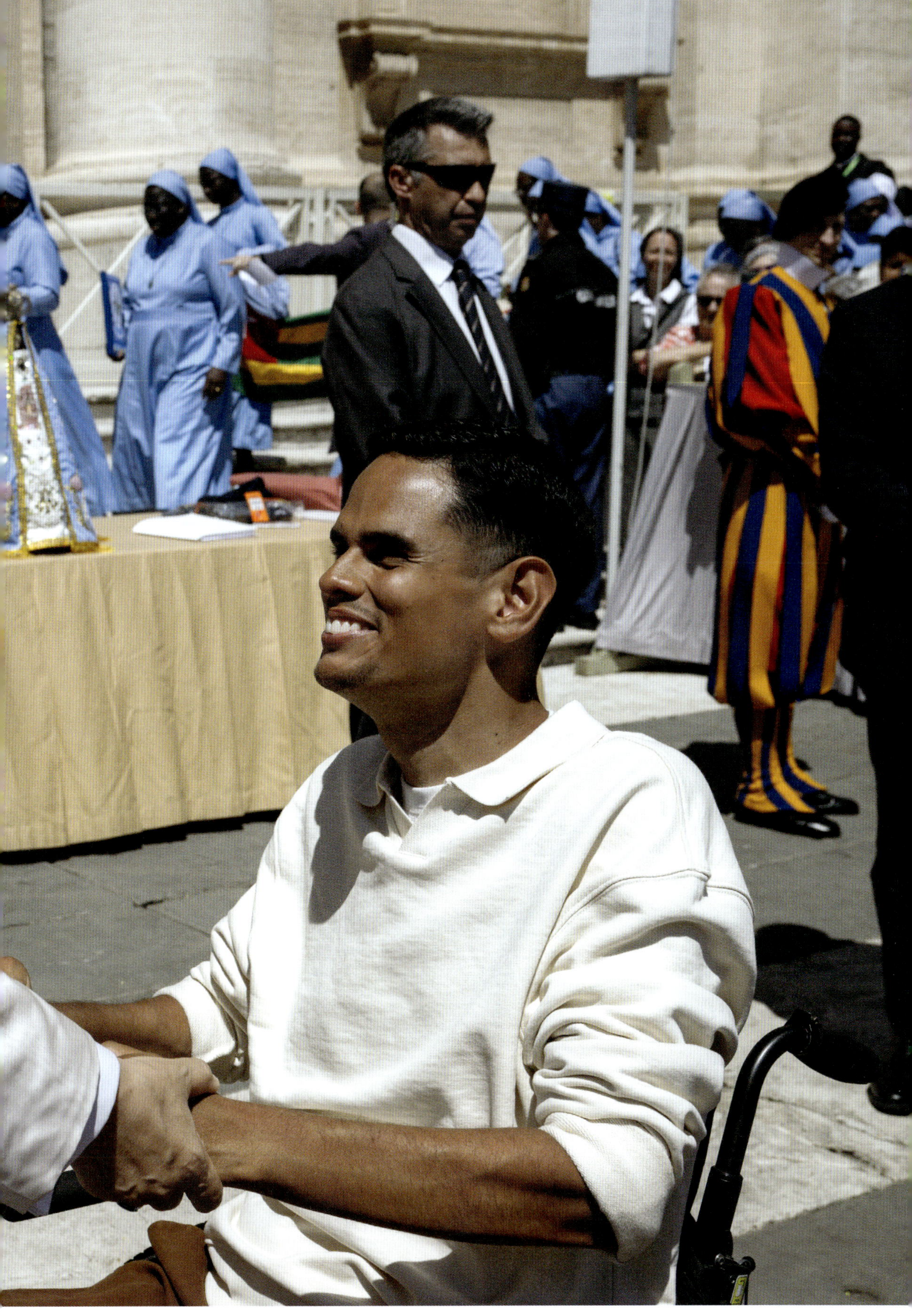

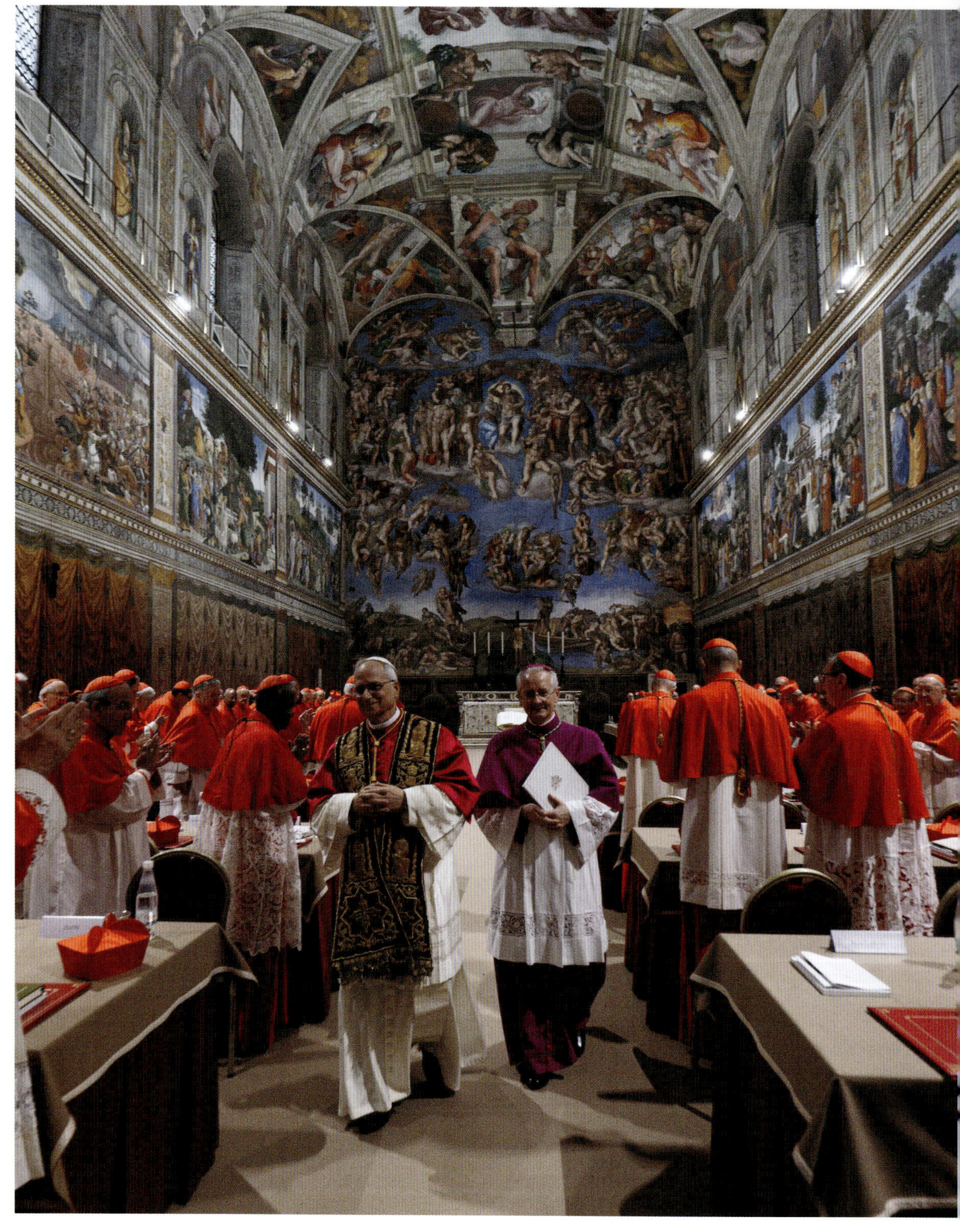

ABOVE *Leo XIV greeting the cardinals in the Sistine Chapel shortly after being declared Pope.*

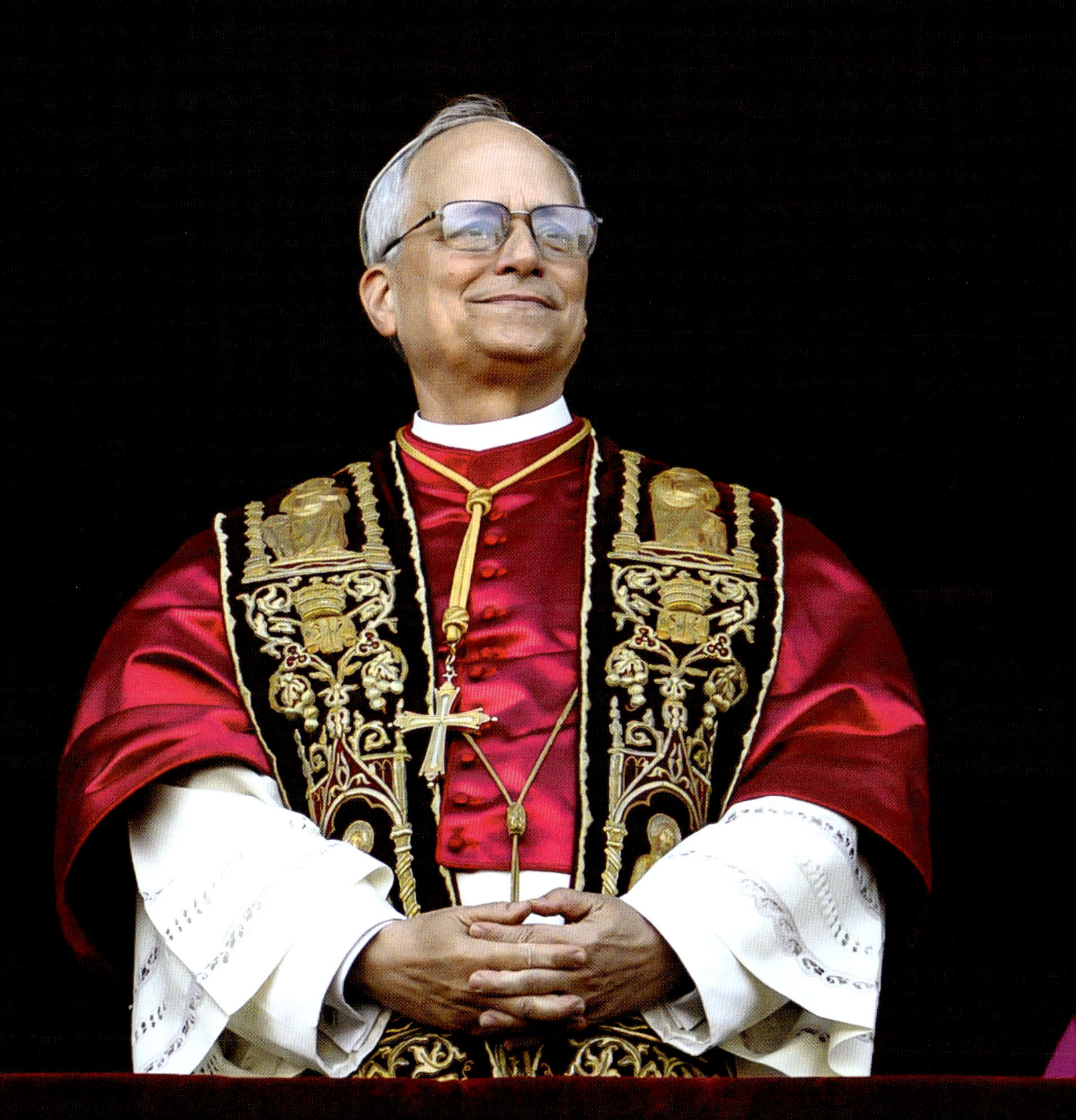

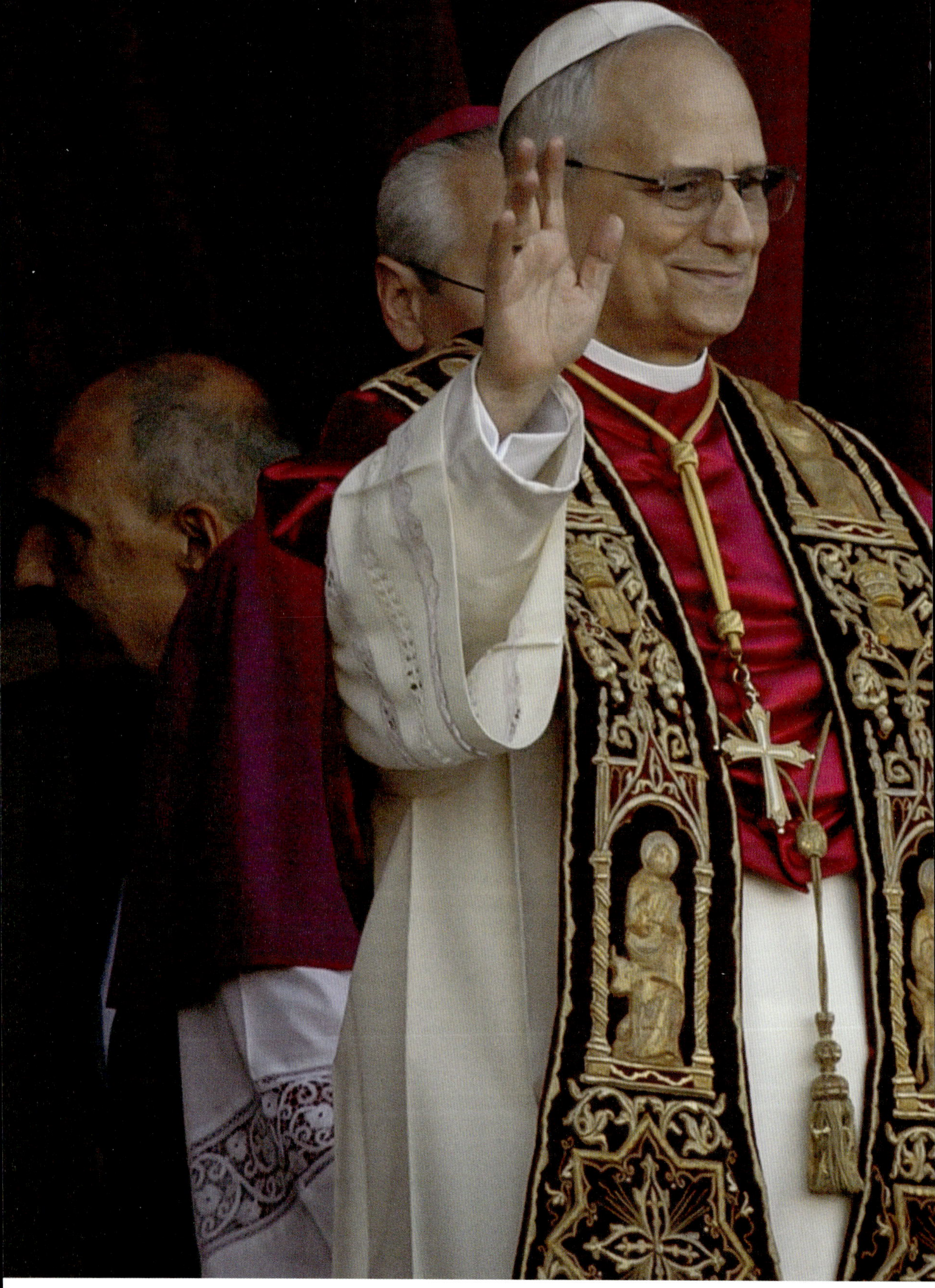

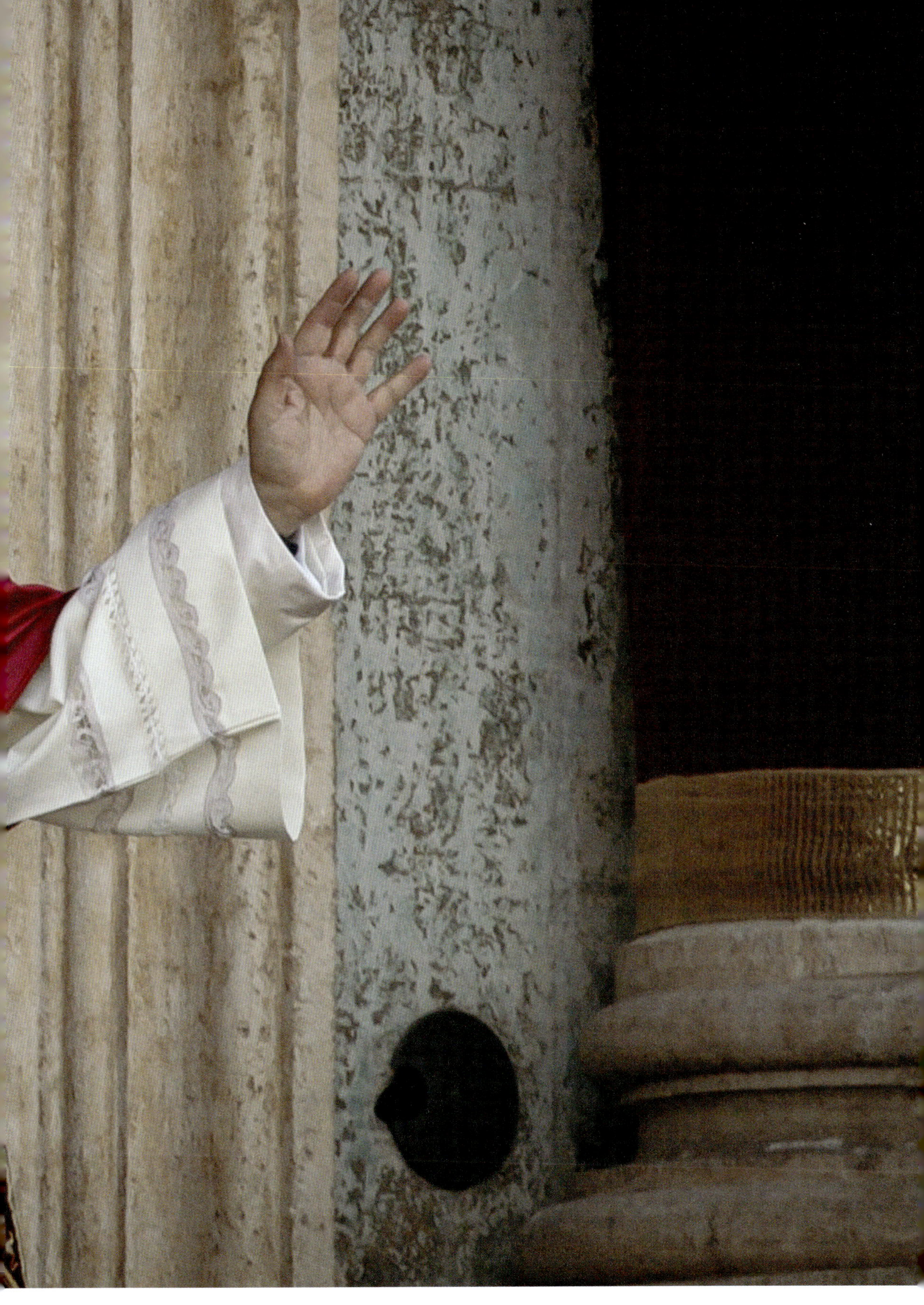

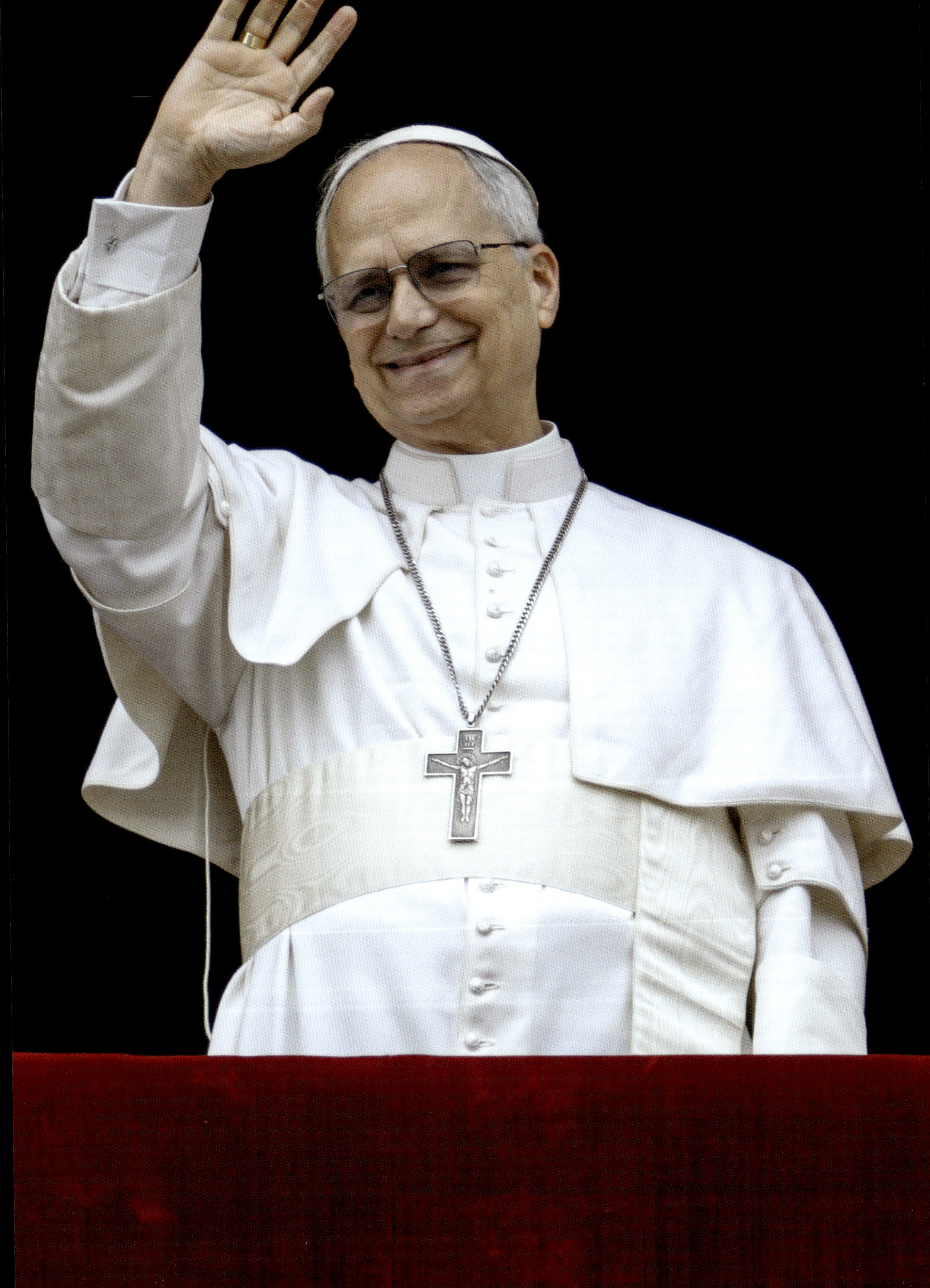

CONCLUSION

A Church That Endures

The journey from the death of Pope Francis to the election and early Papacy of Pope Leo XIV showcased the Catholic Church: steadfast in faith, rich in tradition, and united in hope. Each stage—the tender rituals at a Pope's death, the careful stewardship of the *Sede Vacante*, the dramatic secrecy of the conclave, the triumphant announcement of *Habemus Papam*, the heartfelt first blessings, and the majestic installation ceremony—unfolded with a blend of historical continuity and living faith.

Practicing Catholics can take deep pride in these events. They are not mere pageantry; they are profound expressions of what Catholics believe about the Church and the papacy. The mourning of a Pope is suffused with Easter hope; the election of a new Pope is entrusted to prayer as much as process; the pomp of the inauguration is directed entirely to honoring the mission Christ gave to Peter and his successors. This book, filled with striking photography and reverent commentary, invites you, the faithful, to relive those remarkable weeks. In the figure of Pope Leo XIV—stepping forward from the loggia to bless the world—we see the Church's unbroken line from St. Peter to today. In the rituals described and illustrated, we recognize the wisdom of generations and the touch of the divine in the human.

As Pope Leo XIV begins his ministry, the Church moves forward, *sempre avanti,* always onward, carrying forward the primary mission of Pope Francis that he himself shared with all the Popes who went before him: the safeguarding of Holy Mother Church and Her teachings. The transition has been completed with dignity and devotion. The keys of St. Peter rest in new hands, but the same Lord guides the Church. May this chronicle of that transition inspire in every reader a renewed love for the beauty of Catholic tradition and a hopeful prayer for Pope Leo XIV and the future of the Church he now leads.

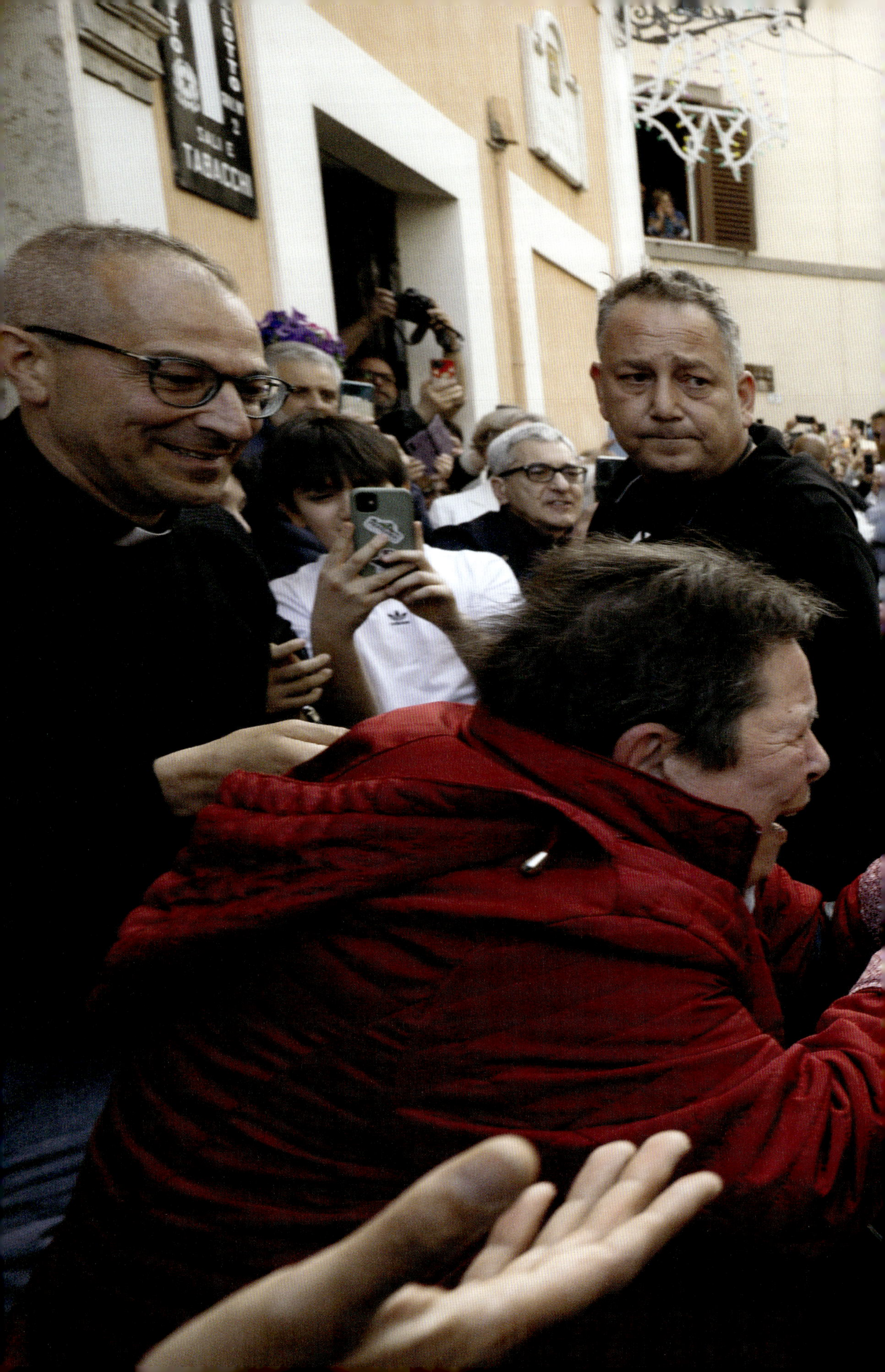
SALI E
TABACCHI

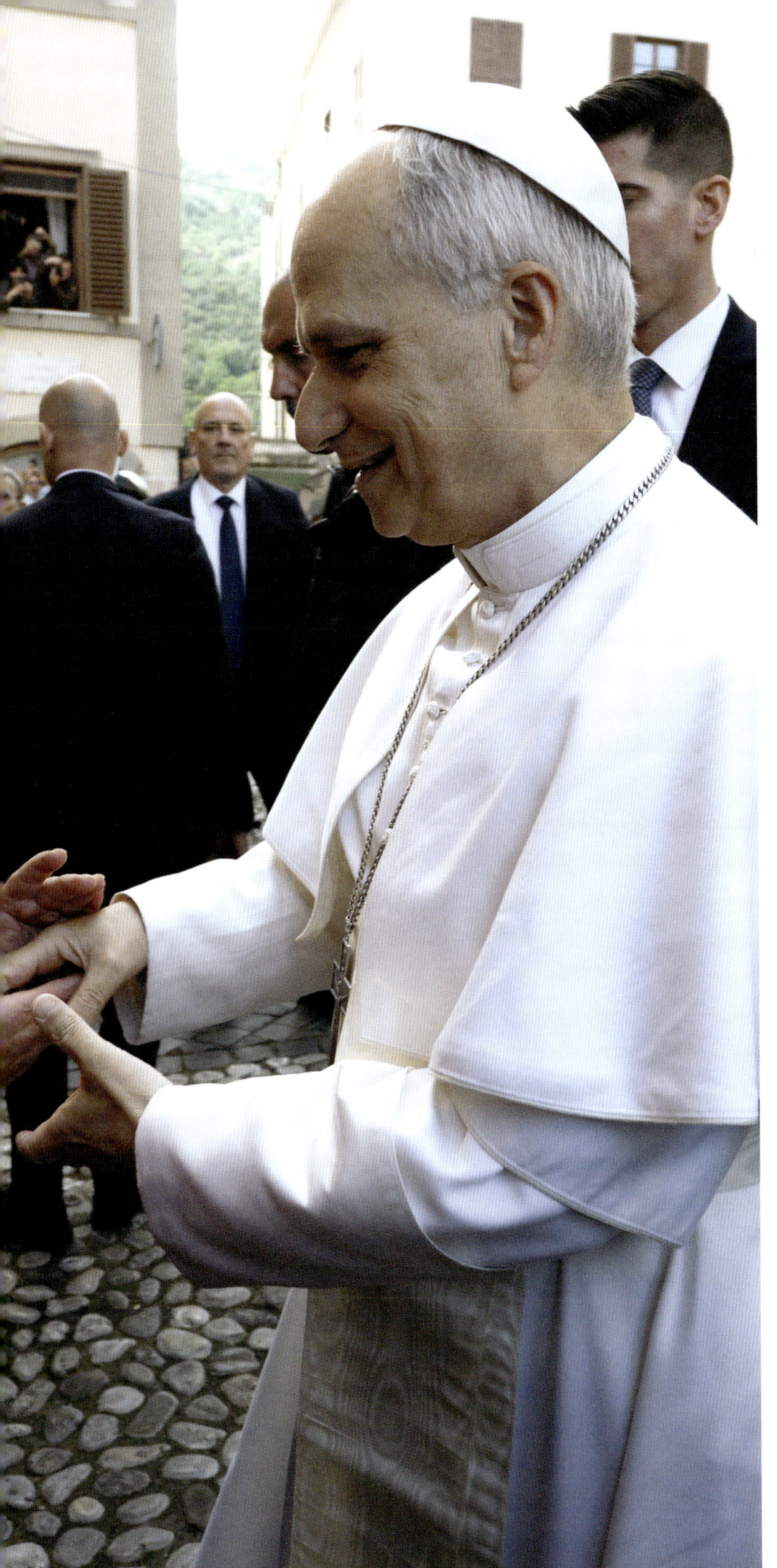

LEFT *Pope Leo greets an elderly woman during his surprise visit to the Shrine of Our Lady of Good Counsel in Genazzano.*

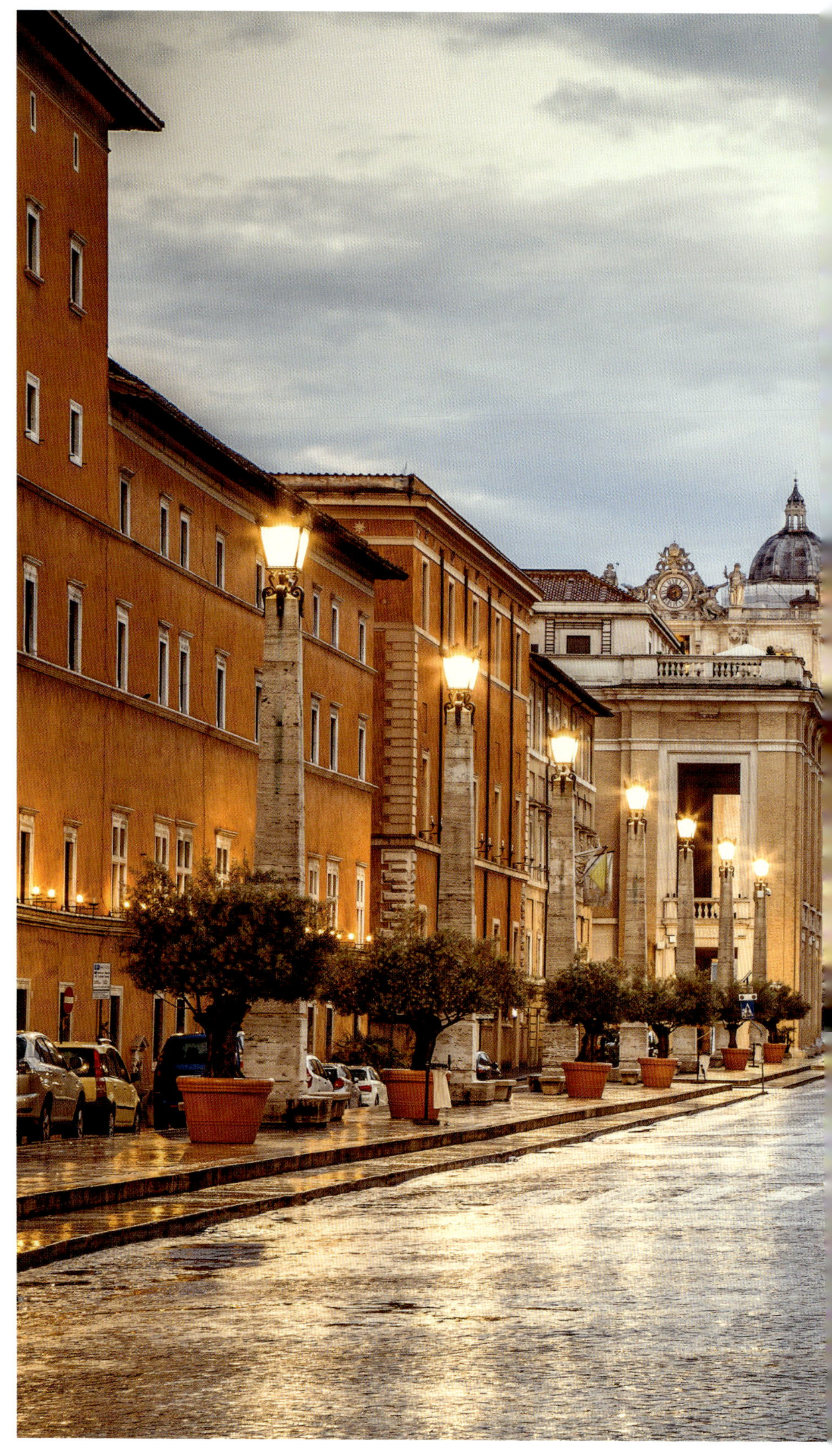

RIGHT *St. Peter's Basilica.*

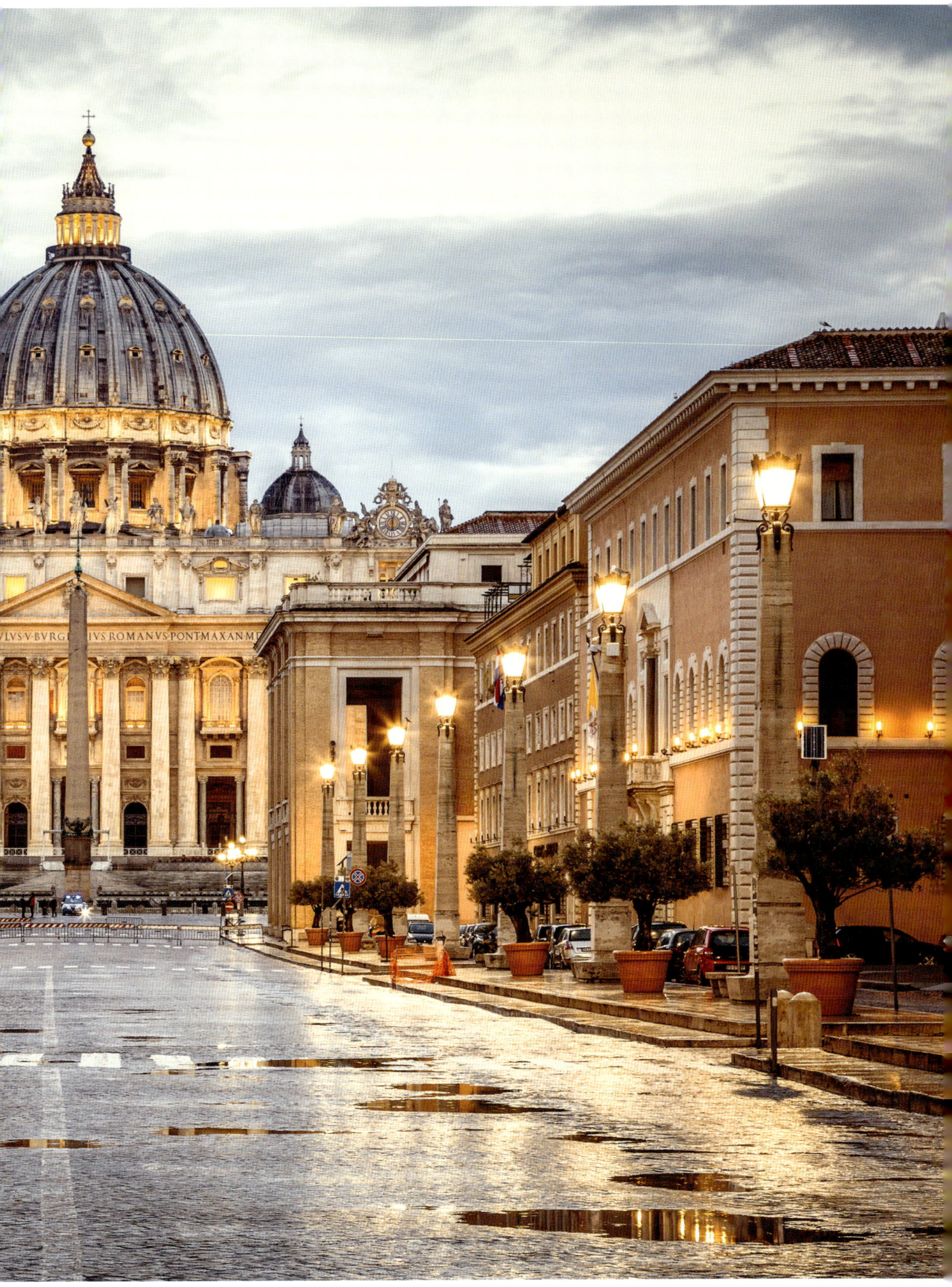
ROMANVS PONT MAX AN

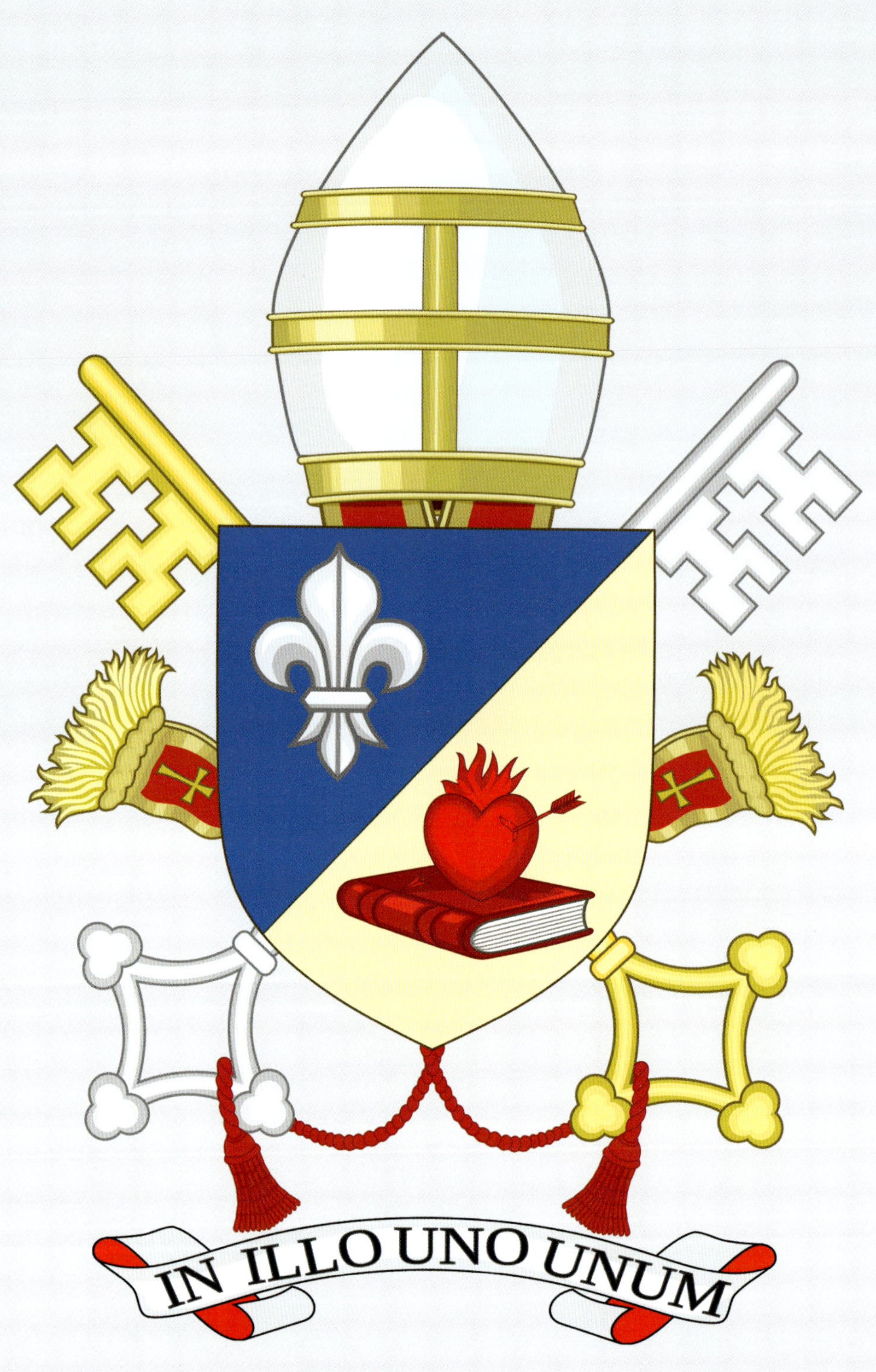
IN ILLO UNO UNUM

APPENDIX I

Pope Leo XIV's Coat of Arms

The Coat of Arms of Pope Leo XIV reveals the essence of his Marian and Augustinian spirituality. The silver mitre has three horizontal gold bands united by one vertical band to represent the Holy Trinity. It conveys his ministry to sanctify, govern, and teach. From this flows two fluttering red infulae (ribbons), portraying Scripture and Tradition, with gold fringes and crosses. The Petrine keys consist of one gold (heavenly authority) and the other silver (earthly authority). The red cord that links them together reflects binding and loosing with love and responsibility.

Pope Leo's shield is divided in half diagonally. The left background is blue, reflecting both Heaven and Our Lady, to whom Pope Leo consecrated his papacy. The fleur-de-lis signifies the Blessed Virgin Mary, grace, purity, beauty, and fidelity. It also symbolizes that Pope Leo was elected on the Feasts of Our Lady of the Rosary of Pompeii and (in the Order of St. Augustine) Our Lady of Grace. Its three petals represent the Holy Trinity. The right background is ivory, a common color for religious orders to convey holiness and purity. It features a flaming red heart, pierced by an arrow. This is associated with the conversion of Augustine, who wrote of his personal encounter with God's Word: "You have pierced my heart with your Word," and, "You have wounded my heart with your love." The book placed underneath the heart represents both the Bible and St. Augustine's writings.

The papal motto is written on a scroll: *In Illo uno unum* ("In Him who is One, we are one"). This recalls Augustine's words (on Psalm 127) that "Christians, with their Head, who ascended to heaven, are one Christ; it is not He one and we many, but, being many in that one, we are one." In these spiritualities, Pope Leo XIV's mission is reflected: to unite the Church in Christ through prayerful listening and communion with Him and knowledge of His Word.

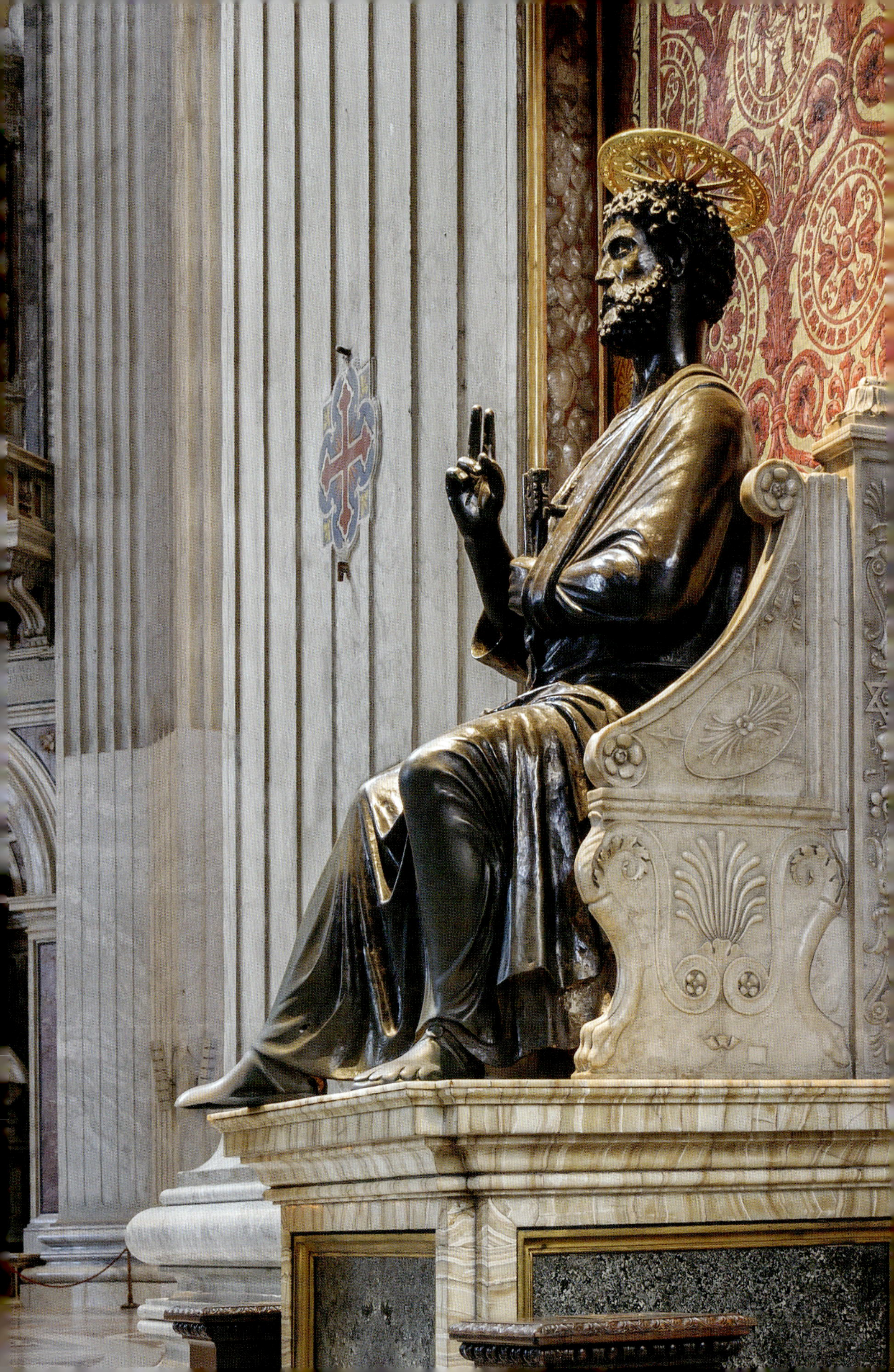

APPENDIX II

Indulgenced Prayer for the Supreme Pontiff

by Pope Leo XIII

O Lord, in union with millions of believers, and prostrate here at Thy feet, we pray Thee to save, defend, and long preserve the Vicar of Christ, the Father of the glorious society of souls, our own Father. Today and every day he prays for us, fervently offering to Thee the sacred Victim of love and peace. Turn then, O Lord, Thy loving eyes upon us, who forgetful as it were of ourselves pray now above all things for him. Unite our prayers with his, and receive them into the bosom of Thy infinite mercy, as a most sweet perfume of that living and efficacious charity, in which the children of the Church are united to their Father. All that he asks of Thee today we too ask for with him. Whether he sorrows or rejoices, or when he hopes or offers the Victim of love for his people, we would be united with him. We desire that the utterance of our souls should be one with his. Mercifully grant, O Lord, that no one of us be far from his mind and heart during the hour of his prayer, and when he offers to Thee the sacrifice of Thy blessed Son. And in the moment that he, our most revered Pontiff, holding in his hands the very Body of Jesus Christ, shall say to the people over the chalice of benediction the words: The peace of the Lord be ever with you, do Thou, O Lord, cause Thy most sweet peace to descend with a new and manifest power into our hearts, and upon all the nations of mankind. Amen.

—*Indulgenced prayer of Pope Leo XIII* (*May 8, 1896*)

LEFT *Arnolfo di Cambio, statue of St. Peter, St. Peter's Basilica, Vatican City.*

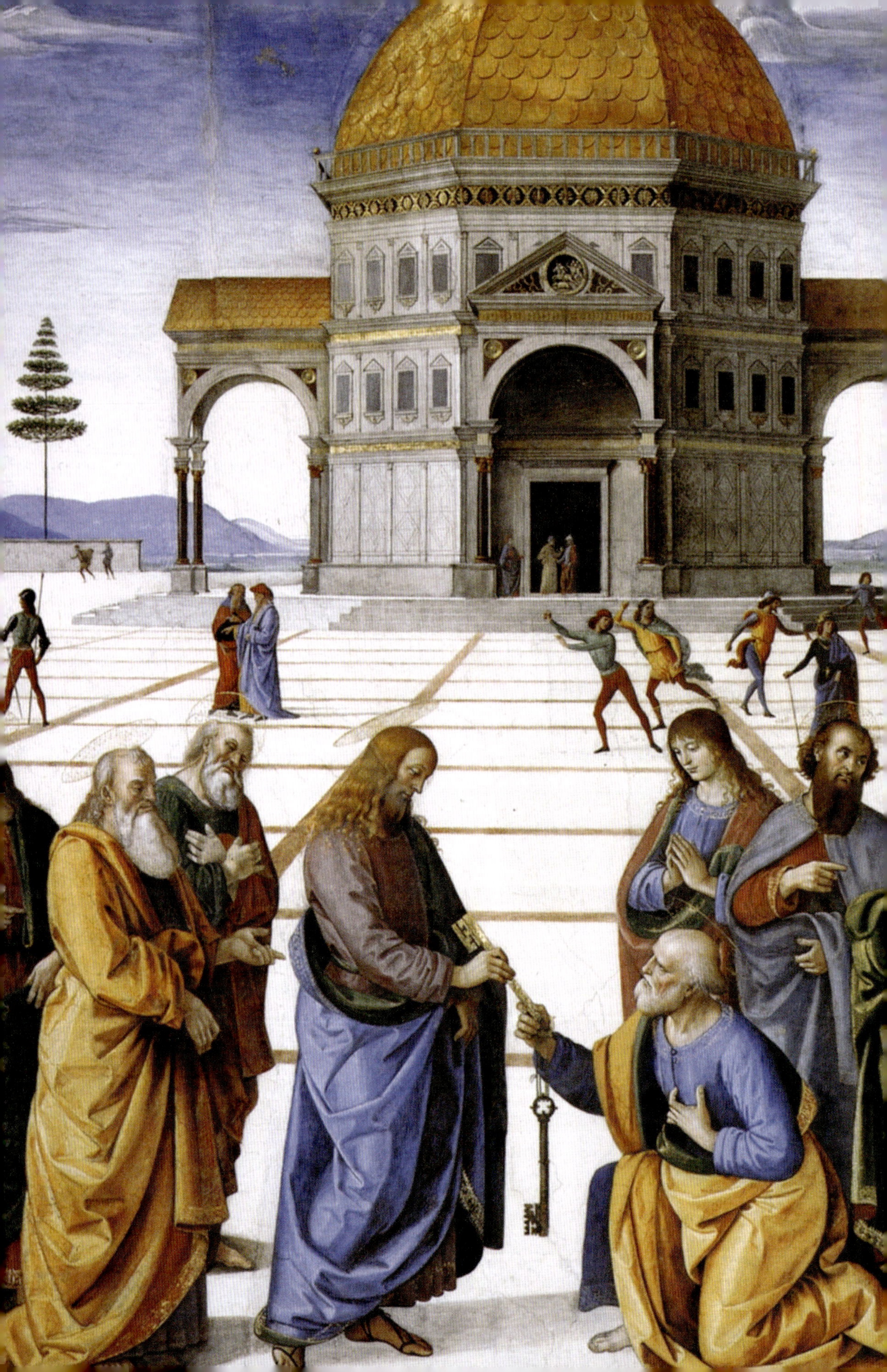

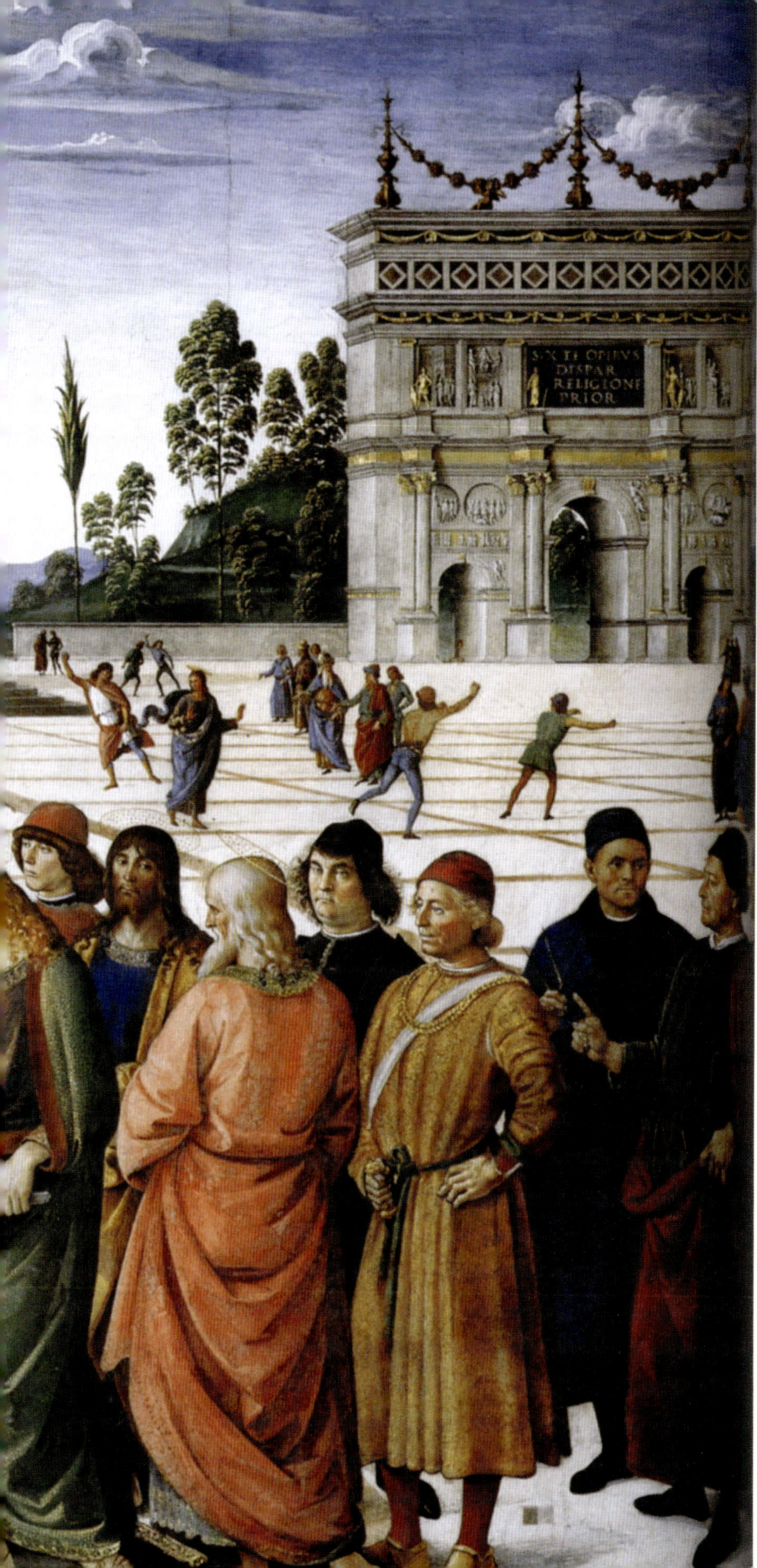

LEFT *Pietro Perugino,* Christ Giving the Keys to St. Peter, *Sistine Chapel, Vatican City.*

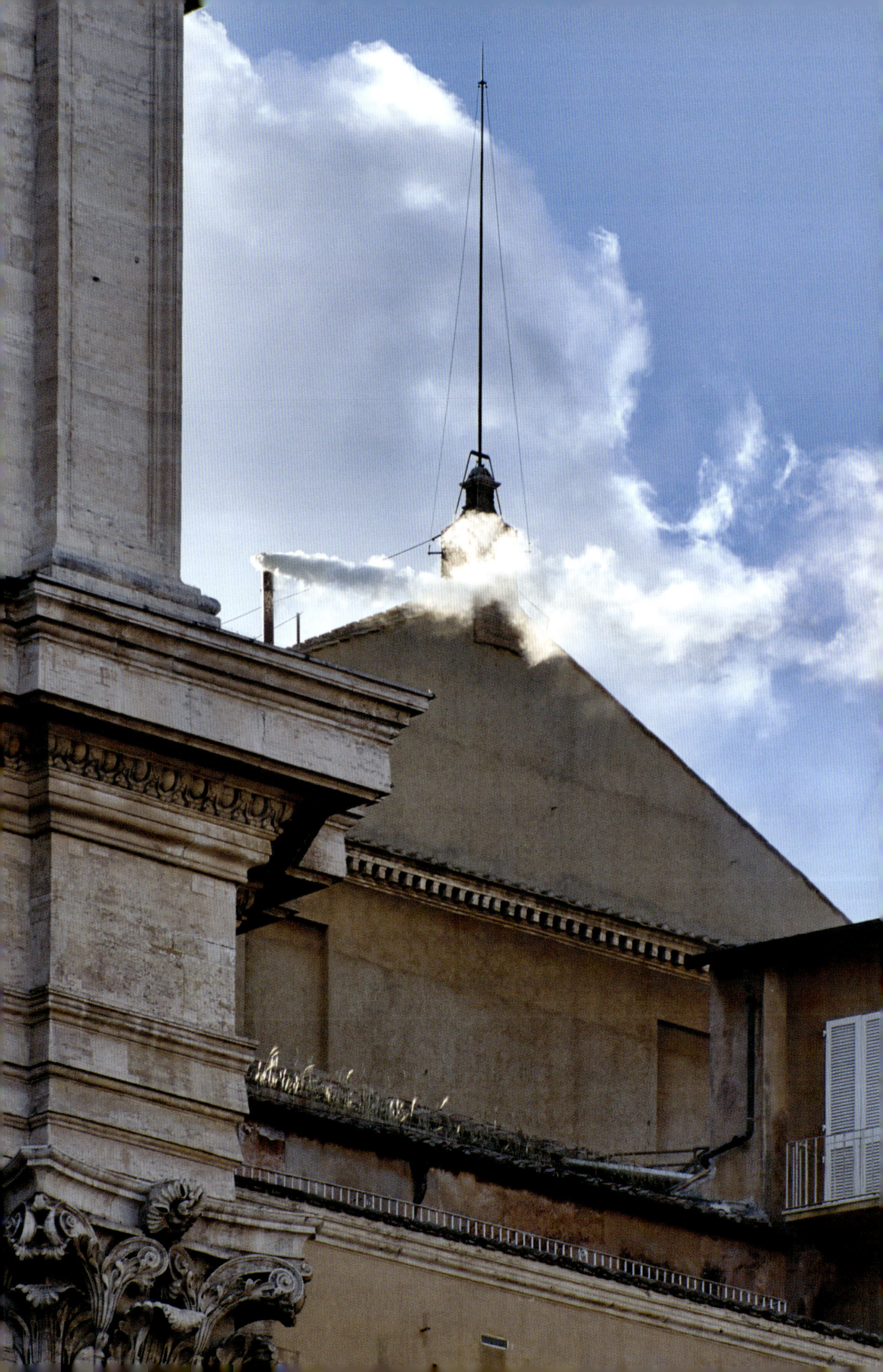

APPENDIX III

Papal Election Timeline

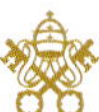

Death of Pope Francis (April 21, 2025)

April 21, 2025

Pope Francis passes away, marking the end of his twelve-year pontificate.

The Cardinal Camerlengo, Cardinal Kevin Farrell, along with members of the papal household, sets a wax seal on the doors of the papal apartments.

Sede Vacante (April 21–May 8, 2025)

April 22, 2025

The first of the General Congregations—the series of twelve meetings in which the cardinals discuss the Church's needs leading up to the election—takes place.

April 23–25, 2025

Pope Francis lies in state inside St. Peter's Basilica.

April 26, 2025

Cardinal Giovanni Battista Re, Dean of the College of Cardinals, presides over Pope Francis' funeral Mass, marking the beginning of the *Novemdiales*—the nine-day period of mourning following the Pope's death.

Pope Francis is laid to rest at the Basilica of St. Mary Major.

May 2, 2025

Workers affix the chimney to the roof of the Sistine Chapel in preparation for the upcoming conclave.

May 6, 2025

The Sistine Chapel is officially sealed off and checked for any recording or communication devices, in order to ensure secrecy.

LEFT *White smoke billowing from the Sistine Chapel chimney, announcing that the Church has a new Pope!*

The Sacred Conclave (May 7–May 8, 2025)

May 7, 2025

The *Missa pro Eligendo Pontifice*—a Mass for the Election of a Pope—is celebrated prior to the start of the conclave.

After processing into the Sistine Chapel, the cardinal-electors each take an oath of secrecy.

The Master of Papal Liturgical Ceremonies, Archbishop Diego Ravelli, utters the famous command, "*Extra omnes!*"

9:00 p.m. (Rome): Following the first round of voting, black smoke emerges from the chimney atop the Sistine Chapel.

May 8, 2025

11:50 a.m.: Black smoke once again issues forth from the Sistine Chapel chimney, indicating inconclusive morning ballots.

5:45 p.m.: After a fourth round of voting, Cardinal Robert Prevost receives the required two-thirds majority and is asked by Cardinal Parolin if he accepts his new office.

6:06 p.m.: White smoke billows out of the chimney, confirming the election of a new Pope.

7:12 p.m.: "*Habemus Papam!*" is declared by Cardinal Protodeacon Dominique Mamberti—"We have a Pope!"

7:23 p.m.: Pope Leo XIV steps out onto the loggia to greet the Universal Church and give the *Urbi et Orbi* blessing.

The First Days of Pope Leo XIV (May 9–May 25, 2025)

May 9, 2025

Pope Leo celebrates his first Mass as Pontiff with the College of Cardinals.

May 10, 2025

Pope Leo addresses the College of Cardinals about the challenges facing the Church.

May 11, 2025

Pope Leo chants the *Regina Caeli* prayer during his first public recitation.

May 18, 2025

Pope Leo celebrates his inaugural Mass as the Bishop of Rome and the Supreme Pontiff of the Catholic Church.

May 25, 2025

Pope Leo takes formal possession of the papal basilica of St. John Lateran.

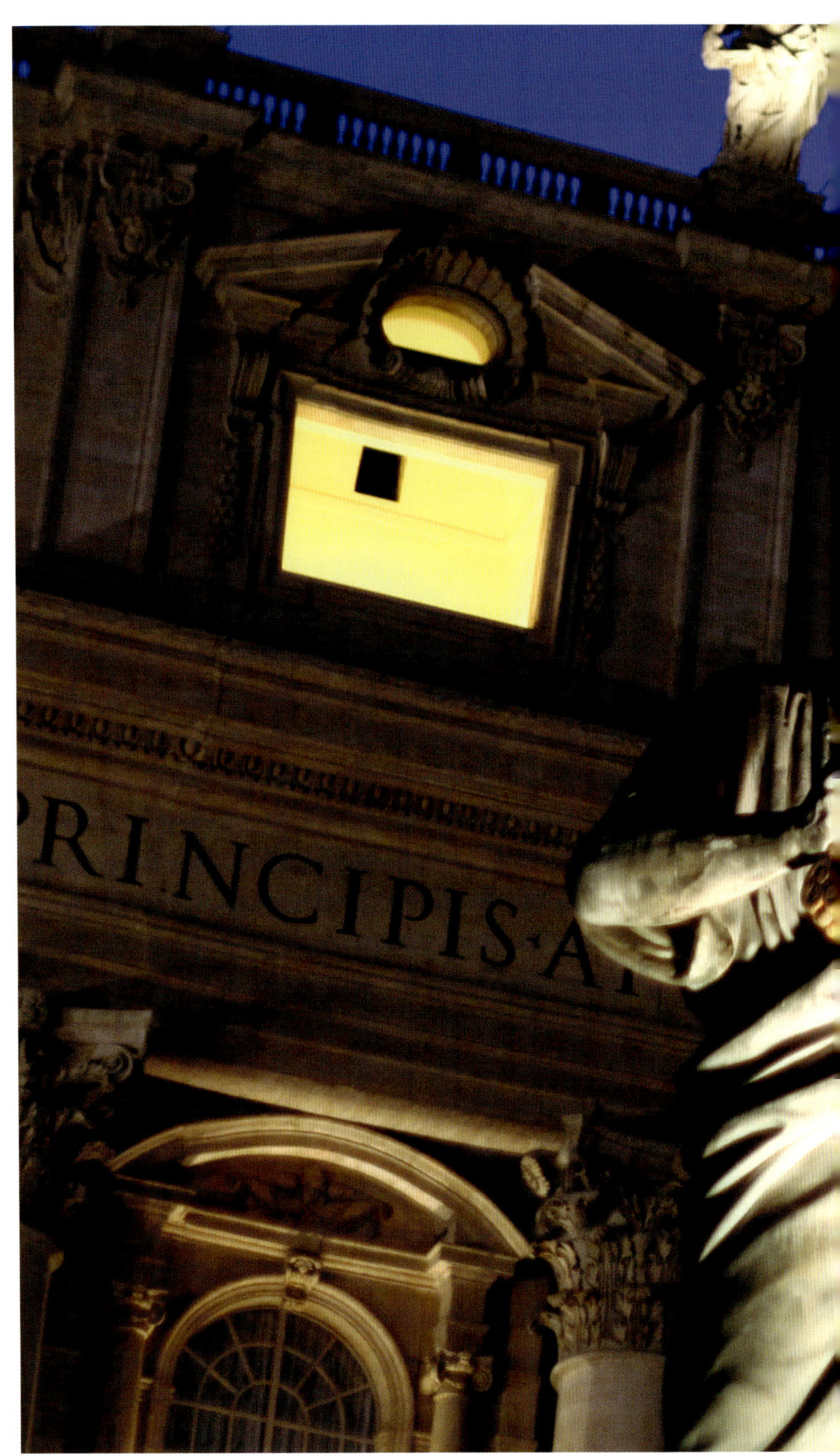

RIGHT *Giuseppe De Fabris, statue of St. Peter, St. Peter's Square, Vatican City.*

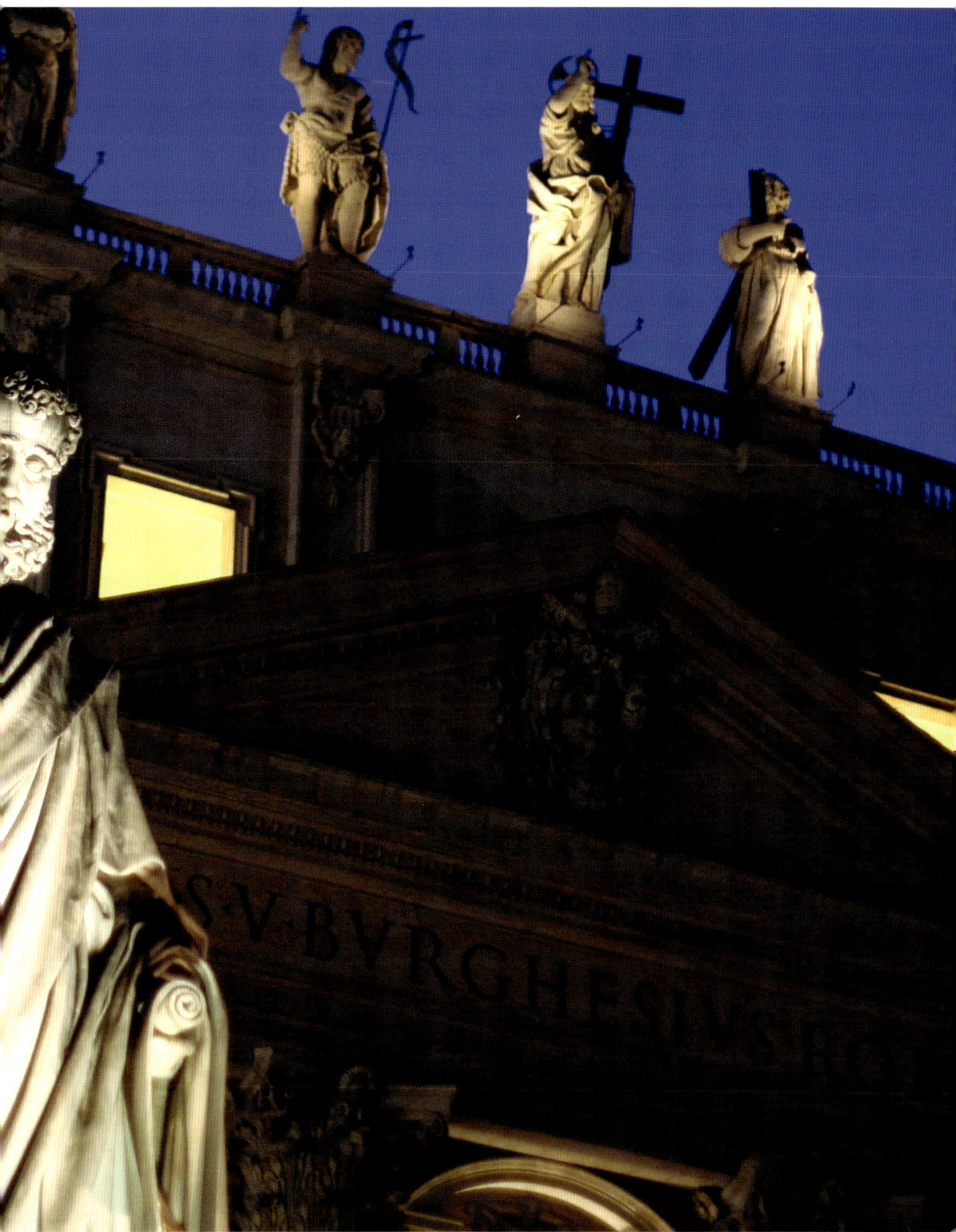
S·V·BVRGHESIVS

Image Credits

Credits given in order of appearance. Asterisks mark images used on the back cover.

32221042025 (Vatican Media)
519090 (Catholic Photo Press)
255523042025 (Vatican Media)
270923042025 (Vatican Media)
2594120565 (Shutterstock)
Holy Rosary for the Pope EWTN Daniel Ibáñez *
Funeral Mass EWTN Daniel Ibáñez
9221042025 (Vatican Media)
Sedevacante Coat of Arms (commons.wikimedia.org) SajoR CC-BY-SA-2.5
1621042025 (Vatican Media)
121042025 (Vatican Media)
519529 (Catholic Photo Press)
466376 (Catholic Photo Press)
75222042025 (Vatican Media)
329124042025 (Vatican Media)
1685229042025 (Vatican Media)
1655628042025 (Vatican Media)
1687929042025 (Vatican Media)
230437 (Catholic Photo Press)
520737 (Catholic Photo Press)
521389 (Catholic Photo Press)
2574107052025 (Vatican Media)
Holy Rosary EWTN Daniel Ibáñez *
2342007052025 (Vatican Media)
2342707052025 (Vatican Media)
2344007052025 (Vatican Media)
2588607052025 (Vatican Media)
2585807052025 (Vatican Media)
White Smoke EWTN Daniel Ibáñez *
2576907052025 (Vatican Media)

48808052025 (Vatican Media)
62008052025 (Vatican Media)
69408052025 (Vatican Media)
1208052025 (Vatican Media)
708052025 (Vatican Media)
73508052025 (Vatican Media)
Visit to the Tomb of St. Paul EWTN Daniel Ibáñez
First Regina Caeli EWTN Daniel Ibáñez
Outside of St. John Lateran EWTN Daniel Ibáñez
11016052025 (Vatican Media)
First Regina Caeli EWTN Daniel Ibáñez
220610052025 (Vatican Media)
301310052025 (Vatican Media)
Visit to the Tomb of St. Paul EWTN Daniel Ibáñez
3690721052025 (Vatican Media)
16312052025 (Vatican Media)
85208052025 (Vatican Media)
11416052025 (Vatican Media)
Holy Mass for the beginning of a Pontificate, Pope Leo XIV EWTN Daniel Ibáñez
133115052025 (Vatican Media)
Installation of Pope Leo on the Episcopal Seat EWTN Daniel Ibáñez
Pope Leo during a General Audience EWTN Daniel Ibáñez
Pope Leo Celebrating Mass EWTN Daniel Ibáñez
Holy Mass for the beginning of a Pontificate, Pope Leo XIV EWTN Daniel Ibáñez
First Regina Caeli EWTN Daniel Ibáñez
Holy Mass for the beginning of a Pontificate, Pope Leo XIV EWTN Daniel Ibáñez
Holy Mass for the beginning of a Pontificate, Pope Leo XIV EWTN Daniel Ibáñez
Holy Mass for the beginning of a Pontificate, Pope Leo XIV EWTN Daniel Ibáñez
Holy Mass for the beginning of a Pontificate, Pope Leo XIV EWTN Daniel Ibáñez
474218052025 (Vatican Media)
0452818052025 (Vatican Media)
Holy Mass for the beginning of a Pontificate, Pope Leo XIV EWTN Daniel Ibáñez
423518052025 (Vatican Media)
463118052025 (Vatican Media)
60625052025 (Vatican Media)
245425052025 (Vatican Media)
Installation of Pope Leo on the Episcopal Seat EWTN Daniel Ibáñez

96711052025 (Vatican Media)
333510052025 (Vatican Media)
71108052025 (Vatican Media)
4002828052025 (Vatican Media)
41108052025 (Vatican Media)
69408052025 (Vatican Media)
61008052025 (Vatican Media)
103811052025 (Vatican Media)
299210052025 (Vatican Media)
1218983827 (Shutterstock) *

Pope Leo XIV's Coat of Arms (Sodacan Style) (commons.wikimedia.org) Louis de Lauban CC 4.0

St. Peter's Statue, St. Peter's Basilica, Vatican City (commons.Wikimedia.org) Public Domain

Delivery of the Keys by Pietro Perugino, Sistine Chapel, (commons.Wikimedia.org) Public Domain *

Fumata Bianca (Conclave 2025) (commons.wikimedia.org) Public Domain

St. Peter and the Keys to Heaven, Vatican City, (commons.Wikimedia.org) Public Domain

Additional Elements 353602754 Shutterstock.com

Back cover HOLY ROSARY FOR THE POPE EWTN Daniel Ibáñez